THE OFFICIAL SOCCER BOOK

THE OFFICIAL
SOCCER
BOOK
of The United States Soccer Federation

by Walter Chyzowych

Rand McNally & Company
Chicago · New York · San Francisco

Instructional Photographs by Duomo Photography Group

Contributors

Alan Exley
Bill Killen
Ray Klivecka
Dr. Leonard K. Lucenko
Dr. Joseph Machnik
Bill Muse
Joel Rosenstein, R.P.T.
Nick Zlatar

The publisher and the United States Soccer Federation are deeply indebted to them for their help in the preparation of *The Official Soccer Book.*

Picture Credits
Photographs reproduced courtesy of:
The USSF
The North American Soccer League
The Chicago Sting of the NASL
Pioneer Press, Inc., Wilmette, Illinois
Eugene Chyzowych
The Coca-Cola Company
Steven E. Sutton/Duomo (pp. 175, 186, 225, 226, 227);
   Gale Constable/Duomo (p. 223, top)

Cover photograph by Peter Robinson

Drawings of exercises in Chapters 7 and 13 rendered by Ursula Melendi

Library of Congress Cataloging in Publication Data
Chyzowych, Walter.
   The official soccer book of the United States Soccer Federation.

   Bibliography: p.
   1. Soccer coaching. 2. Soccer. 3. Soccer—United States. 4. Soccer
—Rules. I. United States Soccer Federation. II. Title.
GV943.8.C48   796.33'4'0973   78-7100
ISBN 0-528-81008-1
ISBN 0-528-88125-6 pbk.

First printing, 1978
Second printing, 1979
Third printing, 1980
Fourth printing, March 1981
Fifth printing, November 1981
Sixth printing, 1982

CONTENTS

THE OFFICIAL SOCCER BOOK

INTRODUCTION

Playing soccer requires skill, discipline, speed, stamina, and team effort. But unlike football, basketball, and hockey, soccer does not require exceptional strength or height. Almost any healthy individual with a reasonable amount of coordination, agility, and alertness can learn to play the game, and the degree to which he develops soccer skills need be limited only by his own motivation and the coaching available to him.

The number of soccer players in the United States has risen at a dramatic rate in recent years. Teams have proliferated at all levels, from elementary schools to colleges, from independent clubs to recreational leagues. And with this rise in popularity has come a growing demand for coaching expertise.

To meet this need, the national coaching staff of the United States Soccer Federation (USSF) has developed this manual. It is intended to serve established coaches as well as parents, teachers, and individuals who have accepted the responsibility of fielding a soccer team. It provides specific and detailed information on teaching soccer skills, organizing practice drills, developing team tactics and coordination, and successfully competing in organized games. It also offers conditioning programs for soccer players, advice on nutrition, instruction on dealing with injuries. It is hoped that the manual will answer most questions that arise in training soccer players and in meeting their physical and psychological needs. Parents who want to understand soccer because their children are playing it will find all the basic information here also, and so will those fans who

enjoy watching the game but would like to know more about it.

Though the rules of soccer are the same for all teams belonging to the Fédération Internationale de Football Association (FIFA), or International Federation of Association Football, soccer styles differ among the countries of the world, and there is something to be learned from each. Style of play is determined by such factors as education, climatic conditions, physical facilities, nutrition, temperament, and overall coaching philosophy. For example, in England, where soccer was once played only in the wintertime, participants were forced to keep moving to stay warm. The English style emphasizes hard running, physical contact, long passing, and the ability to play for 90 minutes with all-out effort.

West Germany, Holland, and a few other Western European nations stress technique more, coupled with speed. The players are highly skilled, accept responsibilities well, and play with self-assurance and sophistication. Man-to-man marking, or guarding, has become a popular tactic in West Germany and Holland especially, and this has resulted in a very evident style. Players are given a great deal of individual responsibility, and total game involvement—whether on defense or offense—is expected. Indeed, man-to-man play has introduced a new dimension to soccer.

Another identifiable style of soccer is practiced in Eastern Europe. Here, the game tends to be more stereotyped, and East Germany and the Soviet Union tend to play a more programmed game. The players' physical work rate is high, but they seem to lack flexibility and agility. They also seem limited in imagination and self-expression. A few Eastern European countries have begun to change their approach in recent years. Poland, Czechoslovakia, and Yugoslavia are quite modern in their style, and their teams have excelled in international competitions.

In South America soccer has acquired yet another style. For the most part, the players use a positional game with emphasis on finesse rather than physical contact. Soccer moves at a slower pace, and the players are permitted more time and space.

What is the soccer style of the United States? This is a frequently asked question, and its answer is bound to affect the quality and type of instruction offered to the growing number of young people who play the game in this country. The staff of the USSF has studied the evolution of soccer in the United States for a number of years. Different teaching methods have been observed and evaluated, and communication has been maintained with coaches at all levels. At this point, it seems that an American soccer style is emerging, a style of play that is suitable and comfortable for our players.

Because of the American athlete's sociological and psychological upbringing, he has the ability and willingness to accept challenges, and the mental toughness to carry them through. Thus, man-to-man soccer presents little difficulty for our players, and this style of play seems destined to become the "Ameri-

can style." Transition from defense to offense is perhaps the most difficult aspect of man-to-man play, but American players have shown in recent years that they are capable of positional adjustments and total game involvement.

The soccer season in the United States varies from state to state, and the involvement of players with other sports, especially in schools, often interferes with preparation for the soccer season. Furthermore, the American coach frequently has only a limited time available for pre-season soccer programs. One of the goals of this book is to encourage faster development not only of individual players but also of the team as a whole.

The strong academic background of the American athlete makes him a very coachable individual. He is usually physically and mentally equipped to carry out the difficult assignments of a soccer game. The willingness of the American player to listen and to accept and follow instructions makes him exceptional, and with this kind of material, the future of US soccer is indeed bright.

It is probably *every* coach's dream to develop the potentials of his players and team to their fullest. This manual is intended to help him fulfill that dream. It is also intended to help him develop his own potential as a coach.

PART I
THE GAME
OF
SOCCER

CHAPTER I
THE WORLD'S MOST POPULAR SPORT

Soccer is the most popular team game in the world. More widely played than any other game, it is the national sport of nearly every country in Europe, South America, Asia, and Africa, and it is the only game of the football type to be played in the Olympics. More than 145 countries belong to FIFA, the governing body of soccer. Neither the World Series nor the Super Bowl, which keep thousands of American fans glued to their television screens year after year, can begin to compare to the World Cup—the international tournament, held every four years, that determines the world championship in soccer—in the number of fans it draws or the excitement and fervor it arouses.

To millions of people throughout the world, the World Cup is the ultimate sports event. The best players from nations all over the globe begin competing in the elimination rounds several years before the 24 finalists meet to decide the championship. In the countries whose teams have made it to the playoffs, social and business activities come to a virtual standstill during these games. And not even the Olympic

Games attract a larger audience than the World Cup final. Nearly 1.5 billion television viewers watched Italy defeat West Germany in the culmination of the 1982 World Cup tournament.

Still more overwhelming than the numbers attracted by the World Cup is the intensity of feeling it evokes. A West German leatherworker committed suicide when his television set broke down during a broadcast of one of his country's 1974 World Cup games. Factories in Rio de Janeiro were closed during the games so the workers could watch them on television, and when Brazil was defeated by Portugal, grief-stricken Brazilians lowered their flags to half-mast and flung black carbon paper onto the streets from the windows of office buildings. The defeat of the Italian team prompted an attack upon the team members by a mob of over 500 angry compatriots, and an Italian newspaper commented upon the defeat in a one-word headline: SHAME! Large stadiums in South America are often built with a moat around the playing field to protect referee and players from the wrath of disappointed spectators. President

Mobutu Sese Seko of Zaire sent off his country's team to the World Cup tournament with the parting admonition, "Win or die," an echo of the "Victory or death!" that was chanted by Argentinians at the first World Cup final in 1930.

Though the violence sometimes evoked by soccer matches cannot be explained simply in terms of the excitement of the game, it is certainly possible to account for many of the factors that make soccer immensely appealing to millions of people throughout the world. First of all, soccer is a fast-moving game offering long, unbroken periods of continuous action. While the total action of an American football game amounts to an average of only 15 minutes of actual playing time, a professional soccer game has 90 minutes of action-packed play, divided into two 45-minute stretches by a brief break. Another major factor contributing to soccer's great appeal is the skill and accuracy it demands of its players, which makes the game a joy to watch. Since every player can play either offense or defense, soccer requires maximum flexibility, agility, and thinking fast on one's feet; it encourages creativity on the part of the individual

player. It is a game of precision and stamina rather than brute force, and some enthusiasts have even described it as a kind of poetry in motion. Other factors behind the appeal of soccer are its simplicity and adaptability. The rules of the game are easy to grasp, and it can be played under a variety of weather conditions as well as indoors (in a modified form). Finally, soccer appeals to people's democratic instincts. It does not require unusual physical attributes, nor does it require the purchase of expensive equipment. An entire soccer team can be equipped for the cost of a single football uniform.

With so many factors contributing to the appeal of soccer, it is hard to understand why it has taken so long for the game to become popular in the United States. Is it because of the rowdyism occasionally associated with soccer? Because soccer has been considered a game for immigrants rather than an all-American sport? Because other sports—baseball and football—have usurped the place soccer might have held in Americans' hearts? Whatever the reasons may have been, the situation is definitely changing. Today soccer is the fastest-growing sport in this country. One of the milestones in the growth of soccer in the United States came in 1967, when two major professional leagues were formed—the United Soccer Association (USA), with teams in 12 cities, and the National Professional Soccer League (NPSL), which fielded teams in 10 cities.

Even though the climate of opinion toward soccer was gradually becoming more favorable, big-league soccer in the United States presented many setbacks to be overcome. Among the problems was a lack of well-qualified American players, which necessitated heavy reliance on foreign talent. Low attendance at games resulted in heavy financial losses, and in 1968 the two leagues merged into one, the North American Soccer League (NASL). Slowly but steadily attendance at NASL games began to rise, and by 1973, big-league soccer was on the upswing. Trained in US high schools and colleges, American-born players who had star potential began to emerge, providing fans with heroes they could identify with.

The image of professional soccer in the United States was given a big boost in 1975, when Brazilian superstar Pelé signed a three-year, 4½-million-dollar contract to play with the New York Cosmos. This brought American soccer into the limelight. In addi-

tion to attracting publicity and record crowds, Pelé showed Americans what soccer is capable of being and how the performance of a talented individual can spark the performance of an entire team.

By 1977, American big-league soccer had truly come into its own, with fans thronging into the stadiums in unprecedented numbers. The average attendance at NASL games in 1977 was a substantial 14,640 per game, 29 percent more than the previous year. On August 14, 1977, over 77,690 people watched the New York Cosmos win an NASL playoff in Meadowlands (Giants) Stadium. This was the largest crowd ever admitted to the stadium for any sporting event.

More remarkable than the increase in the popularity of professional soccer in the United States has been the phenomenal growth of interest at schools throughout the country. Even when the NASL matches were still drawing small audiences, the elementary schools, high schools, and colleges were forming teams at an astounding rate as more and more American youths began to discover the rewards of playing the game.

Youth soccer, of course, has been important among FIFA-affiliated countries for years, but though there have been many national and continental championship matches for the Under-19 teams, there was never one comparable in status to the World Cup for senior players until recently. FIFA's first international competition for Under-19 teams, the World Youth Tournament for the Coca-Cola Cup, was held in Tunisia in 1977. Played every two years, the tournament calls for national youth teams to compete in elimination rounds, with 16 finalists contesting for the championship trophy. In 1981 the United States qualified for the first time ever for the final round of the tournament, held that year in Australia. The American team is made up of USSF-affiliated players only.

CHAPTER 2
THE FIELD
AND
THE PLAYERS

THE FIELD

Soccer is played on a rectangular field, traditionally called a *pitch*, which must be between 100 and 130 yards long and 50 to 100 yards wide. For players under 12 years of age, a smaller field is recommended, but it should not be smaller than 40 by 80 yards. Depending on the characteristics of a team, the dimensions of the field can be of great importance. A very fit, fast team with mediocre technique will be more effective on a large field while a less fit and slower team with a high level of technical skill will perform better on a smaller field.

The field is marked off with outer boundary lines. The boundaries that define the width of the field and run its length are called *touchlines* (or sidelines). The *goal lines* are drawn at opposite ends of the field and run its width. To score, the whole of the ball must pass over the goal line between the goalposts and under the crossbar. When the whole of the ball goes beyond the boundary lines at any other point on the field, it is out of play and a restart is necessary. A *halfway line* is drawn across the center of the field to separate attacking and defending zones. It runs parallel to the goal lines.

The Regulation Goal, extending out beyond each goal line, is 8 yards wide and 8 feet high (inside dimensions). For players under 12, smaller goals—7 yards wide and 7 feet high—are recommended. The goal should have a crossbar and two goalposts, with netting attached (preferably nylon) to trap balls after a score is made.

The Goal Area is a rectangular space marked off in front of each goal with lines drawn perpendicular to the goal line, starting on the goal line 6 yards beyond each of the goalposts and extending to a line 6 yards in front of and parallel to the goal line. Goal kicks are taken from this 6-by-20-yard area.

The Penalty Area is a rectangular space marked off in front of each goal with lines drawn perpendicular to the goal line, starting on the goal line 18 yards beyond each goalpost and extending to a line 18 yards in front of and parallel to the goal line. The goalkeeper may handle the ball when he is within this 18-by-44-yard area. (Smaller penalty areas are recommended for players under 12.) In the middle of each penalty area and 12 yards in front of the center of the goal line is the *penalty spot*, from which penalty kicks are taken. The *penalty arc* is drawn in front of the penalty area at a radius of 10 yards from the penalty spot.

The Corner Area is a small arc, or quarter circle, with a radius of 1 yard drawn at each corner of the field. When a ball goes out-of-bounds over the goal line, a corner kick is taken from the nearest corner. A *flag*, on a post at least 5 feet high, is placed at each corner of the field, and these must not be removed when corner kicks are taken. Flags on either side of the halfway line, set back at least 1 yard from the touchlines, are optional. The flag posts should not have pointed tops.

The Center Circle is located in the middle of the field and has a radius of 10 yards from the *center spot*, which is located on the halfway line, midway between the touchlines. Kickoffs are taken from the center spot to start each half and to restart the game after a goal.

All of the field markings and flags are necessary to assist players and referees during the course of a game, and they should be clearly visible at all times.

THE FIELD OF PLAY

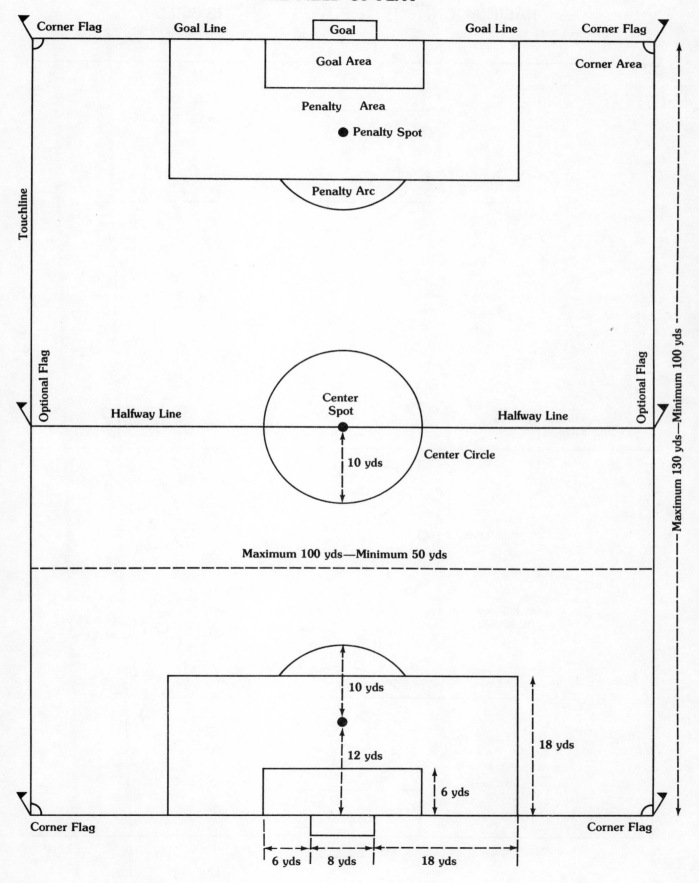

BASIC ALIGNMENT OF PLAYERS ON THE FIELD

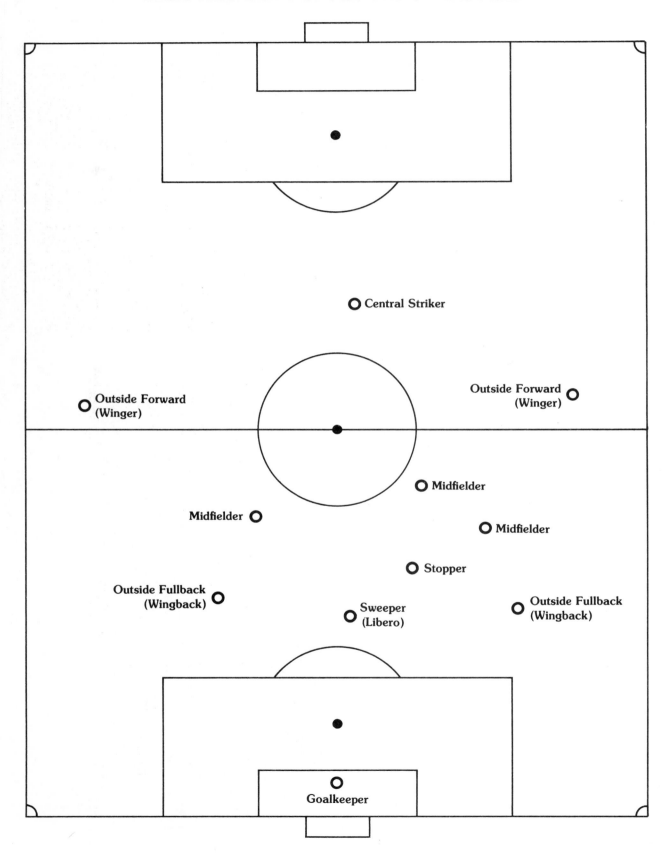

THE PLAYERS

A full team consists of 11 players, one of whom is the goalkeeper. In the modern game of soccer, the positions of field players are no longer strictly defined. Field players must be able to play defensively as well as offensively. They must be able to switch positions instantly as different situations develop in the game. Thus, responsibilities of all players except the goalkeeper are constantly shifting, and positional names serve less and less to define the players' roles.

The traditional lineup included fullbacks, or wingbacks; halfbacks, or linkmen, who controlled the midfield area and effected transitions between defense and offense; and forwards, the key attacking players who scored the goals. The outside forwards were also—and still are—known as wingers, players who move down either side of the field intent mainly on scoring or setting up goal shots. The number of fullbacks, halfbacks, and forwards varied, depending on the formation used and the system of soccer that a particular team played. Rounding out the complement of 11 players, of course, was the goalkeeper, responsible for preventing goals and, usually, for taking goal kicks.

As responsibilities became more fluid, some of the traditional names of the field positions became less meaningful, and in addition to *fullback* and *forward*, the terms used today are *sweeper*, *midfielder*, *striker*, and *stopper*, which come closer to describing a player's function in modern soccer. Let's take a look, then, at the various positions, bearing in mind that the players' functions and responsibilities are more important than their titles.

Goalkeeper

The goalkeeper's first priority is to make saves—prevent the ball from going into the goal. He also is responsible for organizing and assisting the last line of defense. But the moment he gains possession of the ball, he must start the attack by putting the ball back into play in such a way that opponents will not immediately regain possession. The goalkeeper is the only player allowed to use his hands (he is permitted to use them only within the penalty area), so his skills must include catching, throwing, and punching the ball. He is usually the one called upon to take goal

kicks; thus kicking accuracy and power also must be included in his repertory. There is no more important position than that of goalkeeper, and you will find detailed information on learning and teaching the required skills in Chapter 6.

Defenders

As the diagram shows, the defenders, or fullbacks, consist of 2 outside fullbacks (wingbacks), a sweeper (libero), and a stopper. These defenders primarily are interested in preventing goals, although they must be ready and able to launch a counterattack once they come into possession of the ball. They also serve to protect the goalkeeper from overwhelming attack by the opposing team.

The Outside Fullbacks, along with the sweeper, stopper, and goalkeeper, form the last line of defense. They must manage to stay between their own goal and the player with the ball. When a fullback (or any other player) gains possession he must immediately start an attack by passing the ball upfield to an open teammate. Traditionally, fullbacks were the largest men on the team and the strongest tacklers. Today, they need quickness and agility as well in order to stay with fast, attacking forwards in man-to-man or zone play.

The Sweeper, or libero, often finds himself the last defensive hope except for the goalkeeper. He should back up all of his teammates in defensive situations and know how to organize and direct all defensive positions. His special function is to defend against any unguarded attacker who has broken through the defense and is dribbling toward the goal. In today's game the sweeper must be quick enough to move upfield when the team is on the attack and there is less need to provide defensive cover. This gives his team more striking, or scoring, power, especially if he is good at shooting (kicking hard toward the goal with the intent of scoring) from outside the penalty area.

The Stopper, along with the defensive midfielder, is one of the central defenders. The stopper's chief job is to mark, or guard, very tightly, the opposing central striker, the most dangerous man on the field. The stopper must have good tackling ability, the skill

of controlling air balls, and the capacity to get off long clearing passes to the midfielders or forwards on his team. He must be a courageous player as well as a tenacious one because his role is demanding on both the physical and mental levels. Though he is primarily a defensive player, he will move up on occasion to support the attack and may even take a shot on goal.

Midfielders

Usually a team has three types of midfielders, who sometimes are called linkmen or halfbacks. The positions may be referred to as the defensive midfielder, the playmaking midfielder, and the attacking midfielder. Frequently midfielders are also referred to according to their position on the field—right, left, and center. It is up to the individual coach to decide which of these players should serve as attacker, defender, and playmaker. The midfielders as a group act as a link between the defense and the offense, and they must be as adept at initiating plays as they are in breaking up attacks. The midfield area is crucial in soccer tactics, and the team that controls it has a good chance of being the winner. Obviously, strength and stamina are essential to midfielders, who often find themselves in their own goal area when on defense and a few moments later deep in their opponent's territory. All should have goal-scoring potential. The midfielders are the team's workhorses, equally at home on either side of the halfway line.

The Defensive Midfielder usually plays back in the area between the last line of defense and the other midfielders. His job is to mark the opponent with the ball, acting as a defensive screen. When his team is on the attack, he has an important function as a link player, receiving passes from the fullbacks or the goalkeeper and passing the ball to the forwards.

The Playmaking Midfielder is the organizer of the team in the midfield area. He conducts the buildup of an attack and sets the pace by making penetrating passes into the opponent's defensive third of the field. This position requires the talents of one of the best athletes on the team as well as one with superior intelligence and superb technical and tactical skills. Strong leadership qualities are a must for the playmaking midfielder.

The Attacking Midfielder plays an important role in the scoring. His most important responsibility is to provide close support for his forward line when his own team is on the attack. Thus he acts as a link between the forwards and the midfield area. On defense, he is the first to challenge attacking opponents

Illustration of Depth but No Width

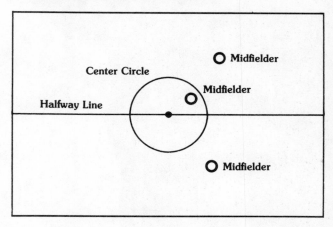

Illustration of Width but No Depth

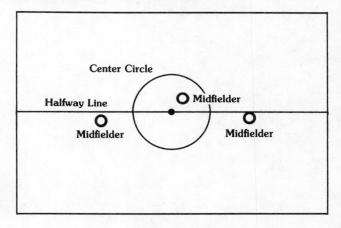

Illustration of Width and Depth

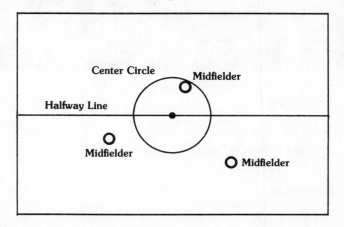

Midfielders must control both width and depth in the central third of the field.

in the midfield area. He often tries to stall an attack by cutting off passing opportunities.

Forwards

The forwards must provide goals for their team. That is their primary job, even though they should be able to switch to a defensive posture when the other team has the ball. Forwards usually are chosen for their speed, quick reflexes, courage, and shooting skill.

The Outside Forwards, or wingers, usually play close to the touchlines in the midfield, forcing the opponent's defense to spread out and opening up more space for the attack. They often make cross passes from the side of the field to teammates in position to score, or they embark on penetrating diagonal

dribbles from the midfield into the penalty area for a shot. On defense the outside forward must be able to apply immediate pressure to any opponent with the ball in his part of the field. He must be able to outplay the outside fullback marking him and be ready to mark the outside fullback in the event of his making an attacking run.

The Central Striker, or central forward, scores most of a team's goals. He must know how to out-maneuver the last man on defense and how to create space for himself or his teammates through intelligent running. The striker must be able to gain possession of the ball, control it, and shoot on goal under heavy pressure. Passing and heading round out a good striker's skills. On defense the striker must im-mediately challenge any player with the ball in the

middle of the attacking third of the field. If the goalkeeper gives the ball to an opposing fullback, the striker should support the forward marking the fullback and be ready to receive a pass from the forward or midfielder who comes into possession.

SUBSTITUTIONS

Under FIFA's laws of the game only two substitutions may be made in international competition and up to five in other matches. No reentry of players who have left the game and no substitutions for players ejected after play has started are allowed. In US college competition resubstitutions are permitted, and the high schools allow unlimited substitutions. Whether limited or unlimited, player replacements may be made, with the consent of the referee, only at the following times:

Prior to a throw-in by your team
Prior to a goal kick by your team
After a goal by either team
After an injury to either team, providing the referee stops play
At halftime

The selection of substitutes is an important consideration for the coach. As a minimum, he should have the following players available for substitutions: goalkeeper, forward, defender, attacking midfielder, and defensive midfielder. One of the other players may change places with the goalkeeper when the game is stopped, provided the referee has been notified beforehand.

Because of injuries, limited substitutions, and the reentry and ejection rules, a team may have to compete with less than the full complement of 11 players. Both the USSF and FIFA recommend that a game should not be considered valid, nor should it be started, if either of the teams has fewer than 7 players on the field.

CHAPTER 3
EQUIPMENT

Compared to other sports, soccer requires very little equipment. A ball of official size and weight and soccer shoes, usually called *boots*, are a must, but no specialized equipment beyond that is mandatory. However, some styles of shirts, shorts, socks, and pads serve better than others, and it is worthwhile to buy these items knowledgeably. Certain coaching aids will prove useful too, and a selected list is provided. The goalkeeper's equipment differs somewhat from that of other players and will be discussed separately. As for the field itself, all that is needed are goals equipped with nets (nylon will prove most durable) and four corner flags.

Balls

Many brands and models of soccer balls are available. They come in a wide range of prices, depending on material and quality of workmanship. If endorsements are printed on the ball, the price usually will be higher in proportion to the fame of the endorser.

For games, a leather ball is recommended. Special coatings may be applied to prevent the ball from absorbing moisture and increase its life if it is used in the rain or on wet fields. Rubber-covered and synthetic balls of official size and weight are becoming more popular, and they are acceptable for practice, although they are not recommended for game use.

For practice, the USSF coaching staff suggests that one ball be provided for each player since 70 to 90 percent of training is done with the ball. Your budget must be your guide in the selection of practice balls, but it is logical that better quality balls will last longer than those of poorer quality. However, if price is an

important consideration, it is better to purchase the most economical ball rather than have too few to go around. Pre-game practice should be performed with the balls to be used in the game or with practice balls of the same type as the game balls.

Balls of different sizes and colors are ideal for technique training of adult players and goalkeepers. Practice with different-size balls should improve agility, and different-color balls can be used to aid concentration. For instance, if a red and a white ball are used in the same exercise, players may be asked to pass with the left foot when they are in possession of the red ball and with the right foot when they have the white ball.

The size, weight, air pressure, and material of the ball are all factors that affect the way it responds in play. For example, a novice with minimal skill will find it easier to control a large, heavy ball inflated to minimum pressure. Smaller, lighter balls are recommended for younger players. The full-size soccer ball is described in the first line of the table below.

For Players	Size	Circumference	Weight
12 and Over	#5	27″ to 28″	14 to 16 oz.
6 to 11	#4	25″ to 26″	11 to 13 oz.
Under 6	#3	23″ to 24″	8 to 10 oz.

Shoes

Great care must be exercised in the selection of soccer shoes, or boots. They should be made of lightweight, soft, flexible leather with protective padding at the heel, arch, and Achilles tendon. A snug fit is necessary for effective control of the ball.

Because traction is so important in soccer, the

studs, or cleats, must be carefully chosen. In general, multistudded models are preferred by most players. These can be worn both on grassy fields and on hard ground. For rainy weather, however, screw-in studs are better because their length can be adjusted. The softer the field and the taller the grass, the longer the studs. The longer, screw-in studs should never be used on synthetic turf, as they might get caught in the fibers and cause serious injury to the ankle or knee. Furthermore, since traction on synthetic surfaces is very limited with long studs, they could result in ineffective play, falls, and scrape burns. On synthetic turf, flat training shoes or specially designed boots with short studs are advisable.

Outdoor technique and tactical exercises should be performed in game shoes. Training shoes, sneakers, or flats should be used for indoor training. Thus each player should have more than one pair of shoes to suit different surfaces and weather conditions.

Shirts

A wide variety of soccer shirts, both long-sleeved and short-sleeved, is available. There are styles with V necks, round necks, and inserted Vs, all available in various color and trim combinations. Shirts are made of cotton, rayon, and a number of other synthetics, including stretch nylon in both light and heavy weights. However, the front-runner among soccer shirts is a combination model consisting of a rayon outer shell lined with absorbent cotton. Under hot and humid conditions, short-sleeved, perforated shirts are strongly recommended. The number of available brands, styles, colors, and fabrics is very large, and since there is no "regulation" shirt, each team should select a model that suits its taste as well as the conditions under which it plays.

Shorts

In shorts the old standby is still around and very popular. It is that heavy-duty Sanforized cotton model with quadruple waistband, innerslip, or built-in supporter, safety cord, pocket, and side slits. It is made by many manufacturers and available everywhere. Since the 1974 World Cup, the nylon satin type has been on the market as well. It is very lightweight, practical, comfortable, and durable. Other materials, including parachute nylon, stretch nylon, and acetate, are available also. The most important consideration in choosing a pair of shorts, however, should be a comfortable fit.

Socks

Today, the most popular style in socks is the full-footed nylon model. It has almost completely replaced old-style cotton socks and the footless, or stirrup, variety that had to be worn with separate sweat socks. Nylon socks come with elastic sewn into the cuff so that they stay up without the aid of tape or rubber bands.

Shin Guards

Shin guards should be worn by all players. They do not hinder movement or the ability to control the ball. But they do protect the shin in case of a direct hit. The latest developments in plastics technology have produced combinations of materials that are thin, lightweight, and inexpensive. Shin guards made of canvas with cane inserts, foam rubber, and rubber-coated materials are also available. In a pinch, a paperback book inserted under the knee sock and attached firmly to the shin will serve the purpose.

Goalkeepers' Uniforms

The goalkeeper in soccer has a special identity, which should be reflected in his uniform. Traditionally, he was outfitted in black, but today many uniforms are available in bright colors and fashionable styles.

At present there are two theories concerning color for goalkeepers' uniforms. One advocates a dark or inconspicuous color so that the forwards of the opposing team will not be able to spot the keeper and consequently will be unable to decide where to shoot. The other recommends bright colors so that the attackers, under pressure to shoot, will aim the ball at the color—and the goalkeeper. No scientific experiments have been made so far, however, to prove or disprove either theory. So you will have to make your own decision.

The goalkeeper's shirt must differ in color from those of his teammates, and it should have padding at the elbows and on the chest. Some keepers, however, prefer to play in shirts without any padding.

The goalkeeper's shorts have padding in front, back, and at the hips. There are two lengths: the standard shorts, generally the same length as those worn by field players, and the longer Bermuda shorts. All top American goalkeepers seem to prefer the shorter style. In recent years, particularly in England, some goalkeepers have begun to wear long pants, no doubt to ward off the cold.

Pads are important protection for goalkeepers during both games and practice sessions. Some goalkeepers like to wear sliding pads as a protection against bruises. Sliding pads and body pads are available for the protection of hips and buttocks as well as kidneys and rib cage. Elbow and knee pads will further help to keep injuries at a minimum. Male goalkeepers also should wear athletic supporters with a plastic cup to avoid injury to the groin and testicles.

Many goalkeepers do not wear gloves for games. They prefer to spray their fingers and palms with sticky substances that prevent the ball from bouncing out of their hands. Many others, however, do prefer to wear gloves, especially in cold and rainy weather. Goalkeeping gloves come in many different materials. The most widely used is leather with pimpled rubber on the fingers and palms. The rubber will cling to the ball and help prevent it from bouncing away. Other glove materials are cotton, vinyl, knit wool, mesh nylon, and stretch nylon. Some of these are pretreated with sticky substances.

Training Suits

A good training or warm-up suit should be part of each player's equipment. Such a suit generally is worn during the warm-up phase of practice and during the cool-down phase after playing. When the weather is cool or cold, a training suit is a must for health reasons and should be worn throughout the practice session.

The preferred material for training suits is a combination of stretch nylon and cotton. The cotton should be on the inside to absorb perspiration. Nylon and cotton also make a very durable combination and promise many years of service. Other materials used for training suits include acrylic, shell nylon, all cotton, polyester, and fleece nylon. All of these are acceptable and usually less expensive than the stretch-nylon/cotton combination.

Rain Suits

Rain suits can be a coach's salvation during rainy games. They also come in handy for inducing heavier perspiration during workouts because they do not allow evaporation. Rain suits usually come in two pieces: a hooded jacket and separate pants.

Coaching Aids

The following is a list of equipment that a coach might wish to acquire to help him train and develop his players. Most of the items are optional, and it is unlikely that any coach will have all of them. However, all are useful and effective either in correcting specific weaknesses or in improving general conditioning.

Small goals with nets can be used for small-sided practice games. They may be constructed from pipes or plastic tubing.

Field markers or cones can be used in grid work as

well as in fitness training and dribbling exercises.

A *pendulum*—a ball suspended from a post by a rope—is useful for technique training of both field players and goalkeepers.

Plastic hoops help to improve agility and develop body rhythm.

A *kickboard* is useful to practice shooting and chip passing.

Flag posts and markers make fine guides for dribbling courses.

Scrimmage vests should be used when teaching group and team tactics.

Hurdles can be set up for dribbling, jumping, and climbing.

A *diving pit* can help to improve heading the ball, volley kicking, scissors kicking, and goalkeeping.

Benches are useful rebound surfaces for give-and-go and other passing exercises.

Plastic dummies can be used to simulate opposing players, especially as a wall (a shoulder-to-shoulder line of players protecting their goal) in restarts and free kicks.

Visors, worn under the chin, will keep players from watching their feet and the ball.

A *magnetic board* helps in teaching tactical theory.

Music makes fitness training and rhythmic movement easier and more fun.

Rope can be used to show angle plays for the goalkeeper.

Jumping rope helps develop quick footwork.

CHAPTER 4
THE GAME

THE OFFICIALS

The game of soccer requires only one referee, who is assisted by two linesmen. The referee controls play on the field, using a whistle and his hands to signal major offenses. He keeps time and a record of the match. He may stop the game in case of injuries or penalties and restart it when ready. The referee enforces the laws (rules) of soccer, determining all penalties, including the expulsion of players, and his decisions are final. Unlike football and basketball referees, who must call and penalize every foul, the soccer referee may refrain from calling a penalty for a violation, having decided it would give an advantage to the offending team. He also has the power to end a game because of bad weather or other adverse circumstances.

The two linesmen are positioned outside each touchline, or sideline, along opposite halves of the field, and they signal with flags. Subject to the decision of the referee, they indicate when the ball is out of play and which team is entitled to the corner kick, the goal kick, or the throw-in. They also assist the referee by signaling fouls that he might not have seen.

DURATION OF THE GAME

In soccer, both a regulation game and the overtime periods are divided into halves. Except by consent of the referee, the halftime interval may not exceed 5 minutes for adults in regulation play and 2 minutes in overtime. Youth players take a 10-minute break between game halves, and the overtime interval is at the discretion of the referee.

The classification of youth groups in the following table reflects skill levels, not biological ages—a 12-year-old, for instance, may be qualified to play with the Under-16 group.

Players	Game Length	Overtime Periods
Adults	Two 45-min. halves	Two 15-min. halves
Under 19	Two 45-min. halves	Two 15-min. halves
Under 16	Two 40-min. halves	Two 15-min. halves
Under 14	Two 35-min. halves	Two 10-min. halves
Under 12	Two 30-min. halves	Two 10-min. halves
Under 10	Two 25-min. halves	Two 10-min. halves
Under 8	Two 25-min. halves	Two 5-min. halves

If a game is ended by the referee before the official time is up, it must be replayed in full unless the rules for a particular competition provide that the score at the stoppage point will stand.

THE GAME IN BRIEF

All competitions between teams in soccer organizations affiliated with FIFA are played under the same rules. Uniformity in the laws governing the game is necessary because there are hundreds of thousands of organized teams, and at the highest level, participation in soccer matches is international in scope.

The Start of Play

A coin toss by the referee decides which team has won the choice of ends and the *kickoff* at the start of the game. After the first half and after a goal, the game is restarted with a kickoff. The kickoff is made with a *placekick* from the center spot. All players must be in their own half of the field and those of the opposing team must remain 10 yards from the ball until it is kicked. The ball must travel into the opponent's half of the field the distance of its own circumference before it is in play. The kicker may not replay the ball until it has been touched by another player, and if he does, the defending team is awarded an indirect free kick. (All penalties are described on a following page.) A goal may not be scored directly from a kickoff, and if the ball goes straight into the opponent's goal, the penalty is a goal kick. The teams change ends for the second half, and the one that did not kick off at the start of the game now does so.

Ball in Play and Out of Play

Once the game is under way, the action is fast, fluid, and nonstop. Moving the ball to a teammate, the players on offense try to advance toward the opponent's goal. Players on defense meanwhile attempt to take the ball away from the attackers by intercepting it or tackling for it. The players move up and down the field, switching back and forth from offensive to defensive roles as the teams gain and lose possession of the ball. There is no slackening of the pace when the defense takes possession, and there are no time-outs. The action stops only when a goal is scored, when the ball goes out-of-bounds, when the referee signals a penalty, and when a player suffers an injury.

The ball is *out-of-bounds* when all of it crosses the goal line—but not between the goalposts—or a touchline either in the air or on the ground. If the ball goes across the goal line, but not between the goalposts, and was last touched by a member of the attacking team, a goal kick is awarded to the defense. If the ball was last touched by a member of the defending team, a corner kick is awarded to the offense. If the ball passes over a touchline, a throw-in is awarded the team whose player did not touch it last.

When the officials cannot determine who last touched an out-of-bounds ball, and after a temporary suspension of play for any other no-penalty situation, the referee restarts the game with a *drop ball*. At the spot where the ball was last in play, he drops it between 2 players, 1 from each team, who vie for its possession after it hits the ground. All other players must remain 10 yards away. A goal may be scored directly from a drop-ball kick. If play was stopped in the penalty area, the game is restarted with a drop ball at the nearest point outside the penalty area.

Offside

A player is offside when he is ahead of the ball as the ball is played by a member of his own team unless he is in his own half of the field; at least 2 opponents (including the goalkeeper) are nearer their goal line than he is; or he received it directly from a corner kick, a goal kick, a drop ball, or a throw-in. For an infraction of the offside rule, an indirect free kick is awarded the defending team at the point where the infraction occurred. However, the penalty is called only if the player, in the opinion of the referee, is interfering with the play or with an opponent or seeking to gain an advantage by being in an offside position. (The historical background of the offside rule is described in Chapter 11.)

Scoring

The team scoring the greater number of goals during a game wins. Each goal counts for 1 point. If the game ends in a draw, in some competitions an overtime period is played. A goal is scored when the whole of the ball crosses the goal line between the goalposts and under the crossbar, provided it was not carried, thrown, or propelled by the arm or hand of an attacking player. If a defending player besides the goalie deliberately deflects the ball with the hands or arms and the ball goes into the goal area, a goal is scored—to penalize the infraction instead of allowing the goal would be to the advantage of the offending team. If the ball does not go in, a penalty kick—which scores a goal most of the time—is awarded to the attacking team.

FOULS AND MISCONDUCT

The referee is the sole arbiter in determining when a violation has occurred, its seriousness, and the severity of the penalty. The linesmen must signal those infringements of the rules they believe he may not have spotted, but the referee always decides what action is to be taken. He alone may judge whether a foul is intentional or one committed within the spirit of the game. Fouls and misconduct fall roughly into four categories: major violations, minor infractions, violations warranting a caution, and serious offenses.

37

EXAMPLES OF OFFSIDE SITUATIONS

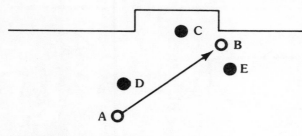

On Clear Pass to Teammate

Player **A** has moved the ball up the field and having **D** in front of him, passes to **B**. **B** is offside because he is in front of **A** and there are not 2 opponents between him and the goal line when the ball is passed by **A**. If **B** waits for **E** to fall back before he shoots, this will not put him on-side because it does not alter his position with relation to **A** at the moment the ball was passed by **A**.

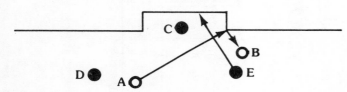

When Ball Rebounds from Goalpost or Crossbar (I)

Player **A** shoots on goal, but the ball rebounds from the goalpost—or crossbar—into play. **B** secures the ball and shoots. **B** is offside because the ball was last played by **A**, a player of his own side, and when **A** shot on goal, **B** was in front of the ball and did not have 2 opponents between him and the goal line.

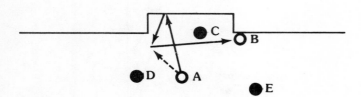

When Ball Rebounds from Goalpost or Crossbar (II)

Player **A** shoots on goal and the ball rebounds from the crossbar—or goalpost—into play. **A** runs to collect the ball and then passes to **B**, who has run up on the other side. **B** is offside because the ball was last played by **A**, a player of his own side, and when **A** shot on goal, **B** was in front of the ball and did not have 2 opponents between him and the goal line. If **A** had made a second attempt to shoot on goal instead of passing to **B**, he could have scored.

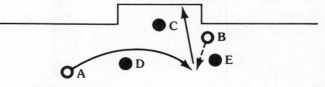

When Running Back for Ball

Player **A** makes a high shot at the goal, but the wind and curve carry the ball back. **B** runs to the ball, collects it, and shoots on goal. **B** is declared offside because he was in front of the ball and there were not 2 opponents between him and the goal line at the moment the ball was played by **A**.

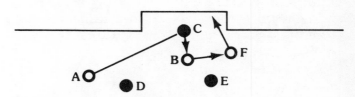

On Shot at Goal Returned by Goalkeeper

Player **A** shoots on goal. The ball is played by **C** and **B** obtains possession, but slips and passes the ball to **F**, who shoots on goal. **F** is offside because he is in front of **B**, and when the ball was passed by **B**, there were not 2 opponents between **F** and the goal line.

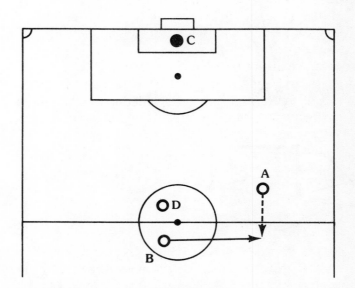

Offside Player Cannot Put Himself On-Side

If player **A** is in his opponent's half of the field of play and was offside when **B** last played the ball, he cannot put himself on-side by moving back into his own half of the field of play.

SIGNALS BY THE REFEREE

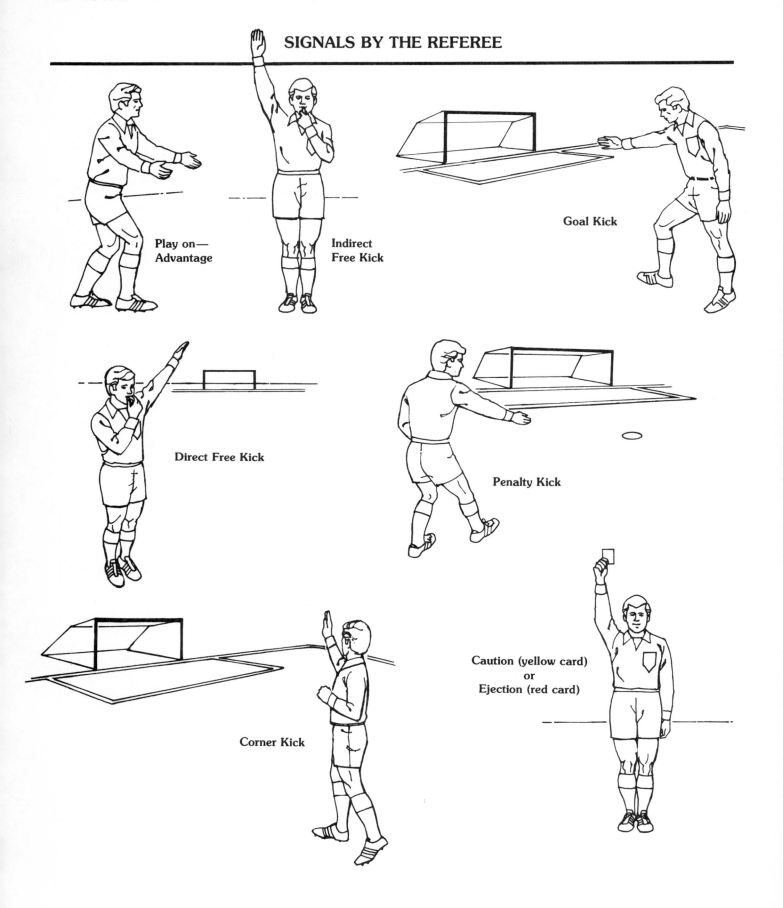

Play on—
Advantage

Indirect
Free Kick

Goal Kick

Direct Free Kick

Penalty Kick

Corner Kick

Caution (yellow card)
or
Ejection (red card)

SIGNALS BY THE LINESMEN

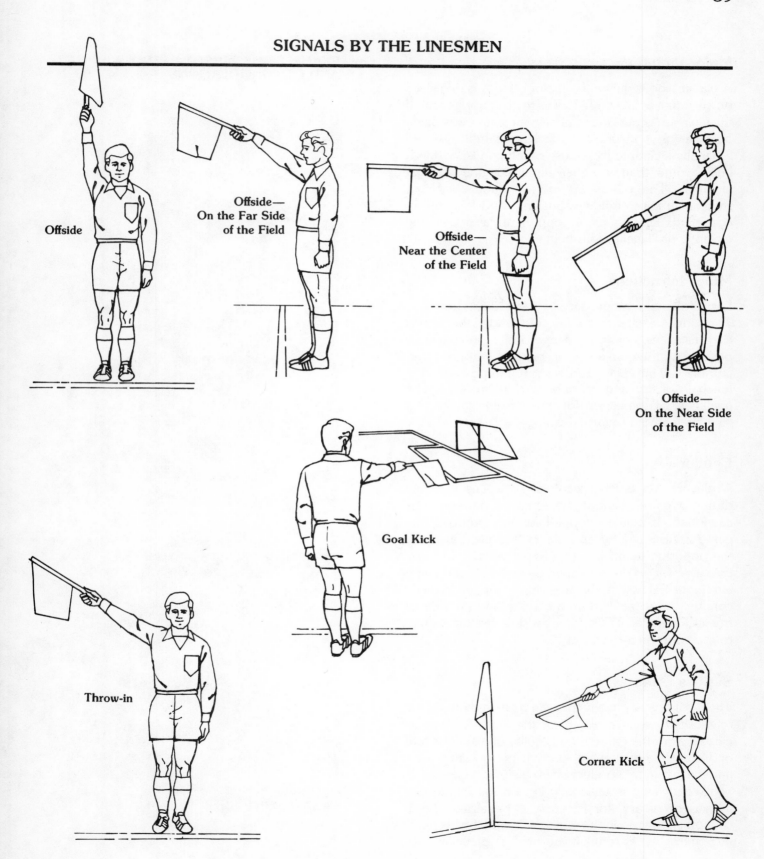

Offside

Offside—
On the Far Side
of the Field

Offside—
Near the Center
of the Field

Offside—
On the Near Side
of the Field

Goal Kick

Throw-in

Corner Kick

Major Violations

A player who is guilty of a major offense is penalized by awarding a direct free kick to the opposing team. If the violation occurs in the penalty area and was made by a defensive player, the attacking team is awarded a penalty kick. Intentional use of the hands, or *hand-balling*, other than by a goalkeeper is deemed a major violation. The others are personal fouls: kicking, striking, tripping, holding, pushing, and kneeing an opponent; leaping at an opponent; and charging violently or illegally from behind.

Minor Infractions

Lesser offenses are penalized by an indirect free kick. They include charging fairly, but under the wrong circumstances; playing dangerously; intentionally obstructing the goalkeeper to prevent him from putting the ball into play; and when not in possession of the ball, obstructing an opponent in the field. The goalkeeper is penalized for time-wasting tactics that give his team an unfair advantage.

Cautions

A player who enters, reenters, or leaves the field during a game without the referee's permission is cautioned. If play is stopped for this purpose, the game is restarted by an indirect free kick taken by the opposing team. If a player persistently infringes the rules, shows disagreement by word or action with a referee's decision, or is guilty of ungentlemanly conduct, he receives both a caution and an indirect free kick penalty. The referee must report the caution to the appropriate authority.

Serious Offenses

The most severe penalty that can be meted out by the referee is to send a player off the field. A player is ejected from the game if he is guilty of a serious foul or violent conduct, uses abusive or foul language, and persists in misconduct after receiving a caution. A goalkeeper who intentionally lies on the ball longer than is necessary, for instance, is penalized with a caution and by an indirect free kick, and if he repeats the offense he is sent off the field. A player is also

EXAMPLES OF PERSONAL FOULS AND OTHER VIOLATIONS

ejected if he is about to be cautioned and before it can be administered commits another offense meriting a caution. The referee must report any serious misdemeanor occurring on or off the field.

PENALTIES

It is the responsibility of the referee to see that no infringement of the rules goes unpunished. Thus when he applies the *advantage rule* and signals that play is to continue—instead of stopping the game to call a violation because doing so, in effect, would be to the advantage of the offender's team—he should make the guilty player aware that his infraction has not gone unnoticed.

The throw-in and every kick described here are in turn subject to an indirect free kick awarded to the opposition if the player taking them plays the ball a second time before someone else from either team touches or plays it.

Free Kicks

There are two basic types of free kicks: a *direct free kick* and an *indirect free kick*. A goal may be scored directly with the first kick, but it cannot be scored with the second unless another player touches the ball before it goes into the net.

Both the direct free kick—when it is specifically so awarded—and the indirect free kick are taken from the position of the ball at the time of the violation. Opponents must be at least 10 yards away from the ball when it is put into play unless the infraction is closer to the goal line than this distance, in which case they must be on the goal line. The ball must be stationary and on the ground and must travel the distance of its circumference before being in play. When the kick is taken within the player's own penalty area, the ball must travel outside that area. All opponents must be outside the penalty area and at least 10 yards away from the ball. If a defender fails to maintain the proper position before a free kick is taken, he is cautioned and the kick is taken again.

The direct free kick does not score a goal too often. A number of defensive players line up to form a "wall" between the kicker and the goal, hoping to block the ball and taking up "space" to make the goal smaller. If the ball is not blocked by one of his teammates, the goalkeeper is usually far enough away

from the kicker to anticipate where the ball is headed and has a good chance to make a save.

The Penalty Kick

A penalty kick is awarded the offensive team if a player of the defending team commits a major violation within his own penalty area. The kick is taken from the penalty spot, 12 yards out from the center of the goal. All players, except the defending goalie and the kicker, must be outside the penalty area and at least 10 yards behind the penalty spot. A goal may be scored directly on a penalty kick. And a goal is scored more often than not, for only the defending goalkeeper can prevent it, and he must guess where in the 8-yard-wide by 8-foot-high goal the ball will be aimed. The goalkeeper must stand with both feet touching the goal line and may not move until the ball is kicked.

The ball must be kicked forward, and it must travel the distance of its circumference before it is in play. If the kicker violates a rule, an indirect free kick is awarded the defending team. If a player of the attacking team, other than the kicker, commits an infraction while a penalty kick is being taken and a goal results, the goal is declared invalid and the kick has to be repeated. If the defending team violates a rule while a penalty kick is taken, the kick is awarded again unless a goal was scored. A player of either team who does not remain at a proper distance before the kick is taken receives a caution.

The Corner Kick

When the ball goes out-of-bounds by passing over the goal line but not between the goalposts and was last played by one of the defenders, a corner kick is awarded the attacking team. The kick is taken from the quarter circle at the corner flag post nearest the spot where the ball crossed the goal line. A goal may be scored directly from a corner kick. Opposing players must remain 10 yards away from the ball until it is in play, and if this rule is violated the kick is retaken.

On occasion a good kicker will attempt to score by curving the ball into the goal. Usually, however, he kicks it in front of the goal, where 4 or 5 of his teammates are positioned, and they will try to head or kick the ball into the net.

The Goal Kick

When an attacking player causes the ball to go out-of-bounds over the goal line or shoots the ball directly into the goal during a kickoff, a goal kick is awarded the defending team. The kick is taken from the goal area, usually—but not necessarily—by the goalkeeper. All opposing players must be outside the penalty area until the ball is in play. The kick must be taken again if the ball does not travel beyond the penalty area or if it is touched a second time by the kicker before it goes out of the penalty area. A goal cannot be scored directly from a goal kick.

The Throw-In

A ball that goes out-of-bounds by completely passing over a touchline is put back into play with a throw-in, awarded to the team whose player did not touch it last. The throw-in is the only time during a soccer game that a field player may use his hands, and the rules are very specific about how it is taken. The thrower must face the field; part of each foot must be on the ground, on or behind the touchline; the ball must be held with both hands; and the ball must be thrown from over the head. If the player makes the throw-in improperly, it is taken by the opponents. If he plays the ball a second time before someone else touches it, the other team is awarded an indirect free kick, but if he plays it again on the field by handling it, the penalty is a direct free kick. A goal cannot be scored directly from a throw-in.

Cautions and Ejections from the Game

When the referee decides to caution a player officially, he holds up a yellow card. When he sends a player off the field, the card is red. The card system of signaling is intended to help curb violent conduct and other serious offenses by calling attention to them and to help in eliminating dissension between referees and players who speak different languages.

A caution is a serious penalty because if the player repeats the original offense or commits another violation, he is expelled from the game. And an ejection from the field of play is the severest of all penalties. The guilty player may not return to the game and may not be replaced. If he is sent off before play begins, he may be replaced only with one of the named substitutes. A substitute who is expelled may not be replaced either.

With substitutes limited to two in international matches and with these needed for strategic purposes or to replace injured players, an ejection in effect penalizes the entire team, for it probably will have to play shorthanded. Every caution and expulsion from a game must be reported to the proper disciplinary committee so that the appropriate action may be taken, and the offense and penalty are recorded. Depending on the seriousness of the misconduct, the player may be suspended for a full game or for three. Repeaters may even be banned for an entire season.

PART II
COACHING
INDIVIDUAL
TECHNIQUES

CHAPTER 5
TEACHING
BASIC
SKILLS

Coaching soccer begins with teaching the individual player the basic techniques, or skills, he will need to deal with the ball under all of the various conditions that occur in a game. The specific skills that must be mastered are ball juggling, passing, shooting, heading, dribbling, tackling, collecting, and, of course, kicking. (In soccer "kick" is a term used only when a player is taking a kick after an infraction has been called and when play is started and restarted with a kickoff. When a player moves the ball with a kick during the game, he is said to be passing or shooting.)

Some of these techniques can be perfected by practicing them directly, as in a game situation. Others must be approached a step at a time, broken down into parts with the aim of eventually putting the parts together. Although the basic skills are initially practiced without the resistance or pressure provided by an opposition, the object is to be able to transfer mastery of them to the total game situation.

The perfection of technique is not an end in itself but rather a means to achieving tactical superiority over an opposing team. This superiority, however, depends on each player's ability to execute the fundamentals of the game. The ultimate goal of technique practice, therefore, is the improvement of the team as a whole and not the perfection of isolated skills.

The coach should be careful not to hasten the process of technique training. If he introduces the element of opposition too quickly, he is likely to encounter problems in subsequent tactical workouts and game-simulating scrimmages. Such problems are especially apt to arise when tactical combinations are attempted. Whenever the coach sees that his players cannot follow through with the more complicated phases of technique and tactics training, he should take them "back to the drawing board" for further practice of the fundamentals.

Coaching basic skills is based on a progressive pattern, beginning with the fundamentals and leading to the more complex methods of dealing with the ball. This progression is as follows: the *fundamental stage*, the *game-related stage*, the *game-condition stage*, and *functional training*.

THE FUNDAMENTAL STAGE

As with all skills in sports (or life), practice is the route to perfection. At the fundamental stage of training, practice takes the form of repetition of individual and group exercises, with emphasis on consistently successful execution. Fundamental technique practice requires a ball for each player so that maximum ball contact is achieved. The objective of this training is to put the player in situations where he must:

Pay attention to his surroundings
Understand the behavior of the moving ball
Develop the ability to track the flight of the ball
Determine accurately where to meet the ball
React to the ball
Look around when receiving the ball
It is important at the fundamental stage to give the

player enough time and space for successful performance. At first, simply serve the ball to the player at varying speeds and trajectories and from various distances. With beginners, the serve may be made by hand for a more accurate delivery. Emphasis should be placed on the player's stability and equilibrium. Do not stress speed, strength, or power until he is

able to execute the basic motions with proper timing.

The fundamental stage of skills training has been broken down into eight distinct parts: *ball juggling*, *passing*, *shooting*, *heading*, *dribbling*, *tackling*, *collecting*, and *pendulum training*. It is essential for a coach to convince his players of the value and importance of practicing and perfecting these basic

skills. Full concentration should be demanded during all phases of technique training.

Ball Juggling

There is no doubt that ball juggling is the best way to develop a "feel for the ball." Beginning players are accustomed to using their hands in sports and life activities, and it is essential that they become accustomed to controlling the soccer ball with their feet and other parts of the body. Ball juggling is the technique of keeping the ball in the air continuously, using the feet, thighs, head, and combinations of these parts. The ball should not hit the ground.

Besides developing a feel for the ball, ball juggling improves concentration and body rhythm. It also helps to eliminate the psychological fear of the ball and thus enhances a player's confidence in making tactical decisions under game conditions. Ball juggling exercises teach the player to control the ball, a skill that allows him to execute all of the other basic soccer skills more efficiently.

Before working on ball juggling, have your players learn to lift the ball from the ground with their feet. They should become equally adept with either foot. Any round ball will do for lifting practice—even a tennis ball. Ask your players to be alert, concentrate, keep their eyes on the ball and their bodies in balance. The ball should not be forced upward, just lifted gently.

A good exercise to help players develop a feel for the ball is to have them juggle the ball with the instep while they are seated.

Ball juggling should be taught in the following progression:

Have players start juggling by dropping the ball from their hands onto their foot or thigh.

When they improve at this, have them start with the ball on the ground, lifting it with their foot to get the ball in motion.

Have players juggle while keeping their eyes on the ball. They should try to remain stationary and keep the ball low. The juggling motions should be easy and rhythmic.

Set goals. Start with 5 juggles and increase the number required as players improve.

When players can juggle well standing in place, have them try juggling as they move across the field.

Ball Lifting to Begin Ball Juggling

—with the Insides of the Feet

—with the Instep

Place the insides of the feet as close to the ball as possible.

Carefully and quickly, scoop the ball up by jumping off the ground.

Point the toes of the lifting foot. Push the instep under the ball.

Carefully and quickly, scoop the ball up by lifting the knee.

Ball Juggling Using Various Parts of the Body

Start juggling on one thigh. Then juggle back and forth between both thighs. Let the ball land on the middle of the thigh.

Point the toes so that the instep is level. Let the ball land on the instep.

Tilt the head back and let the ball hit on the upper part of the forehead. Bend the knees and hit the ball with an upward stabbing motion.

The following ball juggling exercises should be part of each player's training routine:

Stationary ball juggling

With the feet (inside, outside, and instep)
With the thighs
With the head

Ball juggling while moving

With the feet (inside, outside, and instep)
With the thighs
With the head

Combination of stationary and moving juggling

Various combinations using the feet, the thighs, and the head

Ball juggling tips for players

Keep your eyes on the ball.
Maintain your balance.
Place your weight on the balls of your feet.
Keep all areas that contact the ball level; otherwise the ball will bounce away from you instead of straight up and down.

Passing

As with shooting, the object of passing is to strike the ball and propel it in a predetermined direction. Passing and shooting both require timing, accuracy, pacing, power, and deceptive moves.

Passing is the foundation of the game of soccer. All moves that a player learns subsequently entail this basic technique. Passing is the skill of propelling the ball—with either foot or with the head—to another player in such a manner that he is able to control the ball and select an appropriate action to take with it. (See the section on Heading later in this chapter.)

Except for hard, low kicks that are too powerful to be received (and are therefore ideal for shooting), players use the same kicks in passing as in shooting on goal. Passes may be made with the following parts of the foot: the inside, outside, instep, and heel. The inside-of-the-foot pass is the most accurate of these, but it is not as powerful as the others and is therefore not recommended for long distances. The most common pass is the short pass, which can be performed with the inside of the foot (in a *push pass*), the outside of the foot, or the instep (top, inside, or outside). In general, for a long pass the instep is used. When a player wants to send the ball backward, he can do so with his heel (this is called the *heel pass*). In all the kicks, the point at which the player's foot makes contact with the ball determines how high and straight the ball will travel. If contact is made at or above the midpoint of the ball, a low pass will result. If the foot strikes the ball lower, the pass will be higher. When the ball is struck left or right of center, it will tend to "bend" in the opposite direction, creating a *curving*, or bending, *pass* (also called a "banana pass"). It is crucial in teaching passing skills to stress the importance of knee flexion, which gives the ball its power and speed.

There are many other kinds of passes, including the *chip*, or lob, *pass*, in which the ball is kicked steeply over the head of a single opponent or high over the heads of a number of opponents; the *half-volley pass*, in which the ball is kicked just as it bounces up from the ground; and the *volley pass*, in which the ball is kicked before it touches the ground. (See the section on Shooting for a discussion of how to execute the basic volley kick, which is used both to pass and to shoot on goal.)

The wall, cross, and through passes are tactical plays involving other passing skills. In the *wall pass*, or give-and-go, the receiver is used as a "wall" to redirect the path of the ball. The player in danger of being tackled makes a short pass to a nearby teammate, then sprints into open space to receive a return pass. In a *cross pass* the ball is sent from one side of the field to the other or toward the center, usually to set a teammate up for a shot on goal. A *through*, or penetrating, *pass* (also called the "killer pass"), involves kicking the ball between or over the defending players to a teammate who is in a good position to shoot. *Combination passes* occur when 2 or more players use short, low passes to keep possession of the ball as they move toward the opponent's goal.

Passes right on target help your team keep possession of the ball. Your team cannot score unless it has the ball, and the longer it has possession, the better the scoring chances. Have players practice both long and short passes. Training should include pinpoint passing with the inside of the foot, the outside, the instep, and the heel. As soon as possible introduce passing on the run so players can learn how to pass the ball in a gamelike situation.

Passing exercises

Using the inside of the foot:

The inside-of-the-foot pass is most effective for short distances; although highly accurate, it is not very powerful.

Stopping the ball on the ground and passing for various distances

Direct passing of ground balls (passing without stopping the ball)

Volleying the ball in stationary position

Half-volleying

Passing while running forward and backward at a slow pace

Moving laterally at a slow pace and passing after stopping the ball

As above, but direct passing

Target passing

Combination play, including zigzag and square-patterned passing and straight passing among players making overlapping runs

Inside-of-Foot Pass

Bring the kicking foot back and keep your eyes on the ball. Lock the ankle of the kicking foot and point the toes up toward the knee.

Turn the kicking foot sideways and strike the ball with the inside of the foot, between the big toe and the heel.

As the kick is completed, keep the ankle rigid and follow through toward the target.

Using the outside of the foot:

The outside of the foot may be used for short-, medium-, and long-distance passes, although it is most effective in the short and medium range.

Diagonal passing in pairs in stationary position

Triangular passing in stationary position. Two-touch passing (touching the ball twice), followed by 1-touch passing (touching the ball once)

As above, but more slowly

Combination play

Using the instep for long-distance passing:

For most long-distance passing, the instep (either the top or the inside) should be employed. At times, the outside of the foot may also be used. The power of the kick must be predetermined to make sure that the ball reaches a teammate or is cleared from a dangerous situation.

Stationary passing to a teammate who is 30 yards or more away

2-touch passing on the ground

1-touch passing on the ground

Chipping

Volleying

Half-volleying

Centering, or crossing the ball toward the center of the field

Running slowly and then passing for distance and accuracy

Passing tips for players

When you pass, kick the ball to your teammate's feet. Do not pass too hard or too soft. (The distance you want the ball to travel will determine how hard you hit it.)

Make sure your body is over the ball as you kick it. Do not lean back.

Pick a spot on the ball where you want your foot to make contact. Keep your eyes on this spot until after you have kicked the ball.

Place your balance foot (your nonkicking foot) 6 to 8 inches from the ball, pointing in the direction you want your pass to go.

Hold your ankle rigid when you kick the ball. If your ankle is loose when you make contact, your pass will be weak and off target.

Outside-of-Foot Pass

Put the balance foot ahead and away from the ball so there is room to swing the kicking foot.

Point the toes of the kicking foot down and hold the ankle firm. Kick with the outside of the foot through the center of the ball.

Keep your eyes on the ball and follow through with the kicking foot.

Instep Pass

Bring the kicking foot back and keep your eyes on the ball.

Hold the ankle of the kicking foot firm and point the toes down so that the ball is hit by the top of the instep.

Kick through the center of the ball and follow through with the toes pointed down.

Chip Pass for Short Distances

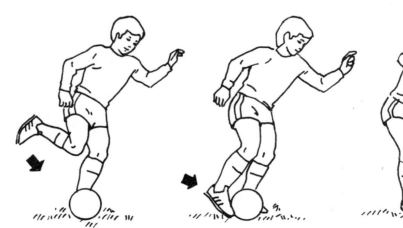

Place the balance foot close to the ball. Flex the knee of the kicking leg as high as possible.

Straighten the kicking leg and strike directly underneath the ball with the top of the instep.

Do not follow through.

Chip Pass for Distances of 20 Yards or More

Place the balance foot away from the ball and kick with a side-swing motion.

Turn the ankle of the kicking foot sideways and hold it rigid. Use the inside of the instep to strike the lower part of the ball.

Kick underneath the ball and give it backspin by holding back on the follow through.

Volley Pass Using the Inside of the Foot

Prepare to kick the ball as it approaches by facing it and pointing the balance foot toward it.

Turn the kicking foot sideways, as in passing with the inside of the foot. Holding the ankle rigid, kick through the center of the ball before the ball touches the ground.

Shooting

Shooting on goal, with the intent of scoring, requires a hard kick or a powerfully headed ball (see section on Heading). Coaching emphasis should be placed on timing, accuracy, power, pacing, and deceptive moves. As with passing, a player should be able to use either foot. Because power is an essential factor in shooting (the harder the ball is struck, the more difficult it is to intercept), the following surfaces of the foot should be used: the inside or outside of the instep, the full top of the instep, and the outside of the foot. For added force, players should be trained to put maximum body weight behind their shots at the goal. The ability to bend, or curve, the ball and to control its loft makes the goalkeeper's job harder and increases the chances of scoring.

The *volley kick,* kicking the ball while it is still in the air, is a valuable technique for scoring goals as well as for clearing balls when on defense. It is not easy to learn, but it is a necessary skill and every player should master it. To execute the volley kick, the player should first step into the path of the ball as though he were going to receive it and control it. With his eyes on the ball and his head down, he leans into the ball as he meets it in the air. Keeping his body in balance, he then kicks through the center of the ball and follows through completely in the direction it is to go.

A variation on this kick is the *high overhead volley,* which is used to send the ball over the head of the kicker. The player strikes the ball when it is about waist level and kicks his leg high, pointing the toes of his kicking foot toward his shin to help curve the ball backward. More difficult than the simple volley kick is the *low overhead volley,* or "scissors kick," which is executed with both legs in the air. As the ball approaches the player, he swings both legs off the ground, leaning backward in an almost horizontal position. When the ball is at about shoulder level, he strikes it with the instep of his kicking foot and puts his hands behind him to cushion his fall. The knee of the kicking leg can be flexed in order to give the kick added power. Both overhead kicks can help players deal with awkwardly moving balls, and both

Shooting with the Instep

Run up to the ball and plant the balance foot 6 to 8 inches from it.

Pointing the toes of the kicking foot down and keeping the ankle rigid, strike through the center of the ball.

Put plenty of weight behind the shot by lifting the heel of the balance foot at the moment of impact.

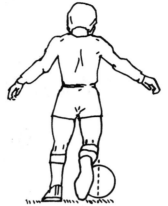 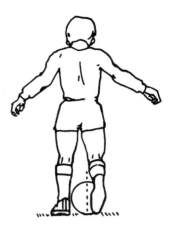

Bending Balls to the Right   and to the Left

To put a clockwise spin on the ball, strike through it a little to the inside of center with the inside or outside of the instep.

To put a counterclockwise spin on the ball, strike through it a little to the outside of center with the inside or the outside of the instep.

---

can be used to pass or to shoot on goal. The chief drawback of these kicks is their lack of efficiency: with his back to his target, the player runs the risk of missing it or sending the ball to an opponent.

Shooting exercises

Stationary shooting of ground balls from various angles and distances

Dropkick shooting from various angles and distances

Volley shooting from various angles and distances

Shooting moving balls combined with short- and long-distance dribbling, beginning slowly then gradually increasing speed

Shooting from passes received from a teammate

Shooting from combination passes

Shooting from cross passes, including ground, half-volley, and volley shots

1-touch shooting from various angles and distances

Shooting while under pressure from a defender

Pressure shooting at top speed

Specialized shooting: bending, or curving, the ball and direct free kicks, including penalty and corner kicks from various angles and distances

Volley Shot Using the Instep

To prepare to kick the approaching ball, face it and point the balance foot toward it.

Point the toes down and keep the ankle rigid, as in instep passing. Strike through the center of the ball. Put plenty of weight behind the shot by lifting the heel of the balance foot at the moment of impact.

Sideways Volley Shot Using the Instep

Prepare to kick the approaching ball by facing it and pointing the balance foot toward it.

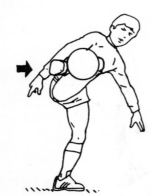

Keeping the toes down and the ankle rigid, strike through the center of the ball.

Pivot on the balance foot in the direction the shot is to go. Put weight behind the shot by lifting the heel of the balance foot at the moment of impact.

Shooting tips for players

Don't waste time. Scoring chances often last no more than a split second. When you have a chance, shoot.

It is best to be in balance when you shoot, but if you are off-balance and have a scoring opportunity, shoot anyway.

Don't shoot blindly into the goal. Try to put the ball out of the goalkeeper's reach. Fixing a target in your mind before shooting helps you to direct the ball away from the goalie.

To get maximum power, put all of your weight into the shot. Good shooters are almost airborne at the moment of ball contact.

Before the kick, fix your eyes on the center of the ball and keep them there during the kick. After the kick, follow through with your foot.

Heading

Heading, or using the head to propel and direct the ball, is unique to soccer. It is an essential technique to learn, for it can be used both to send balls to a teammate and to strike on goal. The forehead, specifically the surface between the eyebrows and the hairline, is the proper area to use. The ball should be struck with the head, not allowed simply to strike the head and bounce off.

The essential factors in heading, to pass or shoot on goal, are timing, accuracy, pacing, and power. The muscles of the abdomen and the small of the back are used to initiate the action, and the neck is held stiff. As the ball approaches, the player must keep his eyes open and trained on the ball. With back arched, knees bent, and heels raised from the ground, he makes contact with the ball and heads through it in the direction he wants it to go. In *jump heading* the player leaps to reach the ball and strikes it while he is in the air, with his back arched to provide added power.

Contact Area in Heading

Tuck the chin into the chest and keep your eyes open at the moment of impact.

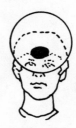

Hit the ball with the upper forehead at the hairline.

Heading exercises

Juggling the ball with the head

Heading a served ball to a partner from a stationary position

Combination heading with a partner (players head the ball back and forth to one another as they move toward the opponent's goal)—1-touch, 2-touch, 3-touch

Moving and heading at a slow pace

Jump heading for accuracy

Jump heading for power

Jump heading using the pendulum

Defensive heading

Heading on goal for accuracy

Heading on goal for power

Playing soccer-tennis using only the head

Heading tips for players

Get into the path of the ball.

Keep your eyes on the ball as it comes toward you. Arch your upper body backward and prepare to head the ball.

Don't be afraid of the ball. You won't get hurt if your head comes forward to hit it.

Watch the ball as it approaches, and watch where it goes after you head it.

Good timing is important. Start to move your head toward the ball when it is about 12 inches away. Hit it with the upper part of your forehead.

Stationary Heading

  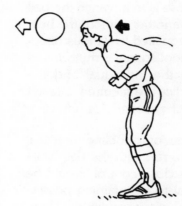

Keep the feet shoulder width apart. Bend the knees and arch back from the hips.

Tuck the chin into the chest and whip your body forward so that the ball is hit with the forehead.

As contact is made, release the chin and follow through with the forehead.

Jump Heading

Keep your eyes on the ball while jumping up to meet it. Arch the back slightly.

At the high point of the jump, meet the ball with the upper part of the forehead.

Follow through with the head and upper body in the direction the ball is to go.

Dribbling

Dribbling is one of the most exciting and creative elements of soccer. Its purpose is to advance the ball from one part of the field to another without the help of teammates. The ball is propelled in various directions by soft touches of the foot so that a rhythm and harmony develop between the individual and the ball. Countless hours of practice are required to teach a player the sensitive touch needed for effective dribbling.

In the fundamental stage of dribbling practice, players should be allowed to run with the ball while free and unchallenged. But close control should be stressed because it is crucial to maintaining possession of the ball under normal game conditions. However, if there are no other players close by, the dribbler may roll the ball out farther, having ample time to regain control of it.

Effective dribbling technique utilizes many feints, or deceptive moves. These are intended to upset the balance of the challenging defender and enable the attacker to dribble past him. Feints, in all cases, should be so convincing that they force the defender to commit himself prematurely, thus allowing the attacker to control the situation. The dribbler also must be able to change speed and direction quickly and smoothly to avoid tacklers and move the ball toward the opponent's goal. *Shielding*, or *screening*, is another way of keeping the ball from an opponent while dribbling. The player does this by putting his body between the opponent and the ball.

Dribbling can be used both to move the ball into advantageous field position and to "beat," or avoid, opposing players. If a safe pass to a teammate is not possible, the player should be able to maintain possession of the ball until a teammate is open, or free. And if the player's path is blocked by an opponent, it is up to him to fake the opponent out in order to avoid his tackle.

Dribbling Past an Opponent

Dribbling exercises

Practice creative dribbling in a restricted area, with the emphasis on change of pace and change of direction

Slalom dribbling (dribbling around or between cones or flags)

Shadow dribbling (using a partner who does not attempt to gain possession but trails the dribbler and imitates the dribbler's moves)

Passive-resistance dribbling, that is, with minimum pressure from an opponent without losing possession of the ball

Dribbling with dispossession, that is, losing the ball to a partner

Dribbling with various parts of both feet

Shielding the ball, with a partner acting as the opponent

Dribbling with convincing feints

Dribbling around a circuit

A repetition of all these exercises at a faster pace

Shielding the Ball from an Opponent

Dribbling with the Instep

Look up and around while pushing the ball with the instep, toes pointing down.

Push the ball with the top of the instep. Do not let the ball get more than 1 or 2 feet in front of the dribbling foot.

Dribbling with the Inside of the Foot

Look up and around while pushing the ball with the inside of the foot, toes pointed up.

Contact the ball midway between the big toe and the heel. Keep it close to the foot.

Dribbling with the Outside of the Foot

Look up and around while pushing the ball with the outside of the foot, toes pointing down.

Do not let the ball get more than 1 or 2 feet ahead of the dribbling foot.

Dribbling tips for players

Dribbling to beat an opponent:

Always keep the ball close to your feet. To deceive your opponent, dribble slowly and straight toward him.

Keep your eyes on your opponent's hips to see which way he is leaning.

Try to fake out your opponent by suddenly dropping your shoulder or leaning to one side.

As soon as your opponent makes his move, take the ball the other way and sprint right past him.

When you have beaten, or successfully avoided, your opponent, look up to determine what to do with the ball. If a teammate is open, pass immediately. Don't give the player you just beat a chance to get back at the ball.

Dribbling to keep the ball:

Dribble in a natural way. Use the instep, the inside of the foot, or the outside of the foot—whichever is easiest and fastest.

Always keep the ball close to your feet. Don't chase it.

Look up and around while you are dribbling. Keep your eyes on where you are going, where your teammates are, and where your opponents are.

Don't dribble just for the sake of dribbling. If there are open teammates, pass the ball. If not, dribble slowly to give them a chance to get free.

Don't run with the ball over longer distances. It is much quicker to pass it.

Shielding while dribbling:

Keep your head up and look around for chances to pass or dribble away from your opponent.

The referee will call you for obstruction unless you keep the ball within playing (touching) distance and your body in a normal upright position.

Keep the ball as far from your opponent as possible. Watch both your opponent and the ball so that you know where to move.

If your opponent tries to charge you or to go around you, move so that you are between him and the ball.

Don't fight back if you think your opponent is getting rough. In a fair game of soccer you play the ball, not your opponent.

Tackling

Tackling is a defensive maneuver designed to dispossess an opponent of the ball. It may result either in ball possession or simply in setting the ball free and

Poke Tackle

making it available to the first player who reaches it. But as a means of gaining possession of the ball, tackling is a technique of last resort.

An important principle of defensive play is to delay an opponent in possession of the ball in order to concentrate numerical superiority in the danger area—the defensive third of the field. Delaying the attacker is accomplished by jockeying, or shepherding, him to a desired part of the field. This done, and the defensive players in good position, the tackler must wait for the right moment to attack the man with the ball.

The dribbler will fake, feint, and otherwise try to induce the tackler to commit himself to a false move. The tackler must learn to reject fake information and wait for the opportunity to steal the ball or move it out of the attacker's reach. Tactical sense and good timing are essential, and good tackling requires discipline and practice.

There are four basic types of tackles: the block tackle, the poke tackle, the slide tackle, and the shoulder charge. In the *block tackle* the defensive player blocks the ball with the inside of his foot at the same time the attacking player strikes it. The defender

and the attacker kick in opposite directions; thus the tackler is attempting to block the ball's path. The *poke tackle* requires the defender to poke the ball away with his toe. It is known as a destructive tackle, as it is used to prevent a score or the development of an attacking play. Poke tackling can be executed from the rear or the side of an opponent. In a *slide tackle* the tackler actually slides into the ball, staying low to the ground and kicking the ball away. For a slide tackle, a defender approaches his opponent from the front, side, or rear. In the *shoulder charge* a defending player uses his shoulder to charge an opponent's shoulder in order to dispossess him of the ball. The contact stops the offensive player's momentum and may put him off-balance, making it easier for the tackler to take the ball away. The shoulder charge is allowed when both players are within playing distance (approximately 6 feet) of the ball. This is the only time that deliberate body contact is permitted in soccer.

Tackling skills should be taught in the following progression:
  Just before the opponent receives the ball
  At the moment the opponent receives the ball
  Immediately after the opponent receives the ball
  After the opponent has received the ball and
    has advanced into the danger area
  Shoulder-to-shoulder contact

Tackling exercises
Delaying the attacker by jockeying
Face-to-face, or frontal, tackling (slide, block)
Tackling from the side (slide)
Tackling from behind (slide, poke)
Tackling while being screened
Group tackling
Tackling when outnumbered by opponents
Shoulder charging

Tackling tips for players
Keep your eyes on the ball.
Maintain a playing distance to the attacker so he cannot accelerate past you.
Do not telegraph your intent.
Do not commit yourself too early. Your opponent may be feinting.
Time your execution carefully.
Rely on footwork rather than force to gain ball possession in executing a shoulder charge.

Shoulder Charge

Charge with the upper shoulder area only.

Push with the shoulder to get the opponent away from the ball or to upset his balance.

Collecting the Ball

Collecting in soccer is the technique of bringing the ball under complete control after it has been received from a teammate's pass, intercepted from an opponent's pass, or gained by tackling. Various parts of the body are used, depending on whether the ball is being collected on the ground or in the air. The most important aspect of collecting is to prevent any rebound so that the ball can be played to a teammate or dribbled immediately. The player's body should give with contact, cushioning the ball and bringing it to a stop. Ideally, the ball is received, stopped, and propelled toward the desired location in one smooth, efficient movement.

For effective collecting, the player must develop a sense of the flight of the ball and be able to anticipate its course as it is heading toward him. Correct timing for contact with the ball is essential. Each player initially should learn to control ground balls while remaining in a stationary position. The inside of the foot, the outside of the foot, and the instep may be used. As skill develops, the player should learn to collect the ball while moving at a slow pace.

In the next phase of training, the player is taught to control the balls that are airborne. Initially, he should learn in a stationary position, with the ball served to him by a partner. The ball should be served at a height of about two body lengths, and the trajectory, speed, and power should vary to expose the player to soft, high-flying balls as well as hard-hit drives. As skill develops, the player may move at a slow pace and serve the ball to himself, controlling it according to the coach's instructions. The player should be taught to control airborne balls using the inside of the foot, the outside of the foot, the instep, the thigh, the abdomen, the chest, and the head.

Collecting exercises

Stationary collecting of rolling balls served underhand from 10 yards (using inside of foot, outside of foot, instep—top, outside, and inside)

Stationary collecting of balls chipped by a partner from various angles and distances (head, thigh, chest, abdomen, inside of foot, outside of foot, instep—top, outside, inside)

Stationary collecting of hard-hit airborne balls served by a partner from various angles and distances (head, thigh, chest, abdomen, inside of foot, out-

---

Collecting Low Balls—with the Inside of the Foot

Move the leg forward and meet the ball with the inside of the foot.

Move the foot back as contact is made to slow the ball down.

Bring the ball far back to control it and stop it dead.

side of foot, instep—top, outside, and inside)

Chipping a ball 30 yards and running to collect it (head, thigh, abdomen, chest)

Running to collect hard-hit balls served by a partner from various angles and distances (abdomen, chest, thigh, outside of foot, inside of foot, instep—top, outside, and inside)

Controlling balls while under pressure from an opponent

Collecting tips for players

Before the ball comes to you, look around. You must know what to do with it and where to pass it after you have control of it.

Keep your eyes on the ball as it comes to you. Move into its path to make sure it does not get past you.

Always meet the ball and cushion it by withdrawing slightly at the moment of contact.

After gaining possession of the ball, be sure to control it on the ground. Do not let it bounce.

Once you have controlled the ball, pass it as soon as possible to an open teammate.

Collecting High Balls—with the Instep

There are two ways of collecting with the instep.

 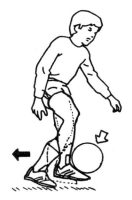

Meet the ball in midair with the top of the instep. Pull the foot, with the ball, to the ground.

Lift the foot a few inches off the ground to meet the ball with the instep. Cushion the ball by pulling the foot back very quickly.

Collecting High Balls—with the Head

Keeping your eyes on the ball, jump up to meet it, tilting the head back to cushion the ball.

Meet the ball with the top of the forehead at the high point of the jump.

Straighten up and let the ball drop to the ground as your body returns to a standing position.

Collecting High Balls —
with the Outside of the Foot

Collecting High Balls—with the Thigh

Meet the ball in midair with the thigh.

Let the ball land midway between the knee and the top of the thigh.

Withdraw the thigh on contact so that the ball drops to the ground.

Collecting High Balls—with the Chest

Prepare to meet the ball with the center of the chest. Arch your body backward to cushion the ball.

Bend the knees to aid in cushioning the ball.

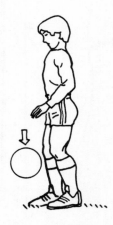

When contact is made, straighten the chest immediately so that the ball drops directly down.

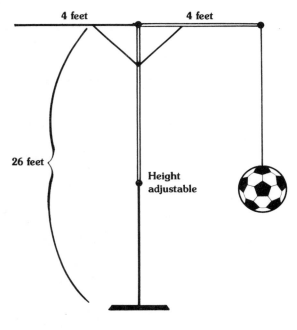

The pendulum (not shown in correct proportions here) may be used for teaching skills as well as for fitness training.

Pendulum Training

The pendulum apparatus is one of the most effective and economical devices available for technique training. It can be used singly or in a series of three or four to improve ball control, passing, shooting, and heading. At the coach's discretion, it can also be used for some types of fitness training. The advantage of the pendulum lies in the quantity of ball contact it provides. The apparatus returns the ball immediately to the player, like a punching bag, and forces him to repeat the action continually. Pendulum training is especially useful to goalkeepers because it provides practice in punching and deflecting the ball and diving for it (see Chapter 6 on goalkeeping). Pendulum exercises can be performed with or without the pressure of an opponent.

THE GAME-RELATED STAGE

At this stage of technique training, group playing situations are contrived to provide practice in specific skills. More concentration is required on the part of the player since he is now exposed to pressure of an opponent, pressure of space, and pressure of time. Additional restrictions can be introduced to improve the player's skill and to prepare him for the demands of the game itself. For example, the coach might allow only low or high passes. This type of training is always designed to reinforce the foundation that was established during the fundamental stage.

The game-related phase requires emphasis on speed and power in approaching the ball and in executing the basic skills learned in the fundamental stage. Initially the pace should be about 80 percent of normal game speed, with eventual progression to top speed. It is obvious that timing now becomes a major factor in the effective execution of technique. This creates more problems for the player, and the coach must schedule an adequate number of repetitions and demand accuracy and consistency of execution.

Game-related training must be approached in a progression relative to each player's abilities. If the player is weak in heading and does not have a good vertical jump, training should involve very little pressure by 1 opponent and balls should be served in such a manner that the player is able to head them without a struggle. As the player's technical competence improves, serves should be more difficult and pressure should be increased. The ultimate goal is to have the player head balls in rapid succession while 1 or more opponents apply maximum pressure. The game-related stage of skill training is considered phase two of teaching technique. The players learn quickly in an economical and efficient manner.

An example of game-related training would be to set up a situation for a player to receive air balls under pressure of an opponent. One player, **A**, serves the ball in the air. Another player, **B**, collects the ball while a third player, **C**, sprints in the receiver's direction, attempting to win the ball from him. This exercise should be done repeatedly, with the positions rotated.

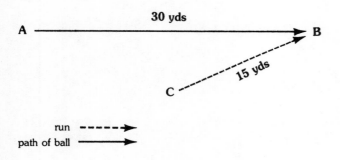

Another example of game-related training would be a passing exercise pitting 5 players against 2 players in a restricted space, or grid. The grid should be 15 by 20 yards. Five outside players play 1-touch or 2-touch, passing the ball to one another. The 2 players in the center apply pressure and try to win the ball from the passers. Concentration may be on any of the passing skills—inside foot only, outside foot only, and so forth.

THE GAME-CONDITION STAGE

Technique training under game conditions requires the continuous pressure that would be present in an actual game situation. The players must learn to perform with efficiency and accuracy while under the pressures of time and space and the constant challenge of an opponent. As the competence level increases, time and space conditions should become more restricted and more opponents should be added, until teams of equal size are pitted against each other, 6 versus 6 (6 V 6), and so on. In addition, each player should be forced to perform his skills while moving at game speed.

A player will learn much faster if he knows whether he is successful or not, and under game conditions he will find this out immediately. If he maintains possession of the ball or achieves whatever he set out to do, his performance has, naturally, been successful, his skill correctly applied. If he loses the ball or fails to accomplish a certain action, then his technique has not been up to par. Here the coach must suggest the appropriate corrections and encourage the player to participate in game-condition exercises. If a player understands the necessity for these exercises and is highly motivated to improve, he will be able to sustain long and repetitive sessions.

An example of a game-condition exercise is to set up a situation of 2 teams of 8 players each (8 V 8). Game rules are in effect, and the entire field is used. The only restriction is that passing may be done with the inside of the foot only. Shots on goal, executed with the instep or the outside of the foot, are allowed in order to hone that important skill. Another exercise might be a 5 V 5 game in which scoring is allowed only by head shots. The objective of such exercises is the improvement of particular skills and the correction of technical weaknesses.

In modern soccer the emphasis is on the total game rather than the restricted interplay among individuals assigned to specific positions. To insure the total involvement of all players, game-condition exercises should be performed by all team members regardless of their stated positions.

FUNCTIONAL TRAINING

Functional training exposes players to specialized training in the particular skills necessary for their positions. For example, outside forwards, or wingers, must perfect their ability to receive high balls when they are next to the touchline. They are confined in a very limited amount of space and subject to great pressure from the rear.

Heading techniques differ, depending on whether a player is an attacker, heading the ball toward the

Functional Training for a Central Striker (Central Forward)

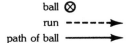

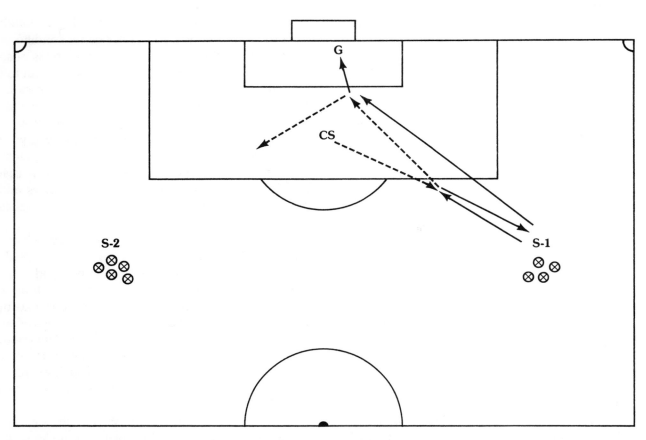

The central striker, **CS**, is positioned in the penalty area. Two servers, **S-1** and **S-2,** each with 5 balls, stand 10 yards beyond the corners of the penalty area. **CS** runs toward **S-1** as **S-1** serves the ball on the ground. **CS** returns the pass and sprints toward the goal. **S-1** passes the ball back to **CS,** who shoots, without stopping the ball, at the goal, which is protected by a

goalkeeper, **G.** Then **CS** sprints toward **S-2** and the exercise is repeated. Variations of this exercise may be devised by repositioning the servers, placing one near the corner area, for instance, and having him serve the next ball for a header shot by the central striker.

goal, or a defender, heading it away from the goal. On the fundamental level of training, the player learned the basic technique of heading the ball. On the functional training level, he learns how to head the ball according to his position on the field and to the tactical situation he is in. In other words, he must learn how to apply the fundamental skills he has acquired.

Functional training usually is performed under game conditions. The player is asked to perform quickly and accurately under pressure. To reduce the pressure somewhat at the earliest stage, the opposing player who is providing passive resistance (minimum pressure) may be moved 5, 10, or 15 yards away. This allows the offensive player to execute his skill at less than game pace. But soon thereafter the oppos-

Functional Training for a Defender Clearing Head Balls

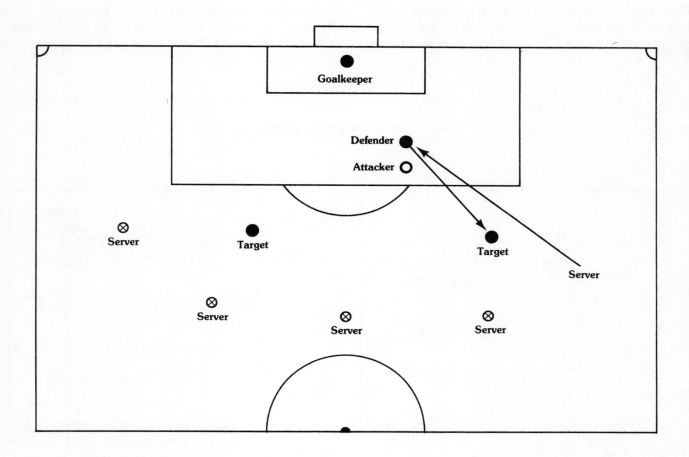

ing player should be positioned closer to simulate actual game conditions.

Functional training also offers the player an opportunity to eliminate flaws in his performance; at this stage exercises become more meaningful. The player can recognize the importance of his actions to the total pattern. He can envision the entire game situation while actually participating in only part of it. He might be practicing receiving high balls next to the touchline, but in his mind he can see himself following up with a pass to a supporting player or feinting to take on an opponent.

The coach must identify the particular weaknesses of each of his players and remedy them under game conditions. If a forward has his shots blocked continually or if he is prone to lose possession while in the opponent's penalty area, it would not be a good idea to work on his shooting technique. Evidently his problem is lack of quickness in shooting while under pressure, and it is this aspect that must be improved. The player must be trained in the penalty area under great pressure by opponents, and he must be asked to create his own opportunities—by feinting, sprinting, passing, or screening—to get his shots off quickly.

Another example of functional training might involve a defender who has difficulty clearing head balls away from the goal area. It would not make much sense to have him engage in heading exercises. Instead, he should be placed in the same situation, again and again, that gives him trouble on the field. He should be served the ball from 30 or 40 yards away, with offensive players providing pressure. The defender must practice not only clearing the ball but clearing it to a target. To refine the exercise further, the coach might set up a situation where 4 or 5 players serve balls to 1 or 2 defenders who must head the balls to 2 target men while they are challenged by 1 or 2 attackers.

In the functional training exercises illustrated in this chapter, it is up to the individual coach to determine how much pressure should be applied.

Functional Training for Midfielders

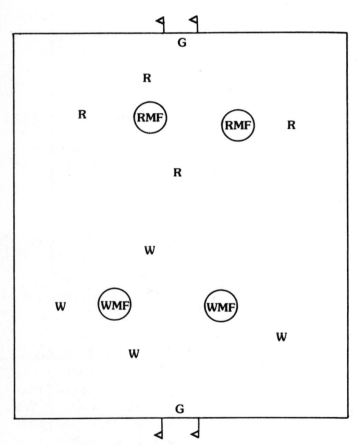

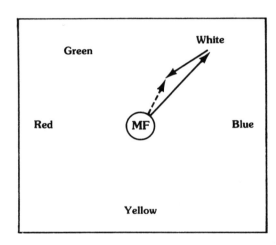

In a confined space, say 20 by 20 yards, position 1 midfielder, **MF,** with 5 players in different-colored vests around him. The vested players move around the space while the midfielder has the ball. When the coach calls a color, the midfielder must pass to that player, move toward him, and then receive and control a return pass.

On a small field, 60 by 40 yards, divide the players into 2 teams, Red, **R,** and White, **W,** with 6 players on each side. Two players on each team are designated midfielders, **RMF,** and **WMF.** The teams play regular soccer against each other, but every second pass must be made to one of the midfielders.

CHAPTER 6
GOALKEEPING

Let it be said once and for all that the statement "One has to be a little crazy to be a goalkeeper" does not apply in soccer. It is true that a goalkeeper needs to possess an unusual degree of courage, for he must frequently face and try to catch balls moving as fast as 80 miles per hour and he must sometimes dive at the moving feet of opponents. The successful goalkeeper, however, will also possess the ability to concentrate, mental toughness, emotional stability, confidence, and the ability to take charge of a situation.

In addition he will have the following physical characteristics: height, agility, flexibility, strength, power, speed, and quickness. It is the responsibility of the coach to structure training sessions in such a way that goalkeepers work on improving both their physical and psychological capabilities.

In this era of "all-purpose players" in soccer, the goalkeeper remains a specialist. Certain situations require him to play the ball with his feet; thus, he must be proficient in kicking skills. And since he is allowed

to use his hands, he is also expected to be an expert in handling the ball. Obviously, training goalkeepers is different from training field players. It requires the personal supervision and special attention of the coach or a qualified assistant for at least 30 minutes of each training session. Too often goalkeepers come to a training session, warm up, and wait for shooting practice to begin. This is a waste of their time and a potential loss to their team, especially if they are asked to do little besides serve as shooting targets. Goalkeepers have specific techniques to master and should be put to work practicing them while the field players are practicing theirs.

With goalkeepers, as with field players, it is important that the coach follow a logical progression in teaching new techniques. Each skill should build on those previously learned. For example, it would not make much sense to have a goalkeeper practice the technique of diving before he has been shown the basic stance for goalkeeping or how to catch the ball. Start with the fundamentals and progress, at the player's own pace, to more complex moves. Demand perfection in the techniques learned and show patience when working on weaknesses. Give cues, analyze the problems, make corrections, and reinforce the positive.

The goalkeeper may have problems due to factors other than skill deficiency. For instance, an insufficient level of fitness may cause him to bend his knees when he comes forward to pick up a rolling ball even though his legs should remain straight to form another barrier. This problem could be caused by the lack of flexibility of his hamstrings and calf muscles. Remember: coaches and players can continue to build only upon a solid foundation of fitness.

Once the goalkeeper is proficient in technique at the fundamental stage of training, he can move on to the game-related stage, which requires the simulation of game conditions with certain restrictions. For example, the goalkeeper, starting from a position on the goal line, is asked to come out of the goal, gather in a high cross shot from the left side, turn, throw the ball to a player on the right side, return to the starting point, and accept a cross from the right side. In this exercise he works on coming out of the goal, judging oncoming balls, catching balls above his head, and then throwing the balls to a target without challenge from field players.

To simulate a game situation, place cones within the goal and penalty areas to present the goalkeeper with obstacles in his path toward the ball. Next, instead of cones, use players who offer passive resistance, or minimum pressure. The goalkeeper's task is being made increasingly more difficult in order to prepare him for the ultimate test of performing at top speed under pressure from field players. In practice

sessions introduce constant variations in the height, direction, angle, speed, and frequency of the balls served him, the position and speed of his movements, the techniques he is allowed to use, the space available to him, and the degree of pressure from opponents.

It is important to remember that a tired body does not learn or execute well. Goalkeeper training should be performed at high intensity for short durations. Stop the exercise when mental or physical fatigue sets in. Ample recovery time should be allowed for the pulse rate to return to normal before you continue with the next exercise. During the recovery period, the goalkeeper may practice another technique at the fundamental level, do a few flexibility exercises, or simply enjoy total rest.

THE GOALKEEPER ON ATTACK

Too often the goalkeeper is viewed only as a player with a defensive role. Yet he also has important attacking responsibilities, calling for techniques that are different from those of the field players. Usually when the goalkeeper plays the ball, he is participating in a transition from defense to offense. His technical execution must be flawless and tactically sound so that the transition proceeds smoothly and to his team's advantage.

Once he has possession of the ball, the goalkeeper is the first line of attack. As he prepares to play the ball, his teammates must position themselves away from the opposition, so that he can initiate the attack by throwing, punching, or kicking the ball to them. How fast, accurately, and far he sends the ball will, in part, determine the success of the counterattack and his team's ability to maintain possession.

Throwing

A goalkeeper throws the ball either by rolling it along the ground in an underhand motion or by throwing it in the air in an overhand motion. Rolling the ball is usually the more accurate technique, but the distance possible with this throw generally does not exceed 30 yards. If a greater distance is required, the goalkeeper should execute the overhand throw. A kicked ball travels even farther, but its delivery is less accurate,

Throwing Exercise 2

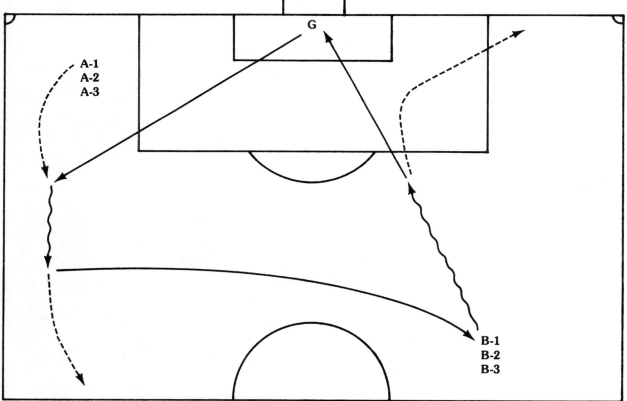

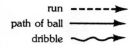

run - - - - ►
path of ball ———►
dribble ∿∿►

and so the ball is subject to loss to the opposition.

Have the goalkeeper begin practice by stepping in the direction of a target man and rolling or throwing the ball to his feet. As the goalkeeper's accuracy improves, the distance to the target man should be increased. The next step in practice is to require the goalkeeper to throw the ball to a moving target man. The keeper should work on his form, pace, and accuracy of delivery.

Exercise 1. The goalkeeper is in the goal. Player **A**, standing to the left of the penalty area, serves the ball to him. The goalkeeper leaves the goal, collects the ball, and using the specified technique (either underhand rolling or overhand throwing), delivers it to player **B**, who is to the right of the penalty area. The goalkeeper returns to the goal to receive the ball from player **B** and deliver it to player **A**. Continue the exercise in this manner.

Exercise 2. A line of players (**A-1**, **A-2**, **A-3**, etc.) is positioned near the goal line to the left of the penalty area. Another line of players (**B-1**, **B-2**, **B-3**, etc.) is to the right of the center circle. The goalkeeper initiates the play by throwing the ball to **A-1**, who is running upfield. **A-1** collects the ball, dribbles to a designated point, passes the ball to player **B-1**, and continues on to a position opposite the **B** group. Player **B-1** collects the ball, dribbles, shoots on goal before reaching the penalty area, follows his shot, and continues on to a position opposite the **A** group. The direction of play is reversed after all the players have received and shot the ball once. The pace can be increased by giving a ball to player **B-1** and having him begin his task as soon as the goalkeeper has released the ball to **A-1**.

Kicking

The goalkeeper must acquire proficiency in kicking still balls and hand-held balls. He needs to know how to kick still balls when he is called on to make goal kicks from the goal area. Kicking from the hands, punting, or drop-kicking can be a potent weapon for clearing balls great distances when he gains possession and the attackers are concentrated near the goal. However, accuracy of delivery always outweighs the advantage of distance. Furthermore, a low kick is always better than a high one since a high-flying ball hangs in the air, and opponents are better able to anticipate its landing spot.

Exercise 1. Two goalkeepers, **G-1** and **G-2**, are located in the corner and goal areas respectively. **G-1** kicks a still ball to the other goalkeeper, **G-2**, who catches the ball and throws it back.

Exercise 2. Players **A** and **B** are positioned along the halfway line, with **A** near the right touchline and **B** near the left touchline. Goalkeepers **G-1** and **G-2** are in the goals. **G-1** punts or drop-kicks the ball, as specified, to player **A**, who collects it, dribbles it, and shoots on goalkeeper **G-2**. **G-2** handles the ball and punts or drop-kicks it to player **B**, who attacks the goal of **G-1**.

THE GOALKEEPER ON DEFENSE

As the last line of defense, the goalkeeper is in a position to make up for tactical errors committed by

Kicking Exercise 2

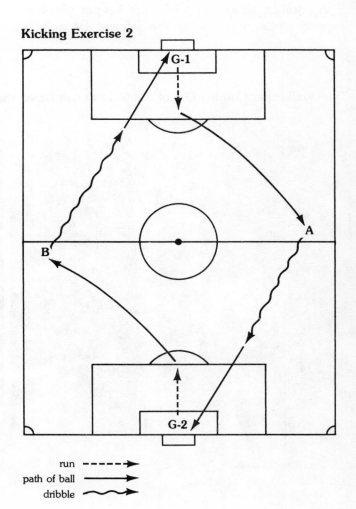

run   - - - - ▶
path of ball   ━━━▶
dribble   ∿∿∿▶

the field players. He himself seldom has a chance to be saved by others. An error by the goalkeeper bears the most embarrassing consequence—a goal. A dropped ball, a poor clearance, a mistake in judgment, and the ball is in the net for all to see. When the attacking team scores, more often than not the field players on the defending team will blame the goalkeeper rather than themselves.

An excellent save, however, brings the fans to their feet and inspires teammates to greater efforts. There is a feeling of relief when the ball is in the goalkeeper's hands. The threat is over; the pressure is off. By maintaining possession and playing the ball slowly, the goalkeeper allows the field players precious seconds to reorganize their thoughts, control their emotions, and get ready to do battle again. Not only has the goalkeeper prevented a goal, he also has given his teammates a psychological boost.

In addition to saving goals, the keeper plays an important role in organizing the defense. Because of his ideal field position, he can read situations and give specific instructions to field players that will eliminate certain dangers. For example, the goalkeeper might tell a teammate to mark the opposing number 9, or he might warn the defense that an opponent is making a blind-side run. A tactically sophisticated goalkeeper is invaluable.

Basic Stance

Since a goalkeeper's moves have to be quick, his basic stance must be comfortable and kinesiologically correct. His feet should be about shoulder-width apart, toes pointed slightly out (not forward), knees and trunk slightly bent, and arms and hands raised to screen the goal. This position keeps him ready for quick action. It should be emphasized that every move is initiated from the basic stance, the goalkeeper's "ready position," which he assumes whenever a dangerous situation develops.

The Goalkeeper Coming Out of the Goal to Cut Down the Angle for the Shooter

The coach should see to it that goalkeepers do not add extraneous moves to the required minimum for making a save. Goalkeepers frequently will move both feet and increase the width of their stance just prior to making a diving save. This means that their weight distribution is no longer ideal, not to mention the reaction time that is lost.

Positioning

Goalkeepers feel most comfortable on the goal line and since traditionally most of their training has taken place there, some might fear coming out of the goal. However, it is impossible to defend the goal by playing only on the goal line. When he is facing a single attacker on a breakaway, the goalkeeper must come out and position himself to obstruct more of the goal from the shooter; in other words, he must confine the attacker's visual target area to the smallest possible part of the goal. This is called ''cutting down the angle to the goal.''

Good positioning will force the attacker to shoot at

How Positioning Cuts Down the Angle to the Goal

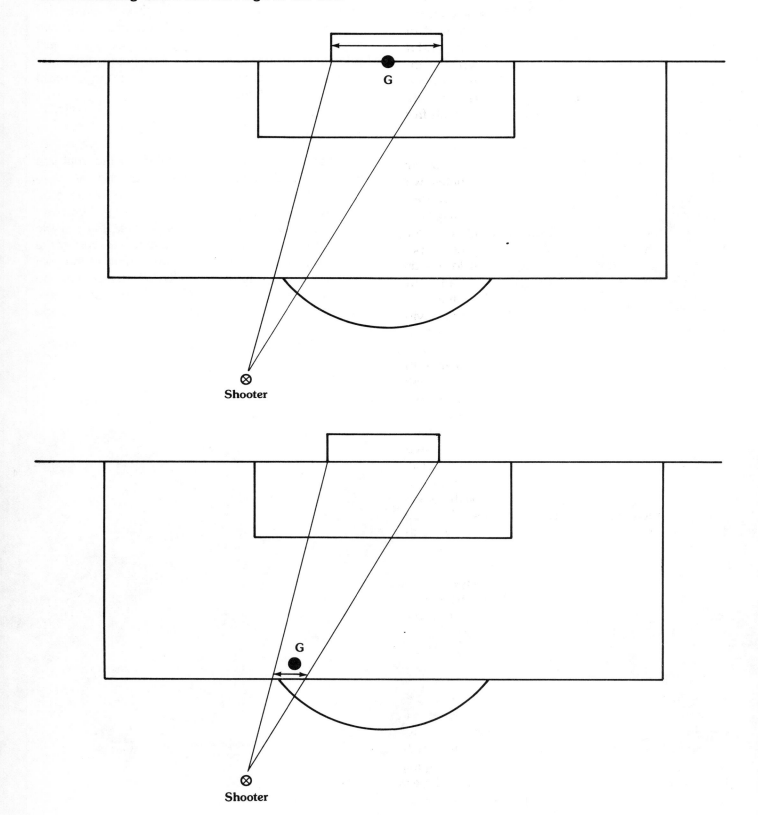

the goalkeeper. The shot might appear to be poor and the save easy, but there is more to it than that. The goalkeeper has read the situation, moved out accordingly, decreased the shooter's options, and reduced the difficulty of the save. Goalkeepers with a sound knowledge of positioning make their job look easy while less knowledgeable goalkeepers are often forced to make acrobatic leaps to prevent goals from being scored.

Coaches may use a variety of methods and equipment, such as videotape, films, photographs, geometry, and marking shot-on-goal angles with ropes, to help goalkeepers visualize and understand how correct positioning reduces shooting angles. Of course, before the goalkeeper moves out to cut down the angle, he must consider a multitude of possibilities: the attacker's position on the field, his distance from the goal, his abilities, the pace of his run, the direction of his run, and his passing options.

To help goalkeepers overcome their fear of leaving the goal, the areas of their responsibility should be defined and included in their training. These areas are: the goal line, the goal area, the penalty area, the penalty arc, and immediately beyond the penalty area. A successful goalkeeper dominates his areas of responsibility. Goalkeepers are allowed to move outside their special domain, but they are not permitted to use their hands when they leave the penalty area.

Exercise 1. Seven players are positioned outside the penalty area, each sitting 5 yards behind a ball, which is inside the penalty area. The coach calls on each player to stand up and shoot on goal. The goalkeeper, starting from the goal line, moves toward the player called, makes the save, and returns to the line.

Exercise 2. The players are placed at various points on the field. On command, 1 player attacks the goal and shoots before he reaches the penalty area. The keeper, starting from the goal line, comes out, makes the save, and returns to the line.

Catching Balls

During a game the goalkeeper must be able to catch balls traveling at various levels—low, medium, and high—and various speeds. His training in catching balls should reflect these game requirements. Catching balls is a fundamental technique of goalkeeping, and a significant amount of training should be done in this area. Besides his hands, the goalkeeper should

set up a second barrier in the path of the ball: his legs, stomach, or chest. His elbows should be kept close to his body to help cushion the impact of the ball.

It is important for the goalkeeper to know the basic "W" position of the hands (thumbs and spread fingers form the "W") and how the hands should be adjusted for balls coming at various heights and from different directions. For balls of medium height that come at the goalkeeper below his waist, the palms should be held facing the ball with fingers pointing down and thumbs pointing away from the body. For balls coming above the waist, the fingers should be held up. The body should be behind the ball to serve as a second barrier and also, if necessary, to cushion the impact of the ball. Obviously, the eyes must be constantly focused on the ball.

When picking up rolling balls, the goalkeeper should keep his feet several inches apart, bend for-

ward at the waist with knees remaining straight, and hold his hands slightly apart with palms facing the ball and fingertips almost touching the ground. He should allow the ball to roll up his palms and forearms, thus bringing it to his chest. Going down on one knee, still done by many goalkeepers, is not recommended since it immobilizes the goalkeeper. It also slows his release of the ball since he must stand up before throwing or kicking it.

Exercise 1. Goalkeepers work in pairs, facing each other 10 to 20 yards apart. One goalkeeper, **G-1**, rolls the ball to the left of **G-2**, who moves directly into the path of the ball and scoops it up. **G-2** rolls it back to the right of **G-1**, who meanwhile has moved directly into the path of the ball. The sequence is repeated without pause.

Exercise 2. The coach, from the penalty spot, shoots or drop-kicks medium-high balls directly at

Rolling Balls Exercise 1

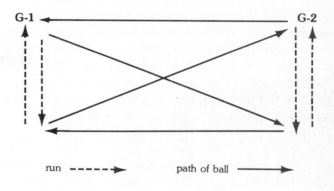

and slightly to the side of the goalkeeper, who attempts to catch each ball.

High balls tend to be a goalkeeper's greatest worry. Not only must he be quick in his judgment and movements but he also must be ready for contact with other players. In order to be the first player on the ball at the highest point possible, he must jump. A takeoff on one foot will give him additional elevation and will also enable him to use his other leg to protect himself from other players. Goalkeepers should be able to jump equally well off either foot. For high catches, the hands should be spread farther apart than for catching medium-high balls. When a goalkeeper is certain of catching the ball, he should call to his defenders that he is about to do so. The defenders then should stop moving toward the ball and begin their transition to attack. Good judgment is required because the opposing forwards will continue to move and may spot a clear path to the ball or the goalkeeper.

Exercise 3. Cones are placed in the goal area as obstacles representing attacking players. Player **A** plays the ball high into the goal area. The goalkeeper,

coming off the line, jumps, catches, and throws the ball to player **B**, who returns a high serve. The routine is repeated, with the goalkeeper throwing the ball to **A**, etc.

Punching

Ideally, the goalkeeper will try to catch any ball that he can reach. However, there are times when it is wiser to punch the ball than to try to catch it. For example, if the ball is slippery or if the goalkeeper would have to displace an opponent who is in a good position to receive the ball, punching is safer and quicker.

The goalkeeper may use one hand or both hands to punch, depending on the situation and his intentions. The two-handed punch is used when the goalkeeper wishes to change the direction of the ball or to send it back where it came from. The one-handed punch is used to make the ball continue on its course, only altering its direction slightly.

For the one-handed punch, the goal-side hand should be used (either hand may be used if both

Catching High Balls Exercise 3

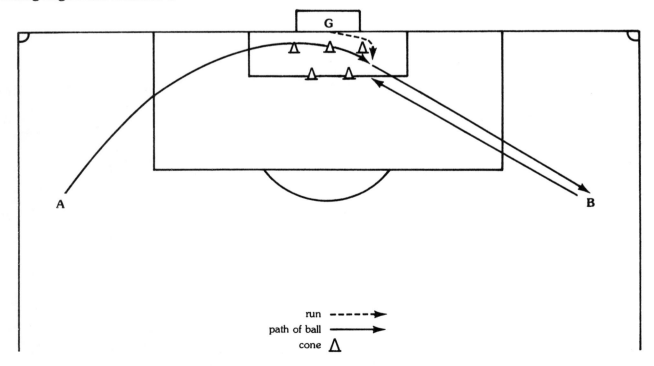

hands are equidistant from the goal), and it is important that the goalkeeper gain maximum elevation. He should punch the ball with a short, brisk stroke, using his fist. If he takes a big swing, he risks making poor contact with the ball. During the punch, the wrists should be firm and power should come from the extension of the elbows.

When the goalkeeper punches the ball, he tries to accomplish three things: to play the ball wide, to play the ball high, and to play the ball deep downfield. Pendulum training can be especially useful in the early stages of punching practice. Punching is primarily a defensive technique, but a good goalkeeper can punch a ball 40 yards or farther with great accuracy and quickly send his team on a counterattack.

Exercise 1. The coach serves 10 high balls from the left side of the field, and the goalkeeper punches each of them to a designated space outside the penalty area. The exercise is repeated from the right side of the field.

Exercise 2. Player **A-1** serves a high ball to the goalkeeper, who punches to target man **B-2**. **B-2** passes to **B-1**, who serves to the goalkeeper. The

goalkeeper then punches to **A-2**. If a two-handed punch is practiced, the goalkeeper punches to **A-2** when **A-1** serves and to **B-2** when **B-1** serves.

Diving

Since diving is a difficult art and may give a goalkeeper nightmares, it is important that coaches proceed with training slowly and logically. At first, the goalkeeper should learn to dive from a kneeling position. Only when he understands the action involved should he progress to the standing position. The movement of the dive starts from the basic stance, although if the goalkeeper has to cover a great distance and if time is available, he may take a sidestep or a crossover step prior to diving.

The goalkeeper should develop an image and an understanding of the various phases of the dive—shifting of weight; lateral bending at the waist; takeoff; position of arms, hips, and legs in flight; catching the ball; landing; and rolling. His lower hand should be in a direct line with the flight of the ball and his upper hand on top of the ball for additional control. The

Punching Exercise 2

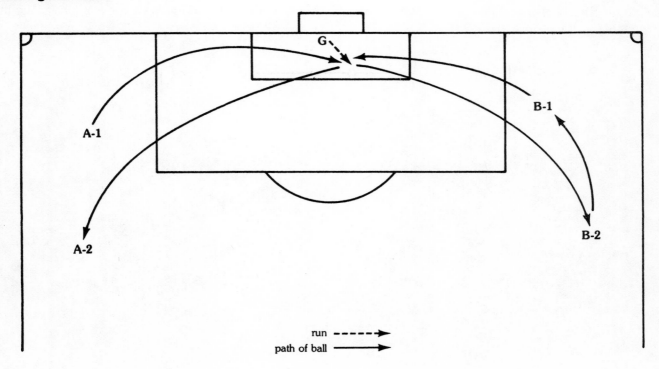

run - - - - ->
path of ball ———>

direction of the dive should be at a 90° angle to the flight of the ball rather than parallel to the goal line. It is important for the goalkeeper to return to his basic stance immediately after a dive and be ready for the next action.

Diving is hard work. It should be practiced for short periods with plenty of rest in between. The coach should try to motivate the goalkeeper. If the player performs below standard, he should go on to something else.

Exercise 1. The goalkeeper stands on the goal line in the ready position. The coach positions himself 12 yards away with 5 balls and tells the goalkeeper the direction his shots will take. With each shot, the goal-keeper dives, saves, and quickly returns to his basic stance to accept another ball. The coach gauges the ability of the goalkeeper and shoots accordingly.

Exercise 2. Ten players with balls stand just outside of the penalty area in front of the goalkeeper. On command, the players shoot on goal in rapid succession, and the goalkeeper makes diving saves. The coach controls the pace with his commands.

Deflections

In certain situations the goalkeeper might not be able to hold onto the ball at the end of his dive, or perhaps the situation is too dangerous for a catch. Since the

motto is "safety first," the goalkeeper may deflect the ball over the bar, around the post, or along the goal line. It is not necessary to strike the ball with power in order to deflect it. Gently guiding it with fingers or palm will do the job. When diving to corners for low or medium-high balls, the goalkeeper should use the bottom hand to deflect the ball around the post. Deflecting balls should be practiced only after the goalkeeper has learned to dive. Practice in deflecting balls can be incorporated in diving exercises, with the goalkeeper deciding which balls he should hold and which he should deflect.

Goalkeeper in a 1 V 1 Situation

As long as the attacker is being contained by a defender the goalkeeper need not come out of the goal. But when the attacker breaks free and the goalkeeper sees that another defender cannot intercept him in time, he must come out and challenge the attacker. The goalkeeper should, however, time and pace his run so that he does not come out too far or too soon. He should maneuver the attacker to one side by slightly overplaying the other side while remaining ready to stop and dive.

The attacker must not be allowed to change his direction, and the defending field players must continue to give pursuit to help force the attacker into the

desired direction. At the last phase of the goalkeeper's run, prior to the dive, he should swerve toward the attacked side. He should dive low, even sweeping his lower leg along the ground, to prevent the attacker from slipping the ball under him.

The goalkeeper must go down on his side rather than on his feet or head. While his lower hand stops the ball, his upper hand aids in controlling it, and his body performs a roll to absorb the impact of the dive and protect the ball. Because of the possibility of injury, a coach should teach this technique step by step and at a slow pace. Only when the goalkeeper understands all of the movements and is able to execute them with confidence can the pace be increased. And only after the goalkeeper has shown proficiency in a 1 V 1 situation should he be exposed to a greater number of opponents.

Still-Ball Situations

In still-ball situations, such as when the corner kick and other direct free kicks are being taken, the goalkeeper should always have the ball in sight and be ready to make a save. He should not be burdened with organizing the defense—setting up the wall of defenders when a free kick is being taken, for instance. These are tasks to be assigned to specific field players. Positioning himself appropriately, the goalkeeper should watch the kicker's approach and the part of the foot that strikes the ball to determine in which direction it will bend.

Scouting reports on the opposition collected prior to a game provide useful information for the goalkeeper and the field players on set plays that the opponents might use. This is especially true for direct free kicks, when the opposing team is likely to use decoy runs and passes. The goalkeeper must participate whenever his team holds still-ball practice.

The most taxing still-ball situation for a goalkeeper is the penalty kick. He is the sole defender to keep a goal from being scored. The distance of the kick is short, and the restrictions of movement do not favor the goalkeeper. It takes the ball approximately ½ second to travel the 12 yards to the goal, and the goalkeeper must stand on his goal line without moving his feet until the ball has been kicked. The psychological warfare between the goalkeeper and the shooter begins the moment the whistle is blown. It

Coaching Goalkeeping Skills

is important for the goalkeeper to remain calm and watch the kicker's approach to the ball. If he has observed his opponent during the game, the goalkeeper should have gathered useful information, such as which foot the shooter prefers, which part of the foot he uses, and whether he is a good feinter. On the other hand, the goalkeeper can only guess where the kicker is aiming the ball, then dive and hope for the best. However, before diving, he should always feint with his upper body and arms in the opposite direction of his intended dive. Making saves from penalty kicks is especially rewarding and should be practiced a lot for the benefit of both goalkeepers and field players.

CHAPTER 7
EXERCISES
TO IMPROVE
TECHNIQUE

This chapter is devoted to exercises, often in the form of games, that will help develop and improve the individual player's technique in passing, shooting, heading, dribbling, and collecting. The exercises may be used as presented, or they may be modified by the coach to suit particular needs. The coach also is encouraged to devise his own ball exercises and games to meet the specific requirements of his team and of each player.

It is important to teach individual technique in a logical progression. The coach must remain constantly alert to the faulty execution of any skill and be ready to correct errors as well as to repeat more basic exercises if necessary. In the passing, shooting, collecting, and dribbling activities, be sure that players practice with both feet. In the collecting exercises, use of the thigh, chest, and head should be included.

The exercises in this chapter will put your players into motion as quickly as possible, while teaching and reinforcing basic skills. Many of the activities will have strong appeal, especially to younger players, simply because they are fun. All of them will improve the player's technique, which eventually must be applied on the soccer field.

Passing with the Outside of the Foot . . .

And the Follow-Through

PASSING EXERCISES

Players should use the inside of the foot, the outside of the foot, the instep, and the heel in learning this most basic of all soccer skills. Short and long passes, low and high passes, executed with both feet, should be incorporated in the exercises. Wall, cross, and through passes should also be included.

Pass Through the Legs
Players attempt to pass the ball through each other's legs. They score 1 point each time they succeed.

Pass to Your Partner's Ball
Players take turns passing at their partner's ball. Each touch of the ball counts as 1 point.

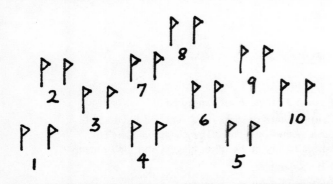

Soccer Croquet
Create a number of "gates" on the soccer field. Assign each gate a number. To score, each player must pass through all the gates in order and finish with a successful shot on goal.

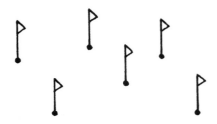

Soccer Golf

Create a number of golf holes in a specific area, and mount a target in each hole. The players must hit all of the targets to finish. Count the number of kicks ("strokes") it takes each player to hit all of the targets.

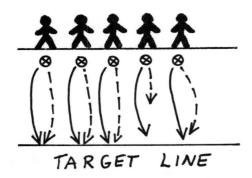

Pass and Run to the Target

Each player must pass his ball toward a target line and then run after it. He must catch up with the ball precisely at the target line. Score 1 point for each successful attempt.

Monkey in the Middle

Players in a circle around 1 or more other players pass the ball back and forth without letting the insider(s) touch it. The number of players can vary from 3 V 1 to 9 V 2. A simpler version of this exercise has nobody in the middle. The players forming the circle try to make as many successful passes as possible within a set time limit.

Pass and Move to an Empty Stick

Set up 2 lines of sticks on a field and have all but 1 player stand by a stick. The player with the ball passes to any of the other players and then runs to the empty stick.

Pass and Follow

The player with the ball passes to any other player and follows the pass as quickly as possible.

Pass and Change Lines (I)

Have players form 2 opposing lines. The first player in 1 line passes to the first player in the other line and then runs to the end of the opposing line. The ball is stopped by the receiver before he passes it. When all the players have changed lines, they begin over again, but now the receiver first-time passes (passes the ball without stopping it).

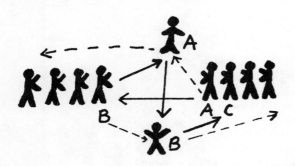

Pass and Change Lines (II)

Players line up as in the preceding exercise but work on a wall pass. Player A passes to B and then runs diagonally away from the line, where he receives a return pass from B, who runs diagonally out from the other line in the opposite direction. A returns the ball to B, who now passes to C. Players A and B change lines.

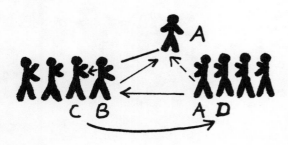

Pinpoint Passing

Players line up as in the preceding two exercises. A passes to B and then runs diagonally away from the line, where he receives a return pass from B. A then passes to C, who passes to D, and D returns the ball to A, etc. The exercise is repeated with each player changing places with A.

Volley Passing Exercises

3 V 1 Shooting at a Stick
Three players, A, B, and C, pass among themselves until one has a clear shot at a stick guarded by a defender who must try to prevent the ball from hitting it.

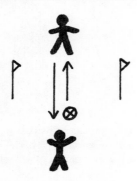

Pass Between the Sticks
Two players must pass back and forth to each other between 2 sticks. First they must stop the ball before passing it; then they must first-time pass. When the exercise becomes too easy, decrease the distance between the sticks or increase the required passing distance.

Passing with 2 Balls
Two players, each with a ball, simultaneously pass back and forth to each other, first in a stationary position and then while moving.

Hot Potato
Players standing in a circle pass the ball back and forth to each other as quickly as they can within a time limit. Whoever has the ball when time is called is eliminated. The last player left is the winner.

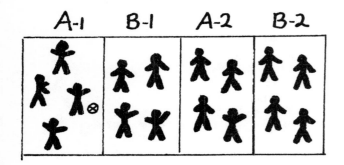

Through the Zones

Players divide up into 2 teams, A and B, with half of each team occupying alternate zones (A-1, etc.). The A players must try to keep possession by passing through the B-1 zone to their teammates. If a B player intercepts the ball, he must try to maintain possession for his team by passing through the A-2 zone. For a variation of this exercise, use 2 balls. If it is too hard, cut down the number of defenders in the 2 center zones.

Man in the Middle

Players standing in a circle take turns passing the ball to the middle man, who passes it back. The ball may be passed after first stopping it or without stopping it.

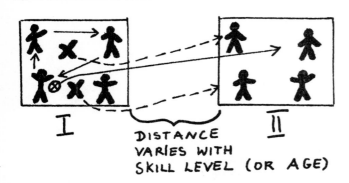

4 V 2 and Run

Position 4 men in each of 2 areas, I and II. In Area I add 2 defenders. As soon as the players in Area I have an opportunity, they must pass to Area II. The 2 defenders run after the ball. If the players in Area II can pass the ball back to Area I before the defenders reach Area II, the defenders must turn and run back. If the defenders make it on time, it is their turn to be attackers and 2 of the other players must become defenders.

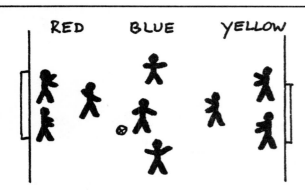

3 V 3 V 3 Passing

Divide players into 3 teams—Red, Blue, and Yellow—with 3 players on a team and the Blue team in the center. The Red and Yellow teams position 2 of their defenders in front of their goals. The Blue team must attack the Red team until it loses possession of the ball. Once the Red team gains possession, its 3 players attack the Yellow team, while the Blue team rests. And when the Yellow team gains possession it attacks the Blue team, while the Red team rests.

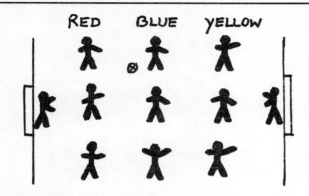

RED   BLUE   YELLOW

4 V 3 V 4 Passing

This exercise is the same as the preceding one except that the 3 players in the 3 teams are lined up and there is a separate goalkeeper positioned at each goal. The Blue team tries to score against the Red team. If the goalie makes a save or the Red team gains possession, it attacks the Yellow team. After the Yellow team gains possession and then loses the ball to the Blue team, the 3 teams change lines. This will assure that plenty of shots are taken.

ATT.

DEF.

Get Free for a Pass

Eight players form a circle around a defender and an attacker, who has the ball. The attacker must get free of the defender before he can pass. He calls a name and passes the ball to that person. Use a time limit or see how long it takes the attacker to pass to everyone. Two defenders may also be used.

Mark Closely

Set up 2 cones a few yards apart. Two players attempt to pass to each other between the cones. A defender tries to prevent this. Score a point for each successful pass. Alternate defenders.

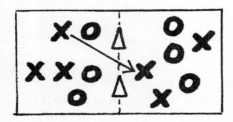

Through the Cones

Form 2 teams of 6 players each. Place 3 players from each team on both halves of a grid and set up 2 cones in the center to serve as goals. Teammates on opposite sides may pass to each other, but every player must stay on his assigned half. If a ball is passed between the cones and received by a teammate on the other side, a point is scored.

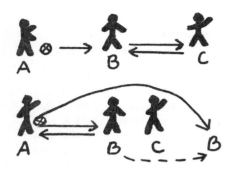

Man-On and Turn

A passes the ball to B, who is positioned between A and C. C has the option of staying back or running in close to B. If C stays back, A commands B to "turn," and B passes to C, who passes back to B. If C runs in on B, the command from A is "man-on." In that event, B passes back to A, who plays a long pass to B, who has turned on the run to receive the ball.

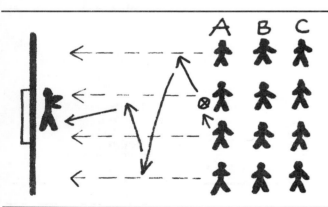

Passing at Moving Targets

Form 2 teams of equal size. The players on the team in possession, while passing among themselves, try to hit their moving opponents with the ball. Each hit counts 1 point.

Pass and Shoot

Form the players into 3 lines of attackers. The first line starts toward the goal—protected by a goalkeeper—but before a shot can be taken, each player in the line must have passed the ball to a teammate at least once. The team that shoots successfully on goal in the least amount of time is the winner. For variation, a player cannot pass to the man next to him, yet each player still must touch the ball before a shot is allowed.

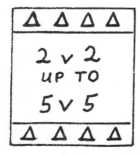

Soccer Cones

Set up cones along a line at each end of a large grid. Teams may consist of any number from 2 V 2 to 5 V 5, depending on the size of the area. The first team to knock down all of its opponent's cones wins.

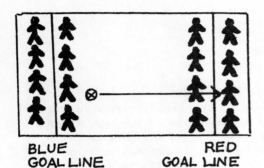

BLUE
GOAL LINE

RED
GOAL LINE

Passing Through a Wall

Have players form 2 teams, the Red and the Blue, with 8 players on a team. Divide each team into 2 groups of 4 players. Four from each team rest behind their own goal line while their teammates form a wall in front of their opponent's goal. A point is scored when the team in possession is able to pass the ball to its resting teammates and receive a pass back from them. On command, active and resting players change places.

NEUTRAL

Passing to the Outnumbered Man

Set up a 3 V 1 situation on both sides of a neutral zone. The object of each group of 3 players is to get the ball to the outnumbered man on the other side of the zone. Each successful attempt scores a point. For a variation, allow only 2 passes per player.

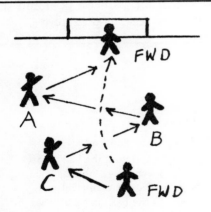

FWD

A

B

C

FWD

Wall Pass and Shoot

Position 2 players opposite 2 other players—but staggered—in front of the goal. The forward (FWD) passes to C, who passes back to the forward, who has run up to receive the ball. The forward then passes to B, and the action is repeated until he receives a return pass from A and finishes with a shot on goal. Repeat the exercise until all players have taken the forward's role.

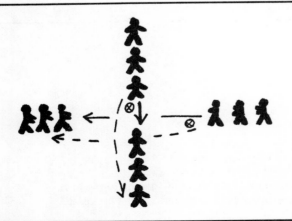

Crisscross Passing

Arrange the players in 4 lines, with 2 lines facing each other. Using 2 balls, they pass to the players in the facing lines, then run to the ends of those lines. The head must be kept up to avoid collisions as the runners cross paths between the lines.

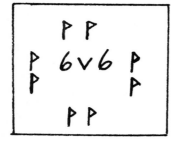

6 V 6 in a 4-Goal Game
Create 4 goals with pairs of flag posts in the center of a field large enough for a 6 V 6 game. A point is scored by passing the ball to a teammate through any of the goals. For a variation, have the teams defend 2 goals and attack the other 2.

SHOOTING EXERCISES

Players should learn immediately to use their *insteps*—the tops, the insides, and the outsides—for shooting on goal and should practice until they become proficient with both feet. Power, accuracy, and timing are essential for shots on goal and should be stressed in all of the following exercises.

Punt and Half-Volley Back and Forth
Have players form pairs and punt the ball (I) back and forth to each other using their insteps. The players should be 8 to 10 yards apart. Still facing each other (II), they kick the ball after it touches the ground (half-volley).

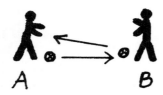

Roll and Shoot
Player A rolls the ball on the ground to player B, who shoots it back to player A, using his instep.

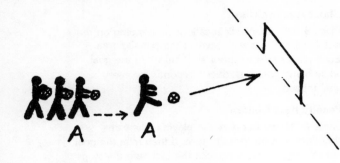

Volley on Goal

Several players line up in front of the goal. Each runs a specified distance forward while holding a ball in his hands, then shoots on the untended goal without letting the ball touch the ground (volley shot).

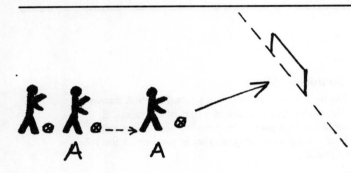

Half-Volley on Goal

Same as the preceding exercise except that the players must drop the ball to the ground before shooting and kick it on the rebound (half-volley).

Dribble and Shoot

Each player dribbles the ball a specified distance, then shoots on goal. The exercise should be.done first with an untended goal, then with a goalkeeper.

Toss and Shoot

In a line of players, have the second player from the goal toss the ball over the head of the first player, who runs after it and shoots on goal.

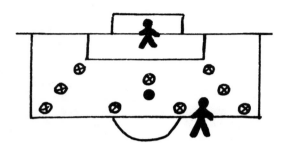

Shoot Against Time

Place 9 balls at specific locations (depending on the skill level of the players) within the penalty area. Each player tries to shoot all 9 balls into the goal while being timed. Deduct 5 seconds for every goal missed.

Penalty Kick Contest

Same as above but now the players take turns shooting from the penalty spot. If they miss the goal but manage to catch up with the ball before it stops rolling, they are allowed to stay in the contest.

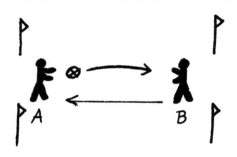

Control and Shoot

Set up 2 goals, using 4 flag posts. Player A throws the ball to B and calls out a part of the body. B must use that part of his body to collect the ball before he shoots on goal. Player A assumes the role of goalkeeper.

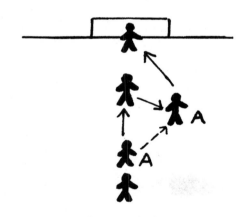

Pass and Shoot

Players form a line in front of the goal. One of them is stationed as a target midway between player A in line and the goal. Player A passes the ball to the target player, then runs out to receive a return pass from him. Collecting the ball while running, player A shoots on goal. The player who shot becomes the next target player, and the person who served as the target goes to the end of the line.

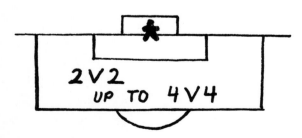

2 V 2 Up to 4 V 4 Against Time

Place 2 teams of from 2 to 4 players in the penalty area. Give each team a ball and have them both try to dribble and shoot on goal. Time limit: 1 minute.

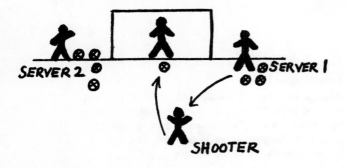

Shooter in the Middle

Position a shooter in front of the goal and place 2 servers on opposite sides of the goal, on the goal line. The servers alternate sending balls to the shooter, who attempts to volley kick on goal.

Correct Form for Making a Shot on Goal

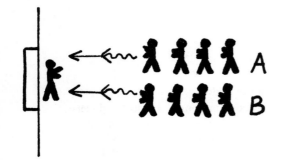

Line Against Line

Arrange players in 2 parallel lines, A and B, facing the goal area. Alternately, the first player in each line dribbles a specified distance, then shoots on goal, with the goalkeeper in position. The line scoring 5 goals first is the winner.

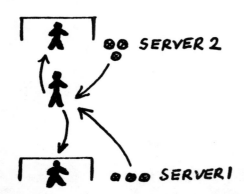

Shoot on Opposite Goals

Set up 2 goals about 30 yards apart on the field, and position a server beside each goal. The servers will alternate sending balls to the shooter, who is positioned midway between the 2 goals. After receiving the ball from one direction, he will turn and shoot in the opposite direction, either collecting the ball before shooting or using the volley kick to shoot directly on goal. After 20 serves, the total number of goals is counted.

HEADING EXERCISES

Three types of heading should be practiced and learned. They are heading for a goal, defensive heading, and heading passes. Each requires basically the same form. Make sure players use the proper area of the head—the forehead, between the eyebrows and the hairline—to strike the ball.

Heading Keep-Up and Head Juggling

A player practices heading against a wall (I), attempting to prevent the ball from touching the ground. Another (II) juggles the ball, using only his head. See how long the players can keep the ball in the air.

Heading Exercises with a Partner

Heading in Pairs

Two players head the ball back and forth to each other. They should be required to do both 1-touch and 2-touch heading in this exercise.

Heading on Goal (I)

Set up 2 flag posts to serve as the goal. The goalkeeper stands in the goal and throws the ball to his partner, who then heads on goal. After 10 attempts, the players switch roles.

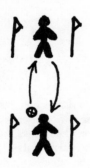

Heading on Goal (II)

Same as the preceding exercise except that 2 goals are used and both players serve as goalkeepers. They alternate heading on goal.

Heading in 3s

Player A heads the ball to B, who heads it back to A. Then player A heads the ball over B to C, who heads it back to B, who has turned to face him. B heads back to C, and C heads the ball over B to A. Repeat.

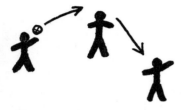

Throw-Head-Catch (I)

Have 3 players form a triangle. The first player throws the ball to the second, who heads it to the third. The third player throws the ball back to the first player, etc.

Throw-Head-Catch (II)

Same as the preceding exercise but the player throws the ball up for himself and heads it to a teammate.

Turn and Head on Goal

Position a player a certain distance in front of a regulation goal. Two other players serve balls to him rapidly and alternately from the sides of the goal area. The player who is shooting must head on goal, quickly turning from 1 server to the other to receive the ball.

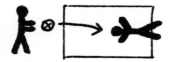

Diving Headers

Using a pole-vault pit, have players dive into it to head a served ball. Make sure to teach the proper technique for landing before commencing this exercise.

Circle Heading

Have players form a circle with 1 man in the center. Players on the outside of the circle take turns throwing the ball to the player in the middle, who heads it back to them.

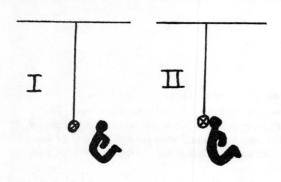

Pendulum Heading / Heading and Stopping

Have players practice heading a ball suspended from a pendulum apparatus (I). After a while they should attempt to stop every other ball dead instead of heading it (II). The players must jump to meet the ball. This will provide excellent training and plenty of ball action.

1 V 1 with Pendulum (I)

Two players jump up competing to head the ball suspended from the pendulum apparatus.

1 V 1 with Pendulum (II)

Same as the preceding exercise except that another player, serving as a goalkeeper, attempts to punch the ball away from both players.

Hold Above Head

One player holds the ball above his head. The other player then jumps and heads the ball out of the first player's hands.

Head and Change Lines

Have players form 2 lines facing each other. The first player in 1 line heads the ball to the first player in the second line and then runs to the end of the second line. The ball is kept in the air while players change lines.

Side-to-Side Heading

One player throws the ball to alternate sides of another player, who runs and attempts to head it, using his inside foot when he takes off.

Two Men in the Middle

Have players form a circle, with 2 defenders in the middle. A player on the outside of the circle tosses the ball to another player on the outside. The receiver heads it back to the thrower while the defenders try to intercept it. Set a time limit.

As the players' heading skills increase, add more defenders in other exercises—in a 6 V 6 situation, for instance. Using half a field, they play regular soccer, but goals can be scored only by heading.

DRIBBLING EXERCISES

There are three purposes for dribbling: to maintain possession of the ball when no teammate is open to receive a pass, to get past an opponent, and to get closer to the goal for a shot. Dribbling should be encouraged because it promotes individualism, which is a positive attribute in soccer. The exercises should incorporate the use of the instep, the inside of the foot, and the outside of the foot.

Tag Ball, Then Heads Up

Everyone has a ball and is dribbling in a limited area. One player is "It" and tries to tag another player. The tagged player then becomes "It." This game may be played for points or for letters, with the winner spelling a word. After the game have the players continue dribbling, changing speed and direction but keeping their heads up. Silently, hold up your hand with a certain number of fingers extended. The players must call out how many fingers you have extended.

Follow the Leader

Three or 4 players follow the first person in line and try to imitate his dribbling moves.

Huntsman

Players follow the leader, but when he says, "Bang," they must try to dribble to a safety zone within a certain amount of time. See how many players he can tag in that time. He must dribble while trying to tag them.

Dribbling in a Circle

Mark off a large circle and place all participants within it, each with a ball. The circle should be crowded. Everyone must dribble at the same time, changing speed and direction often. For a variation, allow the players to kick other players' balls out of the circle. When a player loses his ball, he's dropped from the game. A player is not allowed to leave his own ball to kick another's out of the circle.

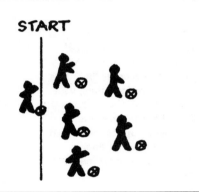

Red Light, Green Light

Place a small number of players on a starting line and give each of them a ball. The player who is "It" stands by the finish line with his back turned to the others, who begin to dribble. When he calls, "Red light," everyone must stop dribbling. He turns quickly, and if he sees anyone move, that player is sent back to the starting line. The person who is "It" turns his back again and calls, "Green light." Everyone resumes dribbling and the game continues. The first to reach the finish line wins.

Duck, Duck, Goose

Have players form a circle and dribble clockwise or counterclockwise. Another player, who is "It," dribbles outside the circle in the same direction. When he calls, "Duck," nobody moves. If he sees someone moving, that person becomes "It." Occasionally the player who is "It" points to a particular person and calls "Goose." The "goose" must chase and try to tag him before he reaches the place the "goose" vacated. Both players are required to dribble during the chase. If the "goose" fails to tag the challenger, he becomes "It."

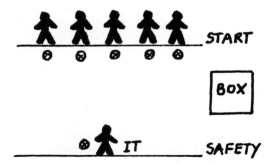

Call and Tag

Mark off a safety zone and a penalty box on the field. The person who is "It" faces the players on a starting line and calls a name or number. The player whose name is called begins dribbling toward the safety zone while "It," also dribbling, tries to tag him. If "It" succeeds, the player goes to the box. Count the players in the box at the end of a time period. Next, use 2 teams. All the tagged players go into the box but can be released by being tagged by a teammate. Count the prisoners from each team at the end of a time period.

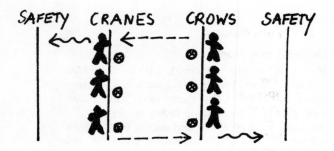

Cranes and Crows

Form 2 lines of players, "crows" and "cranes," a certain distance apart, with safety zones at opposite ends of the field. When you call "Crows" or "Cranes," the players in that line must dribble toward their safety zone while the other line, without balls, tries to catch them. Keep score of the number of players caught.

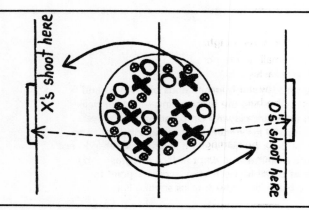

Team Against Team and 1 V 1

Two teams of equal size dribble in the center circle. Each player has a ball. On command, the members of 1 team dribble toward their opponent's goal and try to shoot on goal. The players on the other team leave their balls in the center circle and run to defend their goal. When a member of the defending team captures an attacker's ball, he attempts to dribble it back to the center circle. This exercise creates a number of 1 V 1 situations all over the field. As an additional condition, allow shooting on goal only from the penalty area.

Slap Jack

Have players form a circle. The person who is "It" dribbles around them. When he touches someone in the circle, the 2 of them must dribble around the other players in opposite directions. The first person to get back to the vacant place occupies it, and the other becomes "It."

Tag the Team

Mark off a starting line and a safety zone on the field. Position 3 teams of players—"Jaws," "Tornadoes," and "Kicks"—on the starting line. The person who is "It" faces them and calls the name of 1 team. The players on that team must dribble toward the safety zone while the person who is "It" tries to tag as many of them as he can. The last team to lose all of its players wins. For a variation, designate 1 player from each team to be "It." The 3 players try to tag members of different teams. Each tag counts as 1 point.

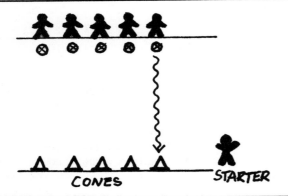

Dribbling to a Baseline

Mark off a baseline with cones, 1 for each dribbler, and have players line up facing the cones. When a person designated as the starter says, "Go," they must dribble to the baseline (using various methods), hit their cones, and dribble back to their starting line. The slowest (or fastest) player becomes the starter.

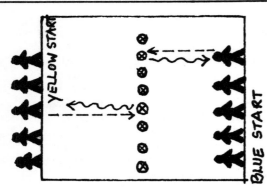

Get Your Ball

Line up teams at opposite ends of the field and place balls along the halfway line—2 fewer balls than there are players. On command, all players must run to the midfield, try to secure a ball, and dribble back to their starting line. The 2 who do not secure a ball may attempt to kick away as many balls as possible. Each team scores 1 point for every ball brought back to its starting line.

Steal the Bacon

Two teams with an equal number of players line up 15 to 20 yards apart. A ball is placed at a midpoint between them. Each team's players are numbered. When the coach calls a number, the appropriate player from each team runs to the ball and tries to dribble it back to his own starting line. Each time a player brings back the ball, his team scores 1 point.

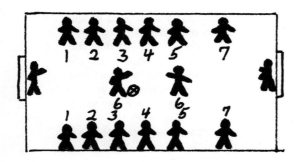

Dribble and Shoot

Line up players and assign them numbers as in the preceding exercise. When you call a number, the 2 appropriate players come out and play 1 V 1 in an attempt to score. Goalkeepers may be used. Each successful shot on goal counts as 1 point. Set a time limit of 20 to 60 seconds for each confrontation.

1 V 1 Through the Zones

Using flag posts, mark off 3 defense zones, each 10 yards deep. Place a defender on the back line of each zone. A forward (attacker) attempts to dribble through each zone, trying to beat the defender, who can move from the back line of his zone only after the attacker enters it. The defender cannot move out of his zone. The forward scores 1 point for each zone he gets through and 2 points for shooting successfully on goal. (This exercise can be varied by changing the size or number of the zones.)

A 6-Zone Game

Mark off the field in 6 zones, with alternating neutral and combat zones. The first combat zone has 3 defenders, the second, 2, the third, 1. Six other players, the forwards, dribble from the starting line and try to get through all of the zones. The defenders cannot enter the neutral zones. Count 1 point for each dribbler who gets through all the zones with his ball. Have players change roles. For a variation, allow the defenders to dribble in the other direction if they gain possession and the forwards must give chase.

Faking Behind the Line

Place cones at both ends of a straight line. Two players, an attacker and a defender, must stay on different sides of the line. The attacker dribbles the ball and feints to try to get his opponent to move out of position. His object is to lose the defender and get to either of the cones first. The defender's job is to stay with the attacker. The defender is not allowed to tackle or to cross the line. Have players change roles after a while.

1 V 1 to a "Goal"

One player dribbles and tries to maintain possession by shielding the ball from his partner, who tries to gain possession. A resting player stands by with his legs apart, and when the second player gains possession he tries to score through them. The scoring player then becomes the "goal," and the other 2 vie for possession. Count 1 point for each successful shot.

1 V 1 to a Ball

Two players attempt to gain or maintain possession of the ball and to hit a stationary ball, which serves as the goal. Count the number of times each player strikes the "goal" with the ball that is in motion.

1 V 1 Around a Stick

One player dribbles around a stick or flag post. The other player tries to tag him. If he succeeds, they exchange roles. For variation, have both players dribble balls.

1 V 1 to 2 Goals (I)

Set up a 1 V 1 situation on the field, with 2 resting players standing with their legs spread serving as goals. The 2 players in the middle vie for possession of the ball and a shot on "goal." After each has succeeded, the resting and working players change roles.

1 V 1 to 2 Goals (II)

Same as the preceding exercise except that instead of playing the ball through the legs of a resting player, each worker must pass to, run toward, and receive a return pass from 1 of them to score a point.

BALL-COLLECTING EXERCISES

Skill in collecting the ball—bringing it under control once possession has been gained—is essential in soccer. For collecting ground balls, the outside of the foot, inside of the foot, heel, and instep (top, inside, and outside) are used. To receive and control airborne balls, players must give with their bodies at the moment of contact, cushioning the ball to prevent a rebound. They must then straighten up, allowing the ball to drop to the ground in a playing position. Airborne balls are collected with the head, chest, abdomen, thigh, inside and outside of the foot, and instep (top, outside, and inside).

Collecting in a Circle
Form a circle of players and flag posts. One player takes a position in the middle. The players on the outside of the circle take turns tossing different types of serves—some low, others high—to the player in the middle. He gets 1 point for every time he succeeds in controlling the ball after he receives it.

Man in the Middle
Form a circle of players and position 1 player in the middle. The outside players each have a ball and take turns serving to the player in the middle. He attempts to collect it and pass it back to the server.

Two Men in the Middle

Same as the preceding exercise but with 2 players in the middle. As the ball is served, 1 of the middle players tries to collect it while the other runs up and attempts to steal it.

Soccer Volleyball

Set up a volleyball net and divide the players into 2 teams of equal size. But instead of directly returning the ball after it has been tossed over the net, the players must first stop it soccer style, control it, then pass it back.

Control and Shoot

Position a player just outside of the penalty area. Players on opposite sides of the goal area serve balls to him, which he tries to control before shooting on goal.

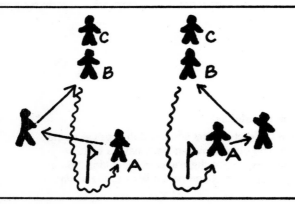

Relay Race

Players form 2 parallel lines, with a flag post 5 yards in front of each line. Two servers, each with a ball, are positioned slightly to the side of the lines. The servers simultaneously throw a ball to the first player (A) in each line. The players must collect the balls, dribble around the flag posts, and return the balls to the servers, who immediately throw to the players next in line. The first line to complete the exercise wins.

A 2-Touch Game

Two players face each other a few yards apart. One player passes the ball to his partner, who must collect it, using his head, chest, thighs, or feet, before returning the pass. Two touches are required.

Throw and Catch

Form players into 2 teams. The ball is thrown back and forth between the teams. Players must receive the ball with their chests or abdomens, giving with it to prevent a rebound, before catching it and throwing it back. If the ball touches the ground, a point is awarded to the other team.

Soccer Tennis

Position 2 players on either side of the net, as in tennis doubles. After the ball is received, it must be controlled before it is returned. If the ball is not received when it is in the air, a point is granted to the other side.

Collect and Change Lines

Form players into 2 lines, A and B, facing each other. The first player in line A throws the ball to the first player in line B. The receiver must collect the ball with a specific part of his body before returning it to the next person in the opposing line and running to the rear of that line. Repeat, with the players changing lines.

Juggling Game
Groups of 4 to 6 players juggle balls. One player in each group has no ball; he darts from one juggler to another, waiting for a loose ball. Whenever a juggling player loses his ball, the player without a ball must immediately try to collect it before the other player can regain possession. The player who lost the ball must now look for another. (With small children, allow 1 bounce between juggles.)

Collecting a Ground Ball with the Inside of the Foot

CHAPTER 8
SKILL TESTING
FOR
YOUTH PLAYERS

The following skill testing program has been devised as a series of contests for which awards—badges, for example—may be given. The skills are all soccer-related and the contests organized according to age groups. A scoring system is provided at the end of the chapter. Although the players will be competing against others in their age group, the emphasis should be on fun and participation.

To set up the skill testing program described here, you will need a playing field at least 80 yards long and 50 yards wide and the following equipment: 3 or

more balls; 4 cones; marking chalk; 2 walls, each 1 yard high and 8 feet long; and a stopwatch. Youngsters can go through the program on their own or under the supervision of a coach or parents. The contests should be an enjoyable way to train for both boys and girls through the age of 15.

DRIBBLE RUN

Set up 4 cones, one at each corner of the goal area or a 6-by-20-yard area—with a goal line and goal clearly

Dribble Run

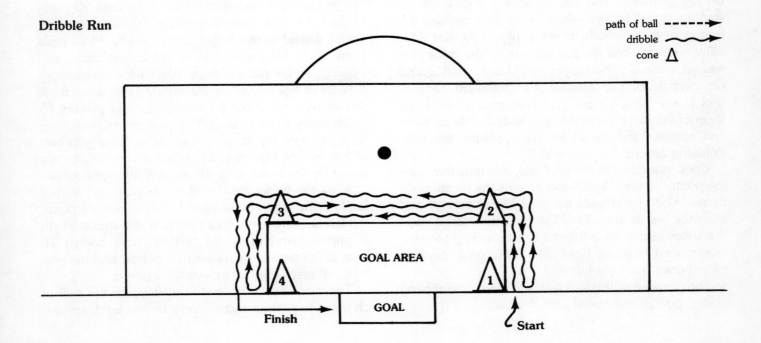

path of ball ------>
dribble ～～～>
cone △

GOAL AREA

3   2

4   1

Finish →   GOAL   Start

Chip at Target

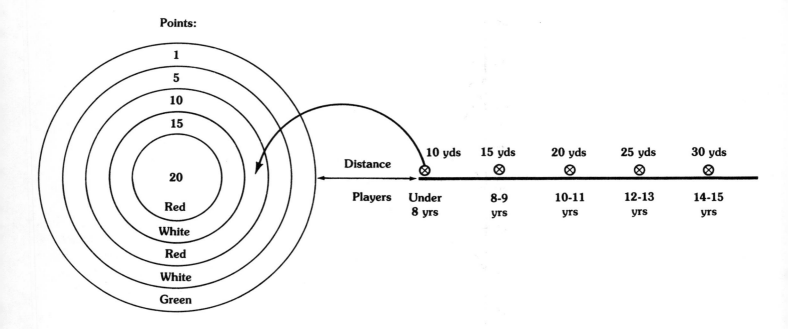

marked for the occasion—anywhere on the field. The player begins with the ball at his feet next to cone 1 on the goal line. The ball rests on the goal line. A starting signal by an official, who also presses the button of a stopwatch, tells the player to start dribbling with the ball on the outside of the goal area toward cone 2. The player dribbles around 2 and on toward cone 3, around 3 and toward cone 4, and finally back to the goal line, parallel to 4. As soon as the ball crosses the goal line, the player turns and retraces the circuit in the opposite direction, dribbling around cones 3 and 2.

Upon returning to the goal line, this time the starting point, he turns again and repeats the circuit once more. When he crosses the goal line at cone 4 and kicks the ball at the side of the goal, the official stops the watch and records the player's time. Right-footed kickers start from the right side of the goal, the left-footed ones from the left side.

The purpose of this skill test is to develop dribbling ability, agility, and speed with the ball.

CHIP AT TARGET

Starting at the center spot, mark off an area 50 yards in diameter with concentric circles 5 yards apart. The circles should form a target, as in archery. Place balls from 10 to 30 yards outside the largest circle, depending on the players' ages. (Balls for players under 8 years of age should be placed 10 yards away from the target area, those for 8-to-9-year-old players 15 yards away from it, etc.) The youngsters must chip their ball into the target area. Each player gets two attempts. The first try is a practice shot and does not count for the score; only the second attempt counts.

Mark the target area in different colors. If the shot lands in the green outer area, the shot scores 1 point. If it lands in the white area next to it, the shot is worth 5 points. Landing in the first red area counts 10 points, the second white area 15 points, and the second red area—the bull's-eye—20 points.

The purpose of this test is to develop the skill of chipping to a target and getting a feeling for distance.

Kick for Distance and Accuracy

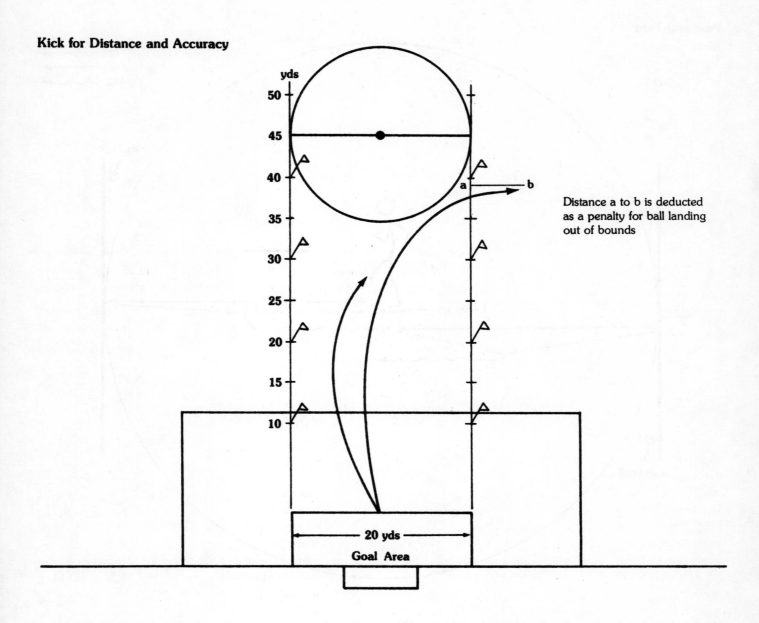

yds

50
45
40
35
30
25
20
15
10

a   b

Distance a to b is deducted
as a penalty for ball landing
out of bounds

20 yds

Goal Area

KICK FOR DISTANCE AND ACCURACY

Using the 20-yard-wide line that marks the front of the goal area as a starting point, a youngster must kick a still ball as far as he possibly can. The ball has to travel in an alley marked by extensions of the sidelines of the goal area. Each player gets one attempt. The distance is marked and scored at the spot where the ball lands on its first bounce. The player will be penalized for a ball leaving the alley: the exact distance that the ball travels outside the boundary will be deducted from the distance it travels inside the alley to determine the score.

The purpose of this test is to develop kicking power while maintaining accuracy.

PASS AND TURN

Set up 2 walls at least 36 inches high and 8 feet long, facing each other and 20 yards apart. Parallel lines

Pass and Turn

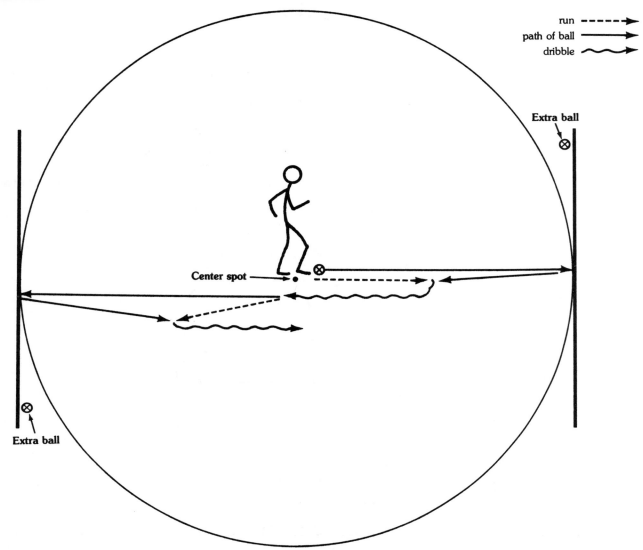

can be drawn tangent to the center circle, which is 20 yards in diameter. A youngster stands on the center spot midway between the 2 walls, with the ball at his feet. When a starting signal is given and a stopwatch has been started, the player passes the ball toward the wall he faces and runs to collect the rebound. Using either foot, he must touch the ball at least once, turn, and dribble it back to the midway point. He then passes the ball toward the other wall and runs to collect the rebound. The player continues turning and passing, each time crossing the center spot before he

kicks. He tries to hit the walls with as many passes as possible by the time 30 seconds have elapsed. In case the ball is lost, a spare ball should be ready next to each wall.

The purpose of this test is to develop passing accuracy and turning ability while improving mobility.

SHOT AT GOAL

At appropriate distances for different age groups, set up 3 balls, 1 directly in front of the goal, 1 at an angle

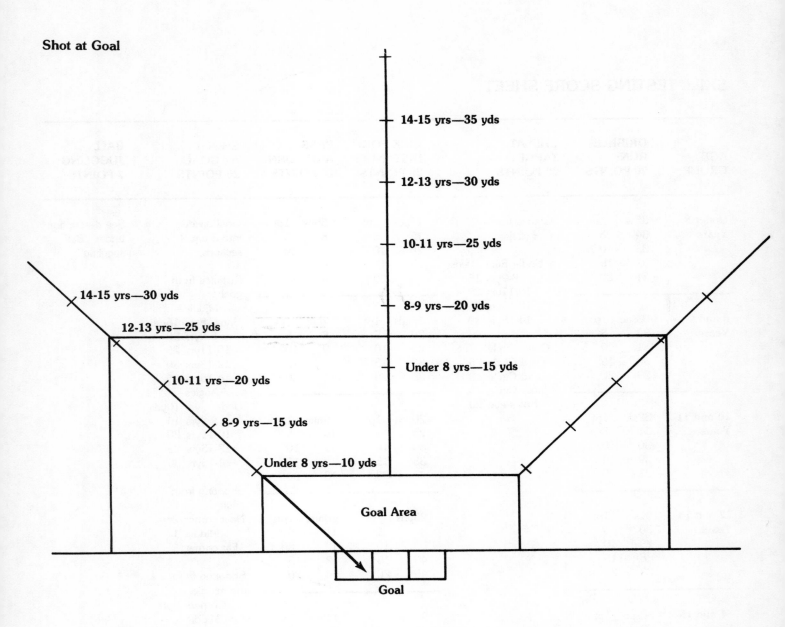

Shot at Goal

14-15 yrs—35 yds

12-13 yrs—30 yds

10-11 yrs—25 yds

8-9 yrs—20 yds

14-15 yrs—30 yds

12-13 yrs—25 yds

Under 8 yrs—15 yds

10-11 yrs—20 yds

8-9 yrs—15 yds

Under 8 yrs—10 yds

Goal Area

Goal

to the right, and 1 at an angle to the left. Each player has one attempt to shoot at the goal with each of the 3 balls. The goal is divided into 3 equal target areas, each 8 feet wide. The ball must cross the goal line between the uprights and under the crossbar without touching the ground.

When shooting from an angle, the player scores 2 points if the ball lands in the near target area, 1 point if it lands in the central target area, and 5 points if it lands in the far target area. When shots are made from directly in front of the goal, both side targets are

worth 5 points, and the center target is worth 1 point.

The purpose of this test is to develop shooting accuracy from different field positions.

BALL JUGGLING

The youngster keeps the ball in the air, juggling it by using different parts of the body. Seven points are scored for successfully completing this exercise.

Players under 8. The player throws the ball in the air, allows it to bounce up from the ground, and be-

SKILL TESTING SCORE SHEET

AGE GROUP	DRIBBLE RUN: 20 POINTS		CHIP AT TARGET: 20 POINTS	KICK FOR DISTANCE: 20 POINTS		PASS AND TURN: 20 POINTS		SHOOT AT GOAL: 20 POINTS	BALL JUGGLING: 7 POINTS
Under 8 Years	35sec	1pt	Distance from outer circle:	10yds	1pt	5hits	1pt	Goal divided into 3 equal sections.	See description under "Ball Juggling"
	34	5		15	5	6	5		
	33	10		20	10	7	10		
	32	15	Under 8yrs 10yds	25	15	8	15	Distance from goal:	
	31	20	8-9yrs 15	30	20	9	20	Middle—	
			10-11yrs 20					Under 8yrs 15yds	
			12-13yrs 25					8-9yrs 20	
8 and 9 Years	33sec	1pt	14-15yrs 30	15yds	1pt	7hits	1pt	10-11yrs 25	
	32	5		20	5	8	5	12-13yrs 30	
	31	10	Outer Circle 1pt	25	10	9	10	14-15yrs 35	
	30	15	Third Circle 5	30	15	10	15	Angles—	
	29	20	Second Circle 10	35	20	11	20	Under 8yrs 10yds	
			Inner Circle 15					8-9yrs 15	
10 and 11 Years	32sec	1pt	Bull's-eye 20	20yds	1pt	9hits	1pt	10-11yrs 20	
	31	5		25	5	10	5	12-13yrs 25	
	30	10		30	10	11	10	14-15yrs 30	
	29	15		35	15	12	15		
	28	20		40	20	13	20		
								Shooting from angles:	
12 and 13 Years	31sec	1pt		25yds	1pt	10hits	1pt	Near corner 2pts	
	30	5		30	5	11	5	Middle 1	
	29	10		35	10	12	10	Far corner 5	
	28	15		40	15	13	15		
	27	20		45	20	14	20	Shooting from the middle:	
								Corners 5pts	
14 and 15 Years	30sec	1pt		30yds	1pt	11hits	1pt	Middle 1	
	29	5		35	5	12	5		
	28	10		40	10	13	10		
	27	15		45	15	14	15		
	26	20		50	20	15	20		

SCORING AWARDS
50-70 pts: Purple Eagle
71-80 pts: Blue Eagle
81-90 pts: Green Eagle
91-95 pts: Gold Eagle
96-100 pts: Red Eagle

gins juggling with the top of the instep. The ball must be struck at least once with the instep, thigh, and head in any sequence. Six touches in succession are needed to score the 7 points.

Players 8 and 9. The player throws the ball in the air, allows it to bounce up from the ground, and begins juggling with the instep. The ball must be struck at least once with the instep, thigh, and head in any sequence. Ten touches in succession are needed to score the 7 points.

Players 10 and 11. Without using the arms, the player lifts the ball in the air and performs 3 successive bounces with the instep, 3 with the thigh, and 3 with the head. Completion in the proper sequence is needed to score the 7 points.

Players 12 and 13. Without using the arms, the player lifts the ball in the air and keeps it there continuously. He must use the instep, thigh, head, and shoulders but cannot use the same part of the body twice in a row. Fifteen touches in succession are needed to score the 7 points.

Players 14 and 15. Without using the arms, the player lifts the ball in the air and keeps it there continuously. He must use the instep, outside of the foot, thigh, head, and shoulders but cannot use the same part of the body twice in a row. He must finish by catching the ball either behind his neck or on the top of his instep and holding it still for no less than 3 seconds. Twenty touches in succession are necessary to score the 7 points.

The purpose of these ball juggling tests is to develop balance, agility, and a feel for the ball.

PART III
COACHING
THE GAME
OF SOCCER

Learning the Game of Soccer Begins with Exercises in Individual Tactics, as Shown in This 1 V 1 Situation and Described in Chapter 10

CHAPTER 9
PRINCIPLES
OF
SOCCER

The basic principles of soccer are not difficult to state. Of course, putting them into practice under game conditions is a more difficult matter. But to meet the rigorous demands and high standards of modern "total" soccer, they should be understood by all coaches and effectively executed by all team members.

The principles can be divided into three basic categories depending on which type of play they affect—*defensive*, *midfield*, and *attacking*. Another principle, *communication*, is vital to successful execution in all soccer situations.

The accompanying table provides a quick, graphic view of the principles of soccer.

DEFENSIVE PRINCIPLES

The moment a team loses possession of the ball, each of its members immediately must think and play defensively. The object is to deny or restrict the opponent's space and time, thus destroying his tactical plans. Structurally, there are three ways to play defense: man-to-man, zone, and both of these in combination.

DEFENSIVE PRINCIPLES
(Deny—Destroy—Develop)

1. Immediate Chase (Pressure)
2. Fall Back and Delay (Retreat, Jockey)
3. Concentration (Funnel), Man-to-Man
4. Balance (Depth, or Support)
5. Control/Restraint (Challenge for the Ball)

VERBAL AND VISUAL COMMUNICATION

MIDFIELD PRINCIPLES
(Build—Connect—Support)

A. Slow Buildup
1. Maintain Ball Possession
2. Dribble into Open Space
3. Combination Passing
4. Total Team Support
5. Change Speed of Ball
6. Change Direction of Ball
7. Develop Attacking Rhythm

B. Quick Counterattack
1. Rush into Open Space
2. Use Through and Cross Passes
3. Accelerated Support
4. Quick Shot on Goal

VERBAL AND VISUAL COMMUNICATION

ATTACKING PRINCIPLES
(Move—Receive—Finish)

1. Mobility (Running into Open Space with and without Ball)
2. Combination Play (Passing for Depth, Width, Penetration)
3. Improvisation (Dribbling)
4. Support (Depth)
5. Finish (Shooting)

Man-to-man defense requires tight, or close, marking (guarding) ball-side (in the vicinity of the ball), and somewhat looser marking by weak-side defenders (those on the half of the field away from the ball). Generally, each defender is assigned a specific opponent, whom he guards and stays with wherever the action occurs on the field.

In *zone defense* players are assigned specific areas of the field instead of specific players. The defender is responsible for his area, picking up attackers as they enter it and relinquishing them to a teammate when they leave. Opponents may be loosely marked, and coverage of space becomes the important factor.

Combination defense demands tight man-to-man marking while an opponent is in the defender's zone. But as the opponent leaves the zone, the defender will "pass off" his man to a teammate and proceed to mark tightly any new man coming into his area of responsibility.

Although man-to-man soccer appears to be the emerging American style of play with the greatest potential for total competitive involvement, the basic defensive principles apply to the other styles as well. Let's look at the fundamental defensive principles of soccer one by one.

1. Immediate Chase

This first principle of defense should begin as soon as ball possession is lost, regardless of where that occurs on the field. The player who loses possession im-

Immediate Chase in Attacking Third of Field

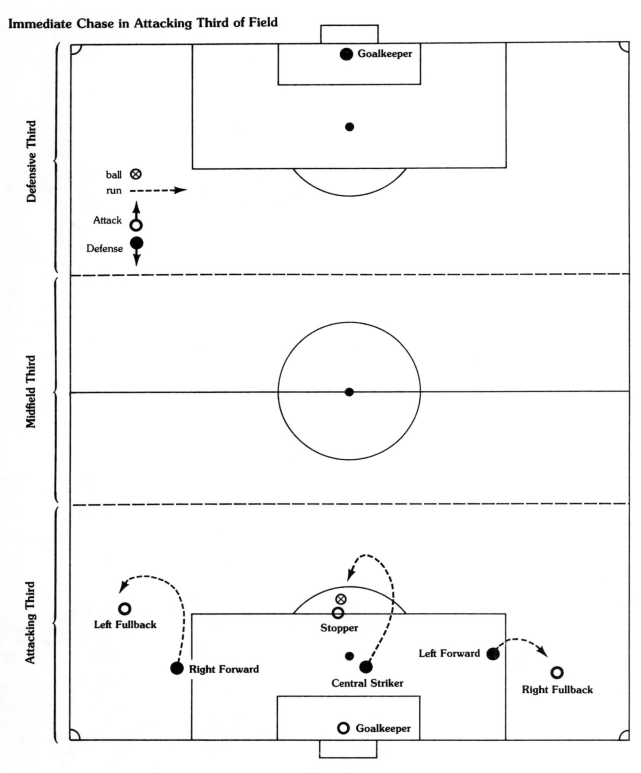

When the forwards lose possession of the ball in their attacking
third of the field (the third nearest their opponent's goal), they
must try to regain possession by chasing their opponents goal-side.

Immediate Chase in Midfield Third of Field

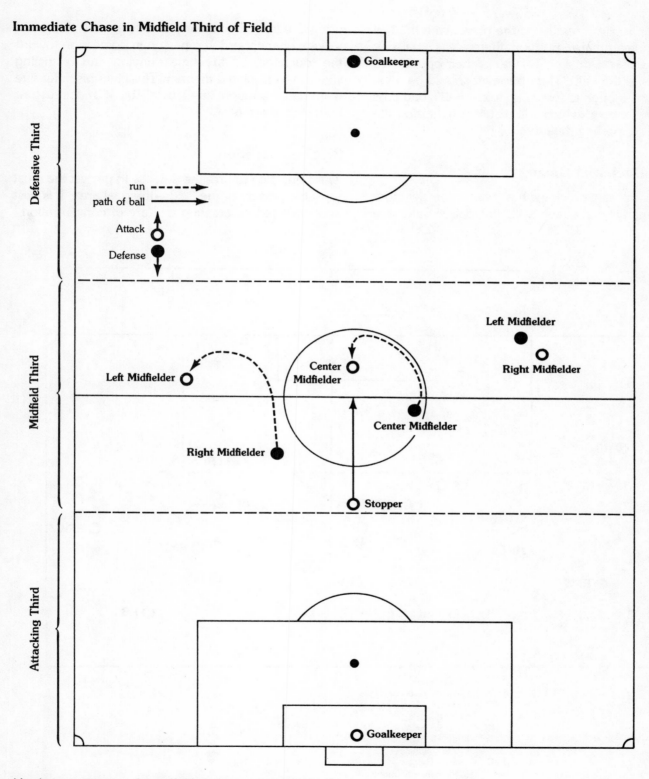

After losing possession, the midfielders must sprint goal-side of their opponents to mark possible receivers.

mediately applies pressure to the player with the ball while his teammates position themselves goal-side (between their team's goal—that is, their opponent's target—and the ball). The opponent should be pressured hard enough to force him to commit a bad pass or a poor dribble, which will result in his losing the ball to a supporting defender.

2. Fall Back and Delay

Once the immediate chase has begun, the defender who is marking the man with the ball should give

ground very deliberately and intelligently. He must jockey, or shepherd, the person in possession toward the touchline, all the time denying and restricting space in a calculated manner. This gives his defensive teammates enough time to fall back and structure their defense goal-side.

3. Concentration

This principle requires the defense to protect the most valuable portion of the field—the goal area. It is best accomplished by creating an "arc of concentration"

The "Arc of Concentration"

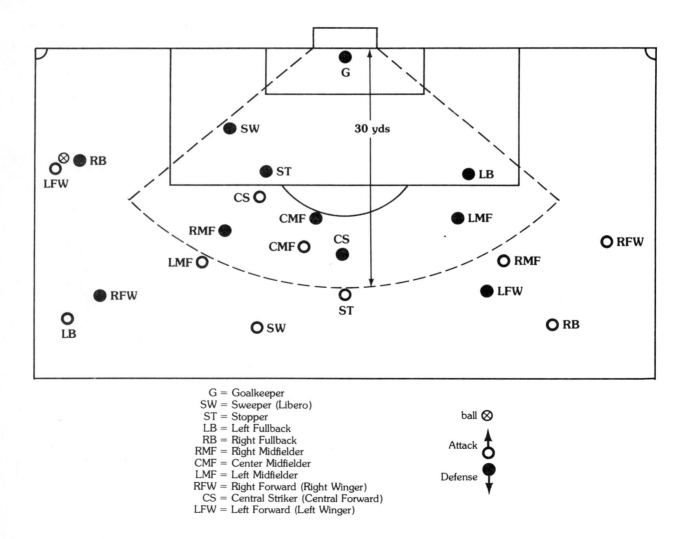

G = Goalkeeper
SW = Sweeper (Libero)
ST = Stopper
LB = Left Fullback
RB = Right Fullback
RMF = Right Midfielder
CMF = Center Midfielder
LMF = Left Midfielder
RFW = Right Forward (Right Winger)
CS = Central Striker (Central Forward)
LFW = Left Forward (Left Winger)

ball ⊗

Attack

Defense

approximately 30 yards from the goal line. As may be seen from the diagram, the angle of the arc should bisect the side of the goal area about 4 yards from the goal line, not on the goal line. The pie-shaped arc of concentration may be likened to an imaginary funnel, within which shots on goal have the best chance of going into the net. The principle of concentration provides heavy defense in this danger area, allowing the opponents only bad-angle shots with a poor chance of succeeding. A further advantage of concentrating the defense in this area is that ball-possession passes by those on attack will take place in front of the defenders, and opportunities for regaining possession will be more frequent.

4. Balance

Balance requires that the player applying pressure to the person in possession be supported, or covered, by teammates. This provides depth in the defense,

which is essential for a balanced team effort. If the player in possession eludes his defender, the supporting defender is on hand to resume the pressure; if the attacker passes, supporting defenders are in position to intercept or immediately mark the receiver.

The general rule for defenders "off the ball" is that the farther away their man is from the ball, the looser they mark him. And by loosely marking him, they can provide more cover. Complete balance is achieved when attackers near the ball are tightly marked man-to-man and goal-side, while attackers farther away from the ball are loosely marked.

5. Control/Restraint

This principle simply means that a defensive player must exercise discipline, or control, in order not to commit himself prematurely when tackling an opponent. Rather than risk being "beaten," the defender should attempt to force a poor pass, shot, or dribble. However, soccer does demand tight man-to-man marking and quick, firm tackling when the opportu-

Balance in Defense

The man in possession of the ball must be marked very tightly. The players immediately around the defender provide him with cover, while the defenders farthest away provide balance by shifting toward the ball side of the field to mark a possible receiver.

Support in Defense

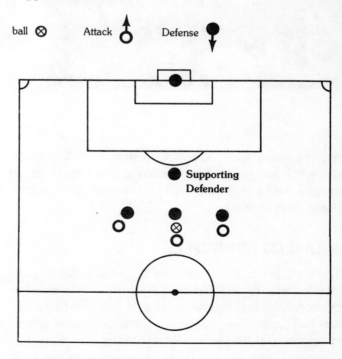

nity presents itself. Control, restraint, and mental discipline are needed to challenge the opponent at exactly the right moment when attempting to regain possession of the ball.

MIDFIELD PRINCIPLES

The midfield is a crucial area both on defense and attack. Indeed, midfield play links these two aspects of soccer. Midfielders must be able to stymie attacks, win ball possession, begin counterattacks, and either strike on goal themselves or set the forwards up for scoring. There are two basic approaches to midfield play: the slow buildup and the quick counterattack. The coach should experiment with both methods to determine which offers his team better results in various circumstances. The most effective teams are capable of using both types of midfield play.

Slow Buildup

In the slow buildup, once a team has gained possession of the ball, it proceeds by dribbling into open space and using combination passes to move the ball toward the attacking third of the field. Total team support is applied in the midfield area. This means that the ball-side teammates of the person in possession move toward him while the weak-side players position themselves to receive passes or make penetrating runs. The application of total team support in the midfield consolidates the players into an offensive unit and helps them to develop an attacking rhythm.

Changes in the speed and direction of the ball also are essential to capitalize on weak spots in the opposition. Midfield space is used to establish tactical superiority, a playing rhythm, and a consolidated attack. Once these objectives have been met, a fast strike on goal is in order.

Quick Counterattack

The quick counterattack may be likened to the "fast break" in basketball. When the team has gained possession of the ball, it is required to switch into an attacking posture instantaneously. The players rush into open space and use 1- or 2-touch through passes to propel the ball as rapidly as possible through the midfield area and into the attacking zone. Cross passes may also be used to move the ball quickly and deceptively. Supporting teammates should play an aggressive role by moving immediately toward the ball and positioning themselves to receive passes and shoot on goal. The quick counterattack, in effect, relies on a small group of players to move through the midfield with maximum speed and to finish with a fast shot on goal.

ATTACKING PRINCIPLES

The moment a team gains possession of the ball, each player must react by beginning the transition to attack. The critical problems are time and space: the ball must be moved to the goal area as quickly as possible. The defense, of course, wants to limit the attackers' space and reduce their time in possession. For the offensive team to succeed, it must adhere to the following principles of attack and thereby solve the problems of limited time and space.

1. Mobility

Mobility in soccer is purposeful running into open space with or without the ball. All offensive players should be in continuous motion during the attack, and the ball should be moved around constantly. This not only makes it difficult for the defense to mark and cover the attackers but also tends to lure the opponents out of position and create weak spots in the defense. Continuous motion by the attackers confuses the defensive players and thus can result in their making critical tactical errors.

In a typical game, a soccer player touches the ball for a total of only 2½ or 3 minutes. The remaining 87½ or 87 minutes of game time are played without ball contact, but mobility during these minutes is just as important as it is during the 2 or 3 minutes when the player has possession.

Here are a few ways to create mobility by using both the width and the depth of the field to stretch out the offensive team and confuse the defense:

Diagonal runs
Blind-side runs (away from the opponent's field of vision)
On-side runs (to avoid being caught in the opponent's offside trap)
Bending, or curving, runs
Checking run (feinting by taking a few quick steps in one direction before turning and sprinting in another direction)

2. Combination Play

Combination play involves 2 or more players using short, low passes—combination passes—to maintain possession of the ball while moving toward the goal. The passes should vary in distance, speed, and direction, and the ball should be switched from one side of the field to the other. The ultimate objective of combination play is to move the opposing team's defense out of position so that a sudden pass can be made to an open man who is in a position to dribble and shoot on goal or to make a through pass to a teammate.

3. Improvisation

Improvisation, or dribbling, at the proper time and in the proper third of the field—the attacking third—can destroy defensive alignments quicker than any other attacking principle. Dribbling also is an excellent delaying technique, which can be used to buy time in the attacking third of the field for the development of team support and the preparation of an attacking unit.

Since all players, regardless of their position, will find themselves in the attacking third of the field at some time during a game, it is important for every team member to be allowed plenty of practice time for dribbling. Competence in dribbling promotes playing confidence and the willingness to take on an opponent, when necessary, rather than look for a pass receiver. This confidence, based on dribbling ability, is important for all field players—fullbacks and forwards alike.

4. Support

This principle of attack also may be referred to as depth. Support requires movement toward the ball so that the player in possession has a minimum of 2 teammates to pass to and, optimally, 3. Total team support, or "compactness," on attack requires that all the ball-side attackers move toward the ball while all of the weak-side attackers make or prepare to make penetrating runs.

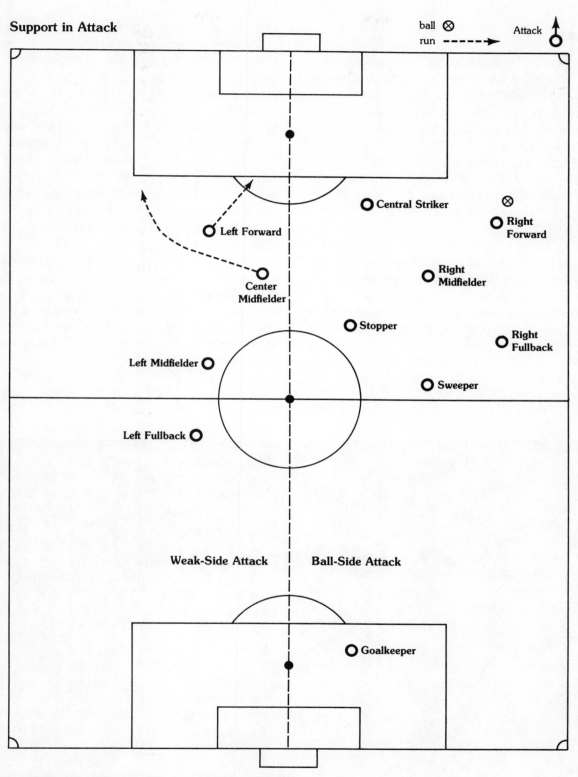

Support in Attack

ball ⊗
run ‑‑‑▶
Attack

Central Striker

Right Forward

Left Forward

Right Midfielder

Center Midfielder

Stopper

Right Fullback

Left Midfielder

Sweeper

Left Fullback

Weak-Side Attack | Ball-Side Attack

Goalkeeper

Attacking support, or depth, requires movement toward the ball by ball-side attackers while weak-side attackers make or prepare to make penetrating runs.

5. Finish

The last principle of attack is to finish, to penetrate the opponent's defense and shoot on goal. This is the culmination of a team's effort to move the ball toward the goal and also the ultimate test of their tactical ability. A successful shot depends on the attacking team's playmaking skills as well as its ability to draw the defense out of position. Ultimately, the finish requires an accurate shot, and much practice time should be spent shooting on goal.

COMMUNICATION

Verbal and visual communication serves as a vital link among players when they are executing any of the three basic soccer principles. Communication extends each player's knowledge of his teammates' and opponents' moves, the position of the ball, defensive weaknesses of his opponents, and his own attacking opportunities. Without communication between players, teamwork cannot reach its full potential.

Verbal communication may take any number of forms. A defender, for instance, might shout "support me" to a teammate, indicating that he is about to commit the play to him. Or he might instruct his teammate, "goal-side of number 7," upon seeing an unmarked attacker. A player on attack, seeing a defender about to tackle the man in possession, might call "man on" to alert his teammate to protect the ball or pass at the first opportunity. "Turn," called by an attacker to a teammate receiving the ball, means that a defender's marking is loose, and the man in possession should turn with the ball and advance toward the opponent's goal.

Arm signals also are useful, and a team may devise special ones for particular situations. For instance, a weak-side fullback might use an arm signal to tell his teammate with the ball on the far side of the field to cross the ball to him as he makes an overlapping run (a run from behind the person in possession to receive a pass from him).

CHAPTER 10
INDIVIDUAL, GROUP, AND TEAM TACTICS

To teach the game of soccer, it is best to start with the smallest unit possible, 1 player versus 1 player (1 V 1), and gradually work up to the entire team situation, 11 players versus 11 players (11 V 11). This progression in the coaching of tactics can be broken down into three major categories:

Individual tactics: 1 V 1
Group tactics: 2 V 1, 2 V 2, 2 V 3, 3 V 1, 3 V 3, 4 V 2, 4 V 3, 4 V 4, 5 V 3, 5 V 4, 5 V 5
Team tactics: 6 V 4 through 11 V 11

In all cases the concept of playing within a restricted space, or grid, should be adopted. This will provide faster action, more ball contact, and the opportunity to observe the success or failure of maneuvers more quickly.

The Coaching Grid

A coaching grid may be marked off in any area of the soccer field or in any other area where there is sufficient space. The grid usually is marked off in either a square or a rectangular shape and is used to work on a particular tactical problem. Grids also can be used to improve skills such as passing and collecting. The size of the grid varies from squares of 10 by 10 yards to areas as large as 40 by 40 yards or even 40 by 75 yards. The size of the grid depends on the objective that is to be achieved in a particular lesson and the technical abilities of the players involved.

A series of 10-by-10-yard grids lends itself well to practicing individual tactics (1 V 1). Two 30-by-20-yard grids are very useful for 2 sets of 3 V 2 tactical exercises.

Often two or more skills can be worked on in a single grid activity. For example, a 3 V 1 exercise performed in a grid 10 by 15 yards in size allows players to practice maintaining possession of the ball and providing support for the attack, while improving their passing and collecting skills.

The use of grids immediately organizes the practice

A series of three 10- by 10-yard grids for practicing individual (1 V 1) tactics

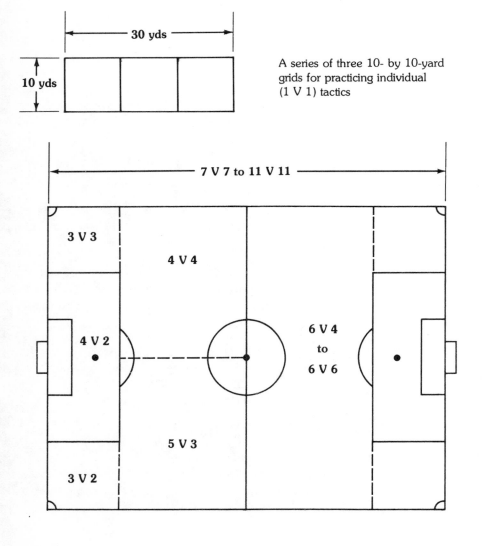

Dividing the soccer field into smaller practice areas, or grids, is an excellent way to teach group tactics. Half the field is used for team tactics with 6 players on a side, and the full field for 7 V 7 to 11 V 11 tactical training.

session and lends it a feeling of order. Players can be told quickly what has to be done, and because the space is restricted, they can perform their tasks with a minimum of direct supervision.

Practice can take place in individual grids or combined grids. Usually, only the inside area of the grid is used. But for certain exercises, such as 1 V 1, the boundary lines may serve as "goals." Players generally are restricted to their grids, but on occasion grids may be used as off-limits areas. For example, in a 3-grid series the middle grid may serve as a barrier that separates the outside grids. Play occurs in the outside grids, and the ball is either passed through or over the middle grid.

How grids are employed is up to the individual coach's discretion. In the final analysis it must be remembered that grids are only one of the tools used in the teaching process. The skills and tactics practiced and learned in the grids eventually must be taken out on the full field, with regulation goals, and practiced there as well.

INDIVIDUAL TACTICS

The object of teaching individual tactics is to improve and develop a player's ability to handle the 1 V 1 situation that is so common in soccer. The basic confrontation between 2 players provides the foundation for tactical understanding. Many of the fundamental principles of play are incorporated in 1 V 1 training.

Each player is exposed to attacking and defensive tactics, as well as to basic skills such as dribbling, shielding the ball from an opponent, tackling, and shooting. The demands placed upon a player in the 1 V 1 situation will demonstrate his capabilities and weaknesses, his fitness, and his mental toughness and alertness. Make sure all of your players receive ample exposure to individual tactics before they progress to group and team tactics. The coaching progression in individual tactics is as follows:

1 V 1 in a 10-by-10-yard restricted area. Players should practice maintaining and getting possession of the ball only; no goal shooting

Add goals within the restricted area

1 V 1 on the regulation-size field with only 1 goal

Add a counterattack goal

Individual tactics exercises

One player dribbles down the field while the other acts as a defender and jockeys the man with the ball in different directions. Alternate the roles.

Place a ball down as a target (goal). The player in possession attempts to strike the "goal."

Two nonplayers act as "goals," standing facing each other at a distance of 25 yards with their feet apart. The 2 players in the 1 V 1 situation try to score by shooting through their "goal's" legs. The 2

"goals" may each hold an extra ball to throw in after a shot to accelerate the action. This exercise lends itself well to interval training: after 1 minute, the players and "goals" change roles.

Two players in a 1 V 1 situation are restricted to the penalty area with a regulation goal and the goalkeeper in position. Either player may score. When the ball goes out of play, you should immediately provide another one.

GROUP TACTICS

During a game, it becomes obvious that the small groups of players that form around the ball are the effective tactical units, both on attack and defense. The location of the ball is the area of greatest action as well as the area of greatest danger and opportunity. Learning what to do in this group situation around the ball is the objective of group tactics.

To begin with, players must be prepared to switch instantly from defense to attack or from attack to defense, always forming new small groups to support each other. A common problem is the inability to switch roles rapidly; too often players are at a loss as to what to do once they or a teammate gains possession. Slowing down or delaying in order to think can be disastrous. The game must be played at high

speed, and decisions, based on experience and ability, must be almost automatic. The coaching progression in group tactics is as follows:

2 V 1 in an area 10 by 20 yards; 2 V 2 in an area 15 by 25 yards; 3 V 3 in an area 20 by 40 yards. Players should practice maintaining and getting possession of the ball only; no shots on goal

Add goals and allow shooting in the restricted areas

Limit each group by requiring 1-touch or 2-touch passing; dribbling past an opponent before passing; a certain number of passes in order to score, etc.

Put groups against each other on the regulation field with 1 full-size goal

Add a counterattack goal

Create small-group tactical exercises in all 3 areas of the field: the attacking third; the midfield, or neutral, third; and the defensive third

Group Tactics on Attack

Once a player has possession of the ball, he is in charge of the situation. With teammates to support him, he becomes very dangerous. Thus, his teammates must immediately group around him at a distance of from 10 to 15 yards to strengthen the potential of his possession. The more teammates he has

around him, the greater his choice of moves and chances for positive play. A 2-player group with 1 of the players in possession is the foundation for the development of attacking group tactics.

In group tactics exercises players work on ball possession and penetration into the opponent's territory by using wall passes, or give-and-go plays. In addition, the basic 2-man overlap play, in which a teammate runs from behind the player with the ball to receive a pass, is introduced and practiced. Tactical considerations such as depth, width, and diagonal-run possibilities should be built into the exercises.

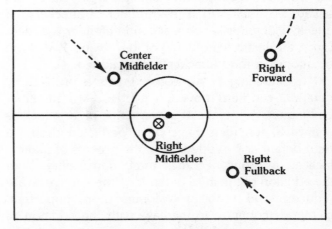

Illustrating the movement of players toward the teammate in possession of the ball

At first, group tactical problems should be presented and solved in grids. Players are allowed to attack, counterattack, and finally shoot on goal. At the outset, the number of defensive players should always be smaller than the number of attackers—2 attack, 1 defends. Then a second defender is added. Once the tactical problems of 2 V 1 and 2 V 2 are overcome, a third attacker can be added.

If maintaining possession presents a problem, 1 defender can be removed, leaving a 3 V 1 situation. Only after the tactical movements of 3 attackers against 2 defenders have been perfected should a third defender be added. Now the process of making tactical decisions becomes more demanding. With the addition of the third defender, time and space are reduced, and mobility becomes more important. Demands continue to increase with the addition of more offensive and defensive players.

Group Tactics on Defense

After the basic attacking moves have been mastered, players must be taught how to defend in the group situation. Each player must understand the importance of facing and staying goal-side of his opponent as well as know how to delay the progress of the man with the ball so that his teammates have time to set up their defense. Only after the defense has been set up should players begin to think about regaining possession of the ball.

Defensive tactics begin immediately upon loss of possession. The player nearest the attacker with the ball immediately assumes responsibility for delaying him. The delaying tactic is an active process in which positioning is a key factor. Defensive positioning must reduce the attacker's shooting and passing space. The closer the defender comes to the man with the

ball, the more he accomplishes this. Yet he must remember that the closer he gets to the dribbler the more risk he runs of being beaten by him.

In a 2 V 1 situation especially, it would be poor tactical play to immediately challenge the man in possession. The second attacker would be free to receive a pass and proceed to penetrate. The defender must learn to play close enough to the man with the ball to gain possession if the attacker makes an error but far enough away to discourage a pass attempt. In all cases, the defender's tactical objective is to interfere with the attacker's progress toward the goal. And when an opponent is within shooting distance of the goal, the defender must make every effort to prevent the attacker from getting off a shot.

As the attacker in possession is being delayed by

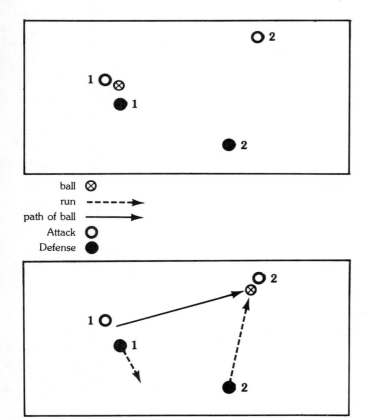

ball	⊗
run	----▶
path of ball	——▶
Attack	○
Defense	●

Illustrating the responsibilities of 2 men on defense when confronted by 2 attackers. The man with the ball is marked closely while the other defender moves into a supporting role.

the closest defender, another defender must sprint toward his teammate to lend support. This creates the "depth" that is crucial to good defensive play. The second defender must determine his angle of support, in relation to a second attacker who is a potential pass receiver, and the distance of his support, in relation to the speed of his opponent. Yet the supporting defender's first duty is to aid his teammate in stopping the man in possession.

The second defender, therefore, has a dual role: first, he must protect his teammate and the area between the attacker and the goal; second, he must watch both the man in possession and his attacking teammates in order to anticipate a pass. If a pass is made to a second attacker, the supporting defender moves toward the receiver to interfere, and the first defender retreats into a supporting role.

Although each defender's basic responsibility is to play man-to-man, a supporting defender must be able to switch to the "zone" concept of covering opponents as well as to a combination of both. All players should be trained in the tactical responsibilities of the first and second, or supporting, defenders. They will have the opportunity to learn these roles by practicing in a 2 V 2 situation within a grid. Small goals should be used at first, next regulation-size goals with goalkeepers, and finally the element of counterattack, with offside rules in effect, should be incorporated.

By adding a third attacker and third defender (3 V 3), the coach introduces the concept of balance on defense. The third, or balancing, defender takes away attacking space and prevents penetration. As the situation changes and he finds himself in the vicinity of the ball, the third defender's role changes too, and he becomes either a first or second defender. Group defensive tactics are to be practiced until all players understand the three basic defensive requirements: stop penetration by delay and confinement; give support; and provide balance away from the ball.

Group tactical exercises

The best way to perfect group tactical movements is to perform them often. The coach should devise games—using opponents to offer resistance, and placing various restrictions on the man in possession—that help players understand how to:

Provide depth support

Provide width support

Provide balance away from the ball

Delay and confine an opponent with the ball
Gain and maintain possession
Make through and wall passes
Make diagonal runs with or without the ball
Use the combination play
Use the overlap play
Finish, or shoot, on goal
Read a situation and choose appropriate action
Make decisions about when to keep the ball, when to make a pass, when to risk a through pass, etc.
Perform with speed and precision

Group tactics exercises usually end when a team has progressed to a 6 V 4 confrontation that utilizes half the field. At this point, the players are ready to begin team tactical training.

TEAM TACTICS

The final stage of tactical training is team tactical development. In teaching team tactics the coach must concentrate on both individual performance and combination play. He must mold a unit of up to 11 players that will have the capability of both attacking and defending.

In team tactics training, each player is taught the responsibilities of his position in all 3 parts of the field. He is also taught to remain constantly aware of the movement of the ball, his teammates, and the opposition. Team tactics exercises involving 7 V 7 up to 11 V 11 should take place on a full field, with both goals being used. For exercises involving fewer players, half the field should be used, with a small goal added along the halfway line.

The use of restrictions is a valuable method of teaching team tactical play. The following restrictions are suggested:

Allow only 1-touch passing
Allow only 2-touch passing
Require players to sprint into space after executing a pass
Allow only 1 team to shoot; the other team must pass the ball 10 times to score 1 point
Require the player with the ball to beat an opponent before passing
Require every third pass to be a through pass

Many other restrictions can be devised by the coach according to the needs of his team. For instance, if players do not move the ball swiftly enough

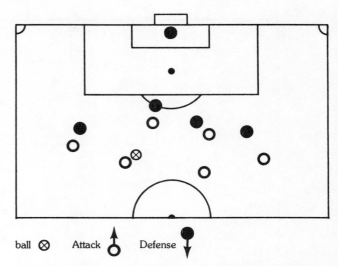

ball ⊗   Attack ◯   Defense ●

Team tactics begin and group tactics end when a team has progressed to 6 V 4 with a goalkeeper on half the field.

and waste time "ball watching," a certain number of wall passes, or give-and-go plays, can be required in order to improve team movement. Another restricted exercise to improve team tactics would use a 6 V 4 or 6 V 5 situation on half the field with 1 goal and a goalkeeper and perhaps a smaller goal at midfield. If the object is to improve attacking ability, the coach times how long it takes to move the ball into free space and counts the number of passes needed to penetrate the defense. If the object is to improve defense, the coach emphasizes support, man-to-man marking, and a general understanding of what constitutes the last line of defense.

Restart Situations

Often in teaching team tactics the coach does not allow enough time for practicing restarts. Statistically, in international play 60 percent of the goals scored result from restart situations such as kickoffs and throw-ins and corner kicks, penalty kicks, and other free kicks. This being the case, the coach should allot a minimum of 15 to 20 minutes of each practice session to training on restarts. Even on game day it is useful to spend some time practicing restarts.

There are many ways of teaching restarts, and the coach must use his imagination to set up training situations that take into account the physical and mental characteristics of his players. He can demonstrate sig-

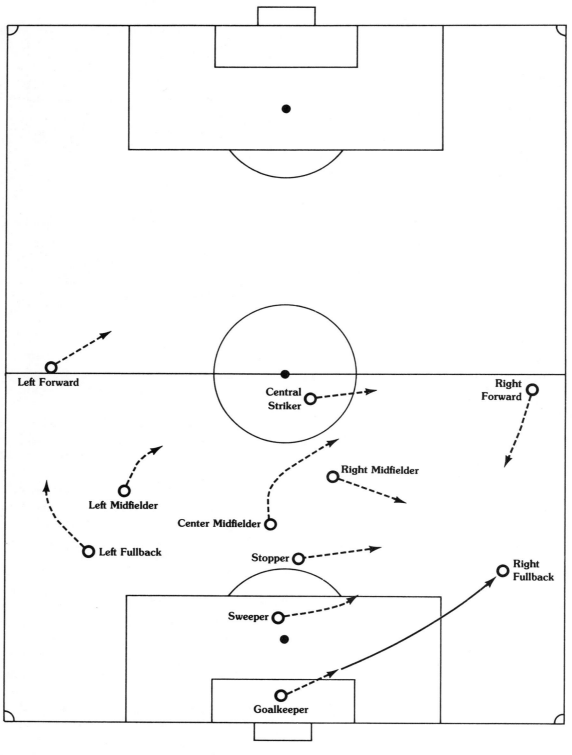

Illustrating the movement of 11 players on the field when their team gains possession. The right fullback receives the ball from the goalkeeper, and all the other players run into tactically advantageous positions in order to start an attack.

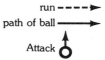

run ----►
path of ball ——►
Attack

nals for them to use to communicate with teammates during restarts; teach low, high, and curving kicks; and show his players how to catch opponents off-balance by making deceptive movements while free kicks are being taken.

To defend against the direct free kick, the primary concern of the coach should be the organization of a defensive wall of players. Each defender's responsibilities must be clearly outlined. This is especially important in the defensive third of the field. The coach must use his own judgment to determine how many players should be included in the wall and whether man-to-man or zone defense should be used. A general recommendation in these situations is to use a minimum of 5 players to form the wall around the penalty arc if the kick is taken close to the penalty area with the goal straight ahead. If the kick is taken from an angle, then the greater the angle the fewer the number of players required in the wall. Those players who are to form the wall should be exposed to the direct free-kick situation in practice. They need courage when hard shots are coming directly toward them.

Organization of 11 Players

Coaches sometimes assume that a soccer formation used by a championship team is right for their team or club. This is not the case. No two teams are alike, for they cannot possibly have players with identical physical and mental characteristics. It is important to assign team positions according to players' abilities.

In most team formations, 4 players are positioned as the last line of defense, 2 as the next line of defense, and 2 as the first line of defense. The same pattern in reverse applies when the team is on the attack. The remaining 2 field players should be positioned where they can be most beneficial to the team. The eleventh player is, of course, the goalkeeper. This suggested organization should serve only as a general guideline. (See Chapter 2 for a diagram of the basic alignment of players on the field.) Today's "total" soccer has done away with rigid positional play, albeit not to the extent that a central striker, for example, finds himself on defense for an entire 90-minute game. The central striker might indeed become a defender on and off during the game but always temporarily.

Team tactics exercises

Using 6 V 4 on half the field:

Train the 6 offensive players to develop an attacking rhythm with no opposition other than the goalie (ghost drill); use 1 goal only

Train the attackers to penetrate against 4 passive defenders (shadow drill)

Train the attackers to penetrate against 4 active defenders

Add counterattack goals for the defenders and add restrictions

Using 7 V 7 or 8 V 8 on the full field:

Use 2 goals without restrictions

Require one team to complete 10 consecutive passes to score a point while the other team is allowed to shoot on goal in order to score its points

Restrict the game to 1-touch, 2-touch, or 3-touch passing

Require the man with the ball to dribble past an opponent (who must challenge for possession) before he can pass to a teammate

Restrict passing to a short-short-long sequence

Add 2 additional goals and play with 4 goals

TACTICAL FUNCTIONS

The goal here is to teach each position to all players so that they understand not only their own but also their teammates' tactical responsibilities both on attack and defense in all 3 areas of the field. In tactical functional training attacking and defending situations are set up in which the different positions on the field are isolated, and the tactical responsibilities of each position are taught. It is important to remember that the concentration should be on one specific position at a time. The proper progression for this type of training is as follows:

The player practices the position with the fewest number of teammates needed and with no opposition (ghost drill)

Passive defenders are introduced (shadow drill)

Active defenders are introduced

Gradually teammates and defenders are added until an 11 V 11 situation is reached under game conditions

See the diagrams of tactical functional training exercises designed to improve attacking ability at specific positions.

The Midfielders' Attacking Tactic

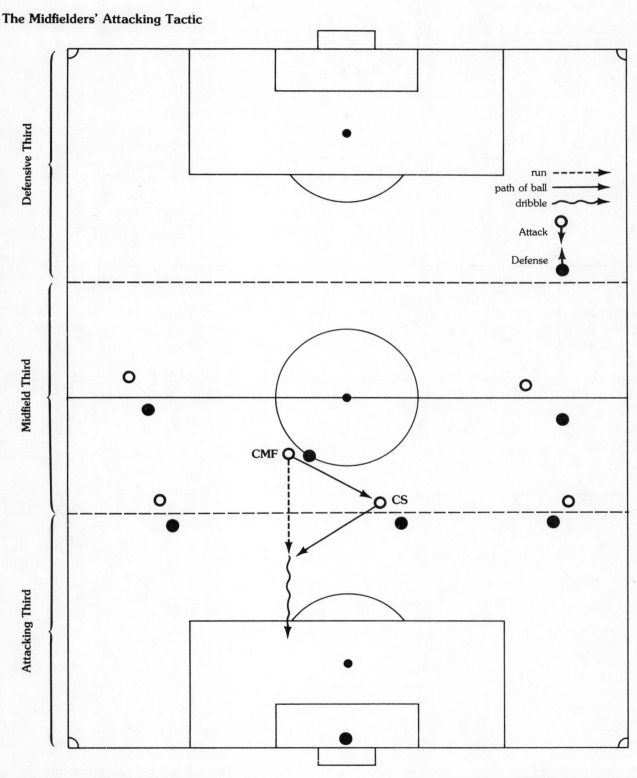

The wall pass and the penetrating run are shown in this example of tactical functional training. The center midfielder, **CMF**, passes the ball to the central striker, **CS**, who 1-touch passes it back to the center midfielder as the latter runs, then dribbles, toward the goal.

The Fullbacks' Attacking Tactic

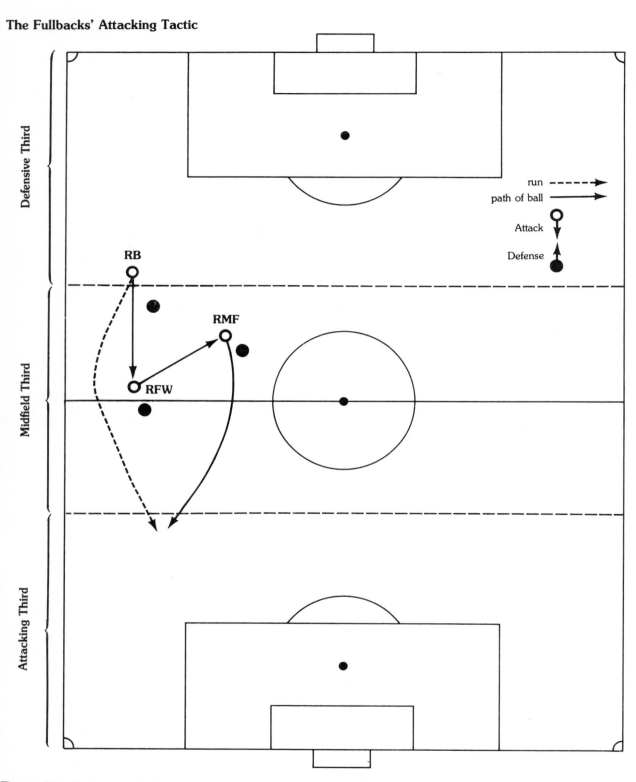

The overlap play is shown in this example of tactical functional training. The right fullback, **RB,** passes to the right forward, **RFW.** The right forward passes to the right midfielder, **RMF,** who chips to the fullback, who has run ahead to receive it.

The Forwards' Attacking Tactic

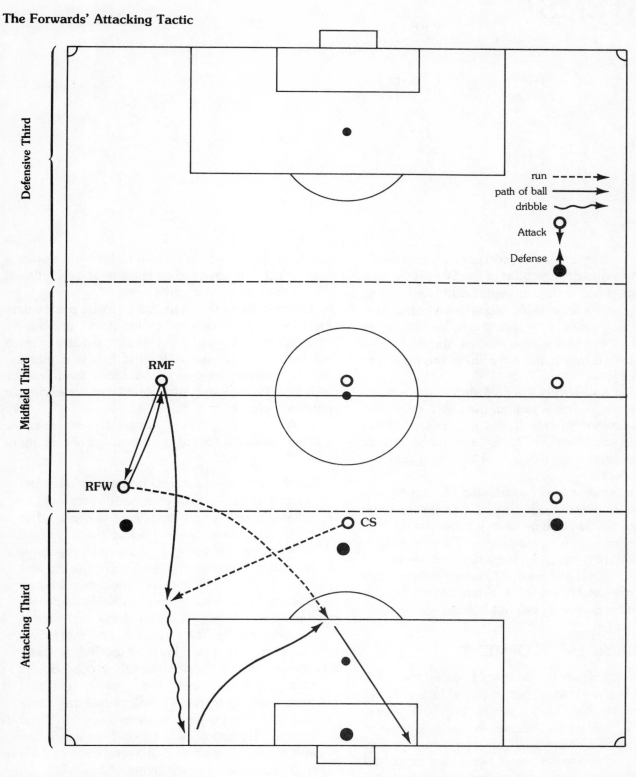

Shooting on goal is shown in this example of tactical functional training. The right midfielder, **RMF,** passes the ball to the right forward, **RFW,** who passes back to the right midfielder. The right midfielder chips to the central striker, **CS,** who has made a diagonal run to receive the ball. The central striker dribbles the ball to the goal line, where he turns it back to the right forward, who has cut to the inside to trail the dribbler. The right forward finishes with a 1-touch shot on goal.

CHAPTER 11
SYSTEMS
OF
PLAY

The term "system of play" in soccer refers to both the arrangement and the functions of the 10 field players. Every system has certain strengths and weaknesses, and no system will, in itself, guarantee victory. Furthermore, a system of play should only be adopted as a general guideline for how players should be deployed during a match and not as a rigid requirement of game action.

Choosing a system is the final step in team preparation. In making his selection, the coach must take into consideration such factors as the physical fitness of his players, their ability to execute the basic techniques, and their mastery of attacking and defending tactics.

Many coaches make the mistake of copying the styles and systems of other teams without realizing that the particular systems or styles they adopt may not be appropriate for their players. Each team consists of different people who have different talents and limitations. It is very important to select a system that suits the players. Unless this is done, the success for which a team is striving will not be attained.

HISTORICAL DEVELOPMENT

England is known as the mother of soccer; the game was nurtured and developed there, although it was introduced to the English people by the Romans. During the early days of soccer, the game was unorganized and there were unlimited numbers of players on a team. The populations of two towns or villages competed against each other, and a game started midway between the two communities. The aim of each side was to kick an object, originally a human skull and later an inflated animal bladder, to the center of the opponent's town. Rules were nonexistent, a fact that often led to considerable bloodshed during the course of a game.

The brutality of soccer increased to the point where the rulers were forced to ban the game, and severe penalties were imposed on those who disregarded the law. Another reason for the ban was that the people preferred to play soccer rather than practice with their bows, which was considered necessary for national defense.

In *A Century of Great Soccer Drama,* John A. Cottrell writes the following chronological account of soccer in England:

> . . . the Romans practiced *harpastum,* carrying the ball game on their conquests as far west as Britain. Soccer of a riotous kind was played in Derby and Chester as far back as A.D. 217, and, while records of the game's more savage days are scanty, we know that an Oxford student was killed by Irish students while playing football (soccer) in the High Street in 1303, that 8 men drowned in daring to play the game on the ice of the frozen River Trent in 1638, and that Oliver Cromwell was a dab-hand at football at Cambridge. Finally, nurtured and developed by the public schools and the universities and pioneered by a handful of clubs, the game emerged as a properly organized sport in 1863 with the formation of the Football Association and the drawing up of a universal code of rules for the regulation of the game of football.

By 1873, team formations were beginning to develop. The more advanced teams lined up in the following manner: a goalkeeper, 2 fullbacks, 2 midfielders, and 6 forwards. Other teams distributed their players this way: a goalkeeper, 1 fullback, 1 midfielder, and 8 forwards. Bunching and dribbling were characteristic of the game, which was played on a field up to 200 yards long and 100 yards wide. There were no crossbars or goal nets; the goalposts were set 8 yards apart and connected at a height of 8 feet by a tape. Until 1875, teams changed ends after every goal, and when a ball went out of play, it was thrown in by the first player to grab it. This is evidence that system played a very minor role in the game.

Gradually, the shape of the team was changed from the 2-2-6 or 1-1-8 formation to an organization of players that provided for a more even balance between defense and attack. Changes in the successive systems were based on the exposure of inherent weaknesses in the defensive system and involved an increase in the number of men for defensive responsibilities.

Introduction of the pass in soccer affected the game much the way the introduction of the forward pass affected American football: many players were caught out of position, and everyone was forced to think about the redistribution or reorganization of the players. Of necessity, soccer teams began to use 2 fullbacks, 3 midfielders, and 5 forwards; that is, the 2-3-5 system. The center midfielder was an attacking player. The other midfielders were given the defensive responsibility of dealing with the opposing outside forwards, or wingers, so that the fullbacks were able to defend the area directly in front of the goal (see Diagram 1).

Diagram 1

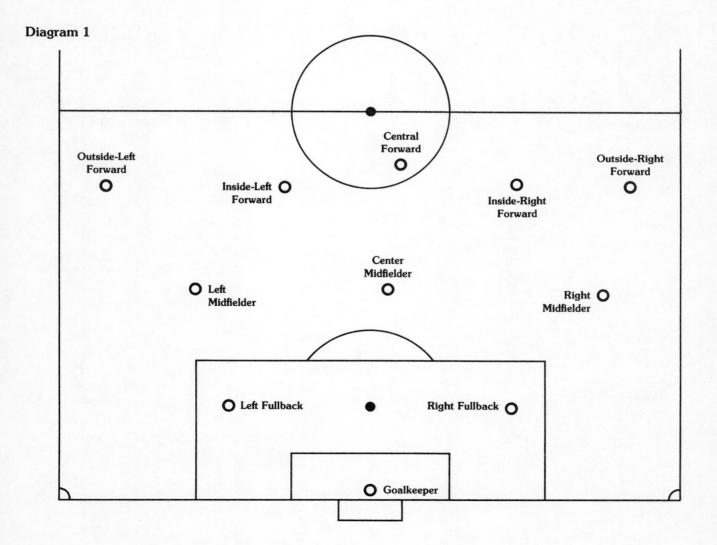

EFFECTS OF THE OFFSIDE RULE

The offside rule, which had a considerable effect on the evolution of playing formations, is probably the least understood aspect of the game. At one time, before there were any regulations governing soccer matches, a team could position 1 or 2 players directly in front of its opponent's goal, and a long pass from a teammate would often result in an easy score. The offside rule was devised to make this unsportsmanlike strategy illegal. An offensive player was declared offside if he ran ahead of the ball in his opponent's half of the field unless there were 3 defensive players, including the goalkeeper, between him and the goal.

Eventually, defenders took advantage of the rule by setting up the *offside trap.* In this maneuver 1 of the 2 fullbacks, playing closer to the halfway line than to his goal area, would dash toward the opponent's half of the field and past an attacker's intended receiver in the defensive half, thus putting the offensive player in an offside position. The result was that most of the action—interrupted by numerous offside calls—took place in the center of the field, and there was so little scoring that fans complained about the dullness of the game.

FIFA took note, and in 1925 the offside rule was changed so that 2 defenders rather than 3 had to be between the attacking player and the goal (see Chapter 4 for illustrations of offside situations). With the offside trap no longer effective in the 2-3-5 system of play then in vogue, there were now too many goals instead of too few. The defense was being

Diagram 2

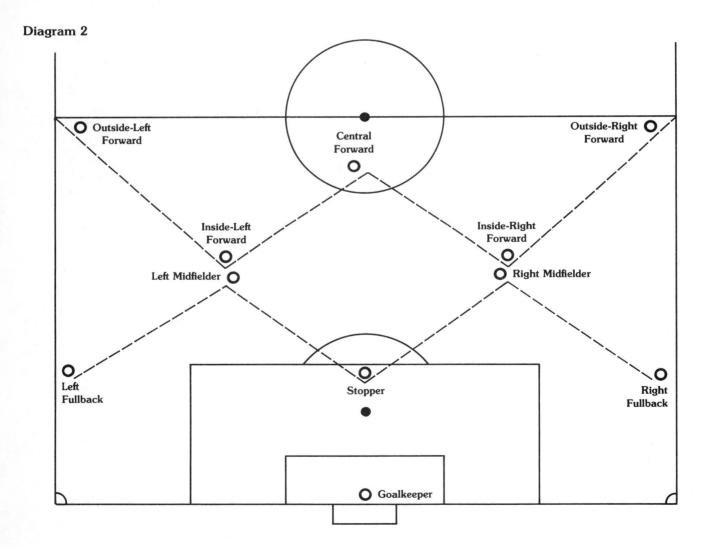

overwhelmed by the offense in the alignment of player positions and functions. Changes in formation were necessary.

THE WM SYSTEM (3-4-3)

Herbert Chapman, manager of Arsenal, one of Great Britain's leading soccer clubs, is credited with the reorganization of the defense and the introduction of the third fullback. The right and left fullbacks were moved out to the flanks and given the responsibility of marking the opposing outside forwards. The center midfielder, or halfback, was relieved of his attacking responsibilities and pulled back to serve as the center fullback, who became known as the "stopper." He was a key player in defense and brought with him

complaints that the art and beauty of the game were being sacrificed to speed and power. The left and right midfielders were positioned much more centrally to control the defensive half of midfield, and the inside-left and inside-right forwards were repositioned to help cover the midfield (see Diagram 2). This arrangement of players is known as the WM system because the players form a *w* and an *m* when they are in position.

Since there are teams in this country that still utilize the WM system, its advantages and disadvantages should be pointed out.

The basic disadvantage of using this system today is that if your opponent is following the 4-2-4 system you have 1 fewer player on defense than the opposition has on offense. The same can be stated about

Diagram 3

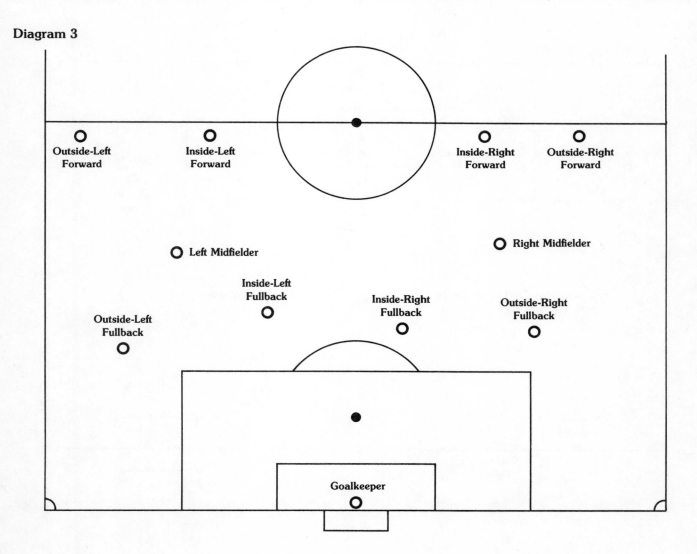

the offense: your 3 attackers are pitted against 4 defenders. In midfield the advantage is clearly with the WM system since there are 4 players. Yet controlling the midfield is of no use unless goals can be scored, and it is difficult to score many goals from the midfield.

The important facts to remember when using the WM system are that the left and right midfielders and the inside forwards must play the dual role of offense and defense. The midfielders must support the offense and concentrate on defensive responsibilities. The inside forwards must support the defense and concentrate on offensive responsibilities with the other forwards. It can easily be seen that endurance is an important requirement for these positions.

4-2-4 SYSTEM

This system provides for 4 fullbacks, 2 midfielders, and 4 forwards. Developmentally, the left midfielder was withdrawn and placed either alongside or somewhat ahead of or behind the stopper and was given strictly defensive responsibilities. The inside-left forward was given the position of the left midfielder. In essence there were 2 center fullbacks. The basic formation is as shown in Diagram 3.

It can be seen that the 2 midfielders are the links between the attack and the defense. When their team is in possession of the ball, they take an active part in the attack by becoming supporting forwards. When the opposition gains possession, these 2 midfielders

Diagram 4

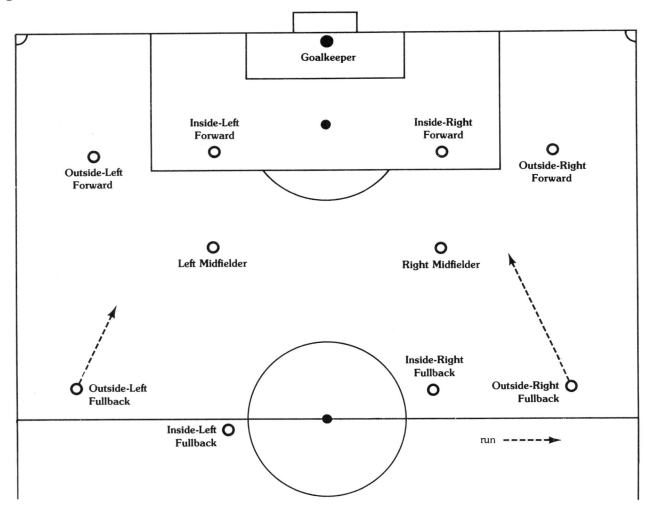

must retreat quickly to assume their defensive responsibilities. In this situation it is very important that the forwards make immediate chase of the ball so they can delay the opposition and permit the midfielders to retreat to the defensive area. A very high work rate is demanded of the 2 midfielders in this system if they are to provide support for the offensive and defensive phases of the game.

Conceivably, it is possible to have 8 men on offense and 8 men on defense if perfect execution can be achieved. Offensively, the 2 outside fullbacks can sprint forward along the flanks to support the outside forwards, or wingers (see Diagram 4).

On a quick counterattack or under constant pressure by the opposition, it is possible to let the fullbacks take part in the attack. They must be disciplined, however, to return at top speed to their positions before the other team can take advantage of its numerical superiority near the goal.

The use of the fullback as an offensive player can be predetermined. As shown in Diagram 5, player number 1, the right midfielder, is in possession of the ball. Forwards numbers 2, 3, and 4 make diagonal runs toward their left, thereby creating open space down the right side of the field, while forward number 5 runs diagonally toward his right. Player number 6, the outside-right fullback, will sprint into the offensive area and receive the ball from the right midfielder. Player number 6 can dribble toward the goal line and will usually have an opportunity to take a shot on goal

Diagram 5

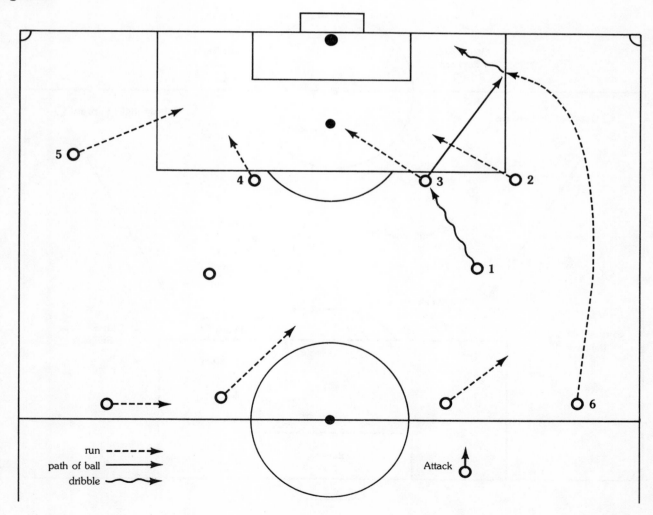

run ----→
path of ball ——→
dribble ～～→

Attack

or to cross the ball to a teammate on the other side of the field.

As the outside-right fullback moves down the right touchline, the other fullbacks drift to the right so that there will be a more even coverage of the field. The right midfielder will tend to stay behind the forwards to support them and be ready to sprint back to cover for the attacking fullback.

This play will work several times during the course of a game, primarily due to the element of surprise. It will work until the opposing outside-left forward moves in to mark the outside-right fullback (see Diagram 5).

Defensively, the outside forwards, or wingers, can be withdrawn backward and to the center to help prevent dangerous situations directly in front of the goal. Double-marking (in which 2 men guard an opponent) of 2 forwards or midfielders is possible if the wingers can be disciplined to play this way. It must also be stressed that the wingers should be able to get back to their offensive responsibilities when their team regains possession of the ball (see Diagram 6).

Switching is another very important aspect of the 4-2-4 system and requires complete concentration and understanding on the part of all players. If a midfielder detects an opportunity to sprint into a spearhead position, 1 of the inside forwards should switch with him and assume his responsibility. The same applies to fullbacks and wingers. The key, however, to successful execution is understanding; all

Diagram 6

run ------>

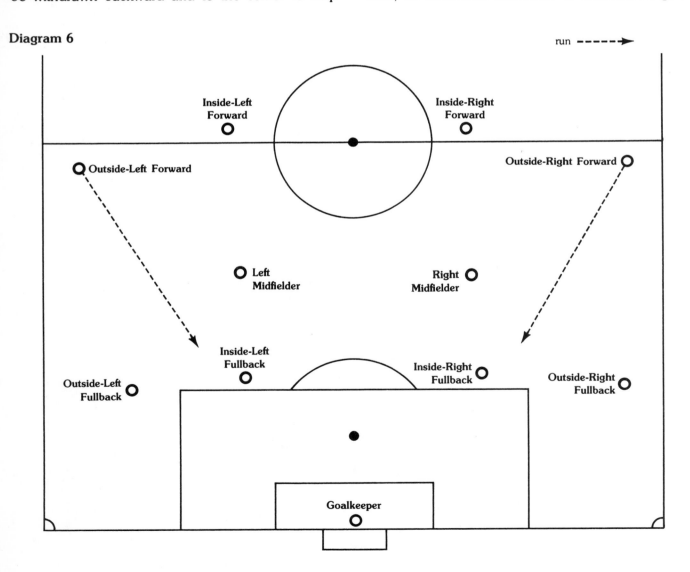

players must completely understand the duties and responsibilities of all members of the team. Switching should not be mechanical but should be spontaneous, as opportunities develop during play. The resumption of normal positions should take place as the context of the game demands. Diagram 7 illustrates the switch between an inside forward and a midfielder. The inside-left forward drops back to assume the normal supporting role of the left midfielder, who has sprinted up to receive the ball from the outside-left forward.

CATENACCIO

The Italians created catenaccio, the most defensively minded formation ever devised in soccer, after they lost 17 of their top players in a 1949 airplane crash. The system incorporates tight, man-to-man marking of opponents, rather than zonal play, and provides for a free man called a sweeper (libero), who usually stands behind the last line of defense and covers every teammate in the defensive third of the field. The sweeper serves as the commander of the defense, directing and organizing the other defensive players. He is responsible for stopping the free man of the opposing side and any other attacker who has broken through the last line of defense. (See Diagram 8 for the typical alignment of the defense in the catenaccio formation.) If the sweeper challenges the opponent of any teammate, that player should switch over to the sweeper's position.

The catenaccio formation can vary. Sometimes there are 3 or 4 attackers, sometimes only 2 or 1.

Against a team that used the 4-2-4 system, the catenaccio formation would be 1-4-2-3 (1 sweeper, 4 fullbacks, 2 midfielders, and 3 forwards) or 1-4-3-2. The 4-3-3 system opponent would be played with a 1-3-3-3, 1-3-4-2, or 1-3-2-4 form of catenaccio. It clearly may be seen that, with discipline, a team using this system can prevent even a vastly superior opponent from scoring. An example of a 1-5-2-2 catenaccio formation is offered in Diagram 9.

Here it is clear that the other team will dominate the action in the midfield, but what often matters more is the activity in and around both penalty areas.

Catenaccio gained popularity in the 1950s, when it was realized that disciplined players, with a purpose, could defeat offensively minded teams. However, more recently it has become less popular because it lacks the excitement of other types of soccer.

Diagram 7

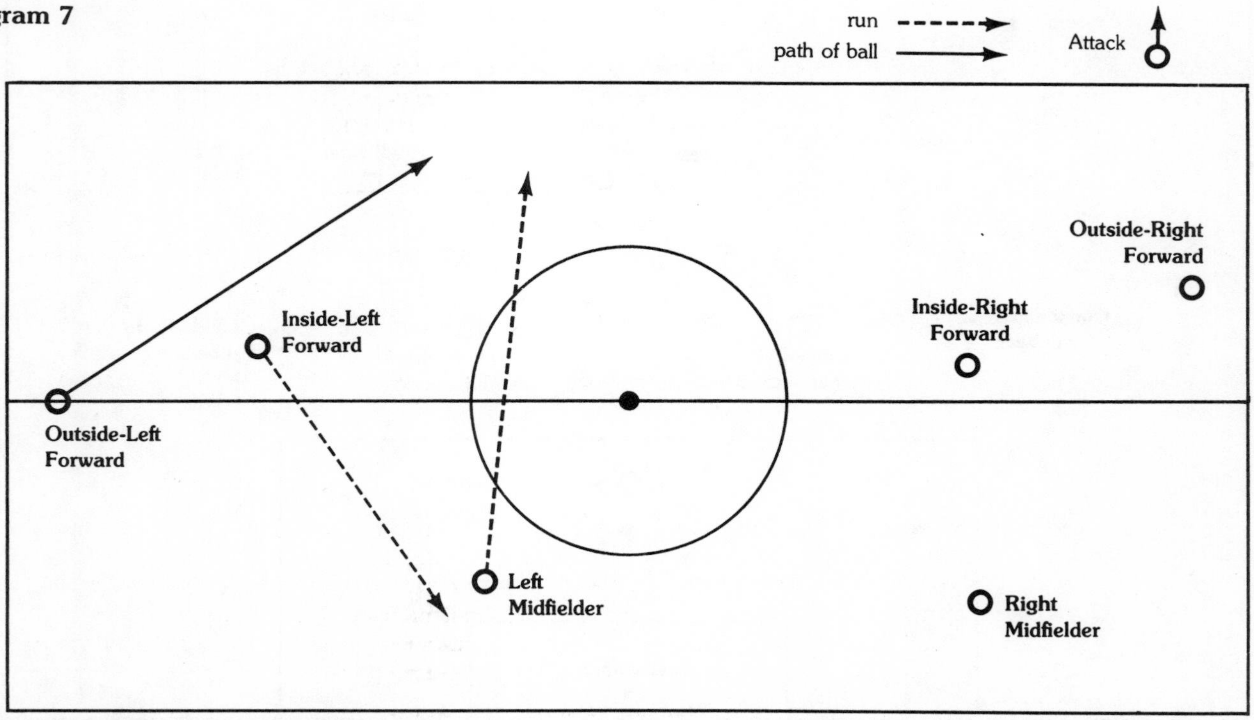

4-3-3 SYSTEM

This is a modification of the 4-2-4 system that is useful when there is need for greater control of the midfield. The natural move is to withdraw a forward to the midfield to strengthen the first line of defense.

The 3 midfield players support the attack at all times, but their primary responsibility is for defense. Diagram 10 shows that defense will be strengthened at the expense of offense unless some adjustment is made. Otherwise, the opposing defense will have numerical superiority and will be able to deal with the 3 forwards without difficulty.

One adjustment that frequently is made is to train the center midfielder to assume a central forward's responsibility when his team gains possession. When the team loses the ball, he must sprint back to take his place with the other midfielders. Diagram 11 illustrates this. As the ball is passed to the left midfielder, the center midfielder assumes a position with the other forwards while the central forward moves to the left to make room for him and the right midfielder moves closer to the center. If possession is lost, the center midfielder must sprint back.

In the 4-3-3 system the fullbacks are encouraged to take part in attacking movements similar to those described for the 4-2-4 formation.

Generally, it can be stated that a team with several good forwards and few good defenders will elect to use this system. The good forwards will score their share of goals regardless of the number of teammates close by, but unless the defense and the midfield are strengthened, the defense will give up more goals than the forwards can score. Consequently, the defense is the area that should be built up. The 4-3-3 system provides for balance over the entire field and

Diagram 8

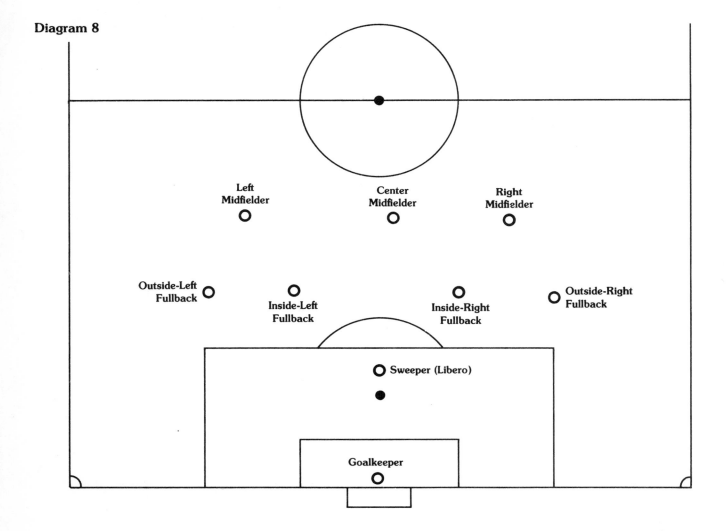

for continuity among the forwards, the midfielders, and the fullbacks.

THE 4-4-2 SYSTEM

Sir Alf Ramsey, England's coach in the 1966 and 1970 World Cups, generally is regarded as the innovator of the 4-4-2 system. The adaptation of the 4-3-3 to a 4-4-2 became necessary because Ramsey lacked world-class wingers on his 1966 team, which, ironically, won the world championship. He therefore decided to withdraw the wingers into the midfield and prepare tactics without using true wingers. In this situation the midfielders and also the fullbacks made "raids" into the orthodox winger positions in attempts to cross the ball into the center of the penalty area.

Another key aspect of this system is that the 2 forwards can be required to make long diagonal runs to the outside of the field to open up the middle. These runs enable the 2 inside midfielders to rush into the central attacking area for scoring penetration (see Diagram 12).

THE FUTURE OF SYSTEMS

It appears that the trend on the international level is toward "total," or positionless, soccer, which first

Diagram 9

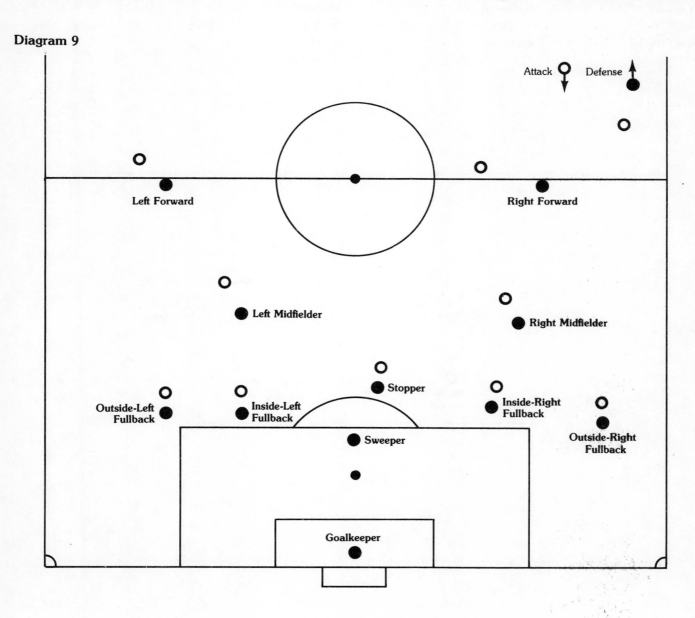

gained attention during the 1974 World Cup playoffs. This method of play was greatly popularized by the Dutch, who used it in the championship match against West Germany. The chemistry among the members of the Dutch team enabled them to attack and defend in mass with great precision while constantly rotating their positions. Whether they were attacking or defending, they always had more players on the ball than their opponents. Also, they managed not to leave any glaring gaps within the structure and balance of the team, in spite of their concentration around the ball. It must be pointed out, however, that the Dutch had players of exceptional skill, tactical understanding, good communication, and endurance.

They appeared to be virtually indefatigable.

The West Germans, who won the World Cup in 1974, demonstrated a similar approach to the game but exercised caution by not committing all 10 field players to the attack. The West German defense was tightly organized, and only about 80 percent freedom of movement was used.

Total movement of all 10 field players will be feasible only when the players are thoroughly trained at all positions. The Dutch were able to use positionless soccer because they had a number of great players who could control the ball under extreme pressure and thus allow other players to push up into the attack with confidence.

Diagram 10

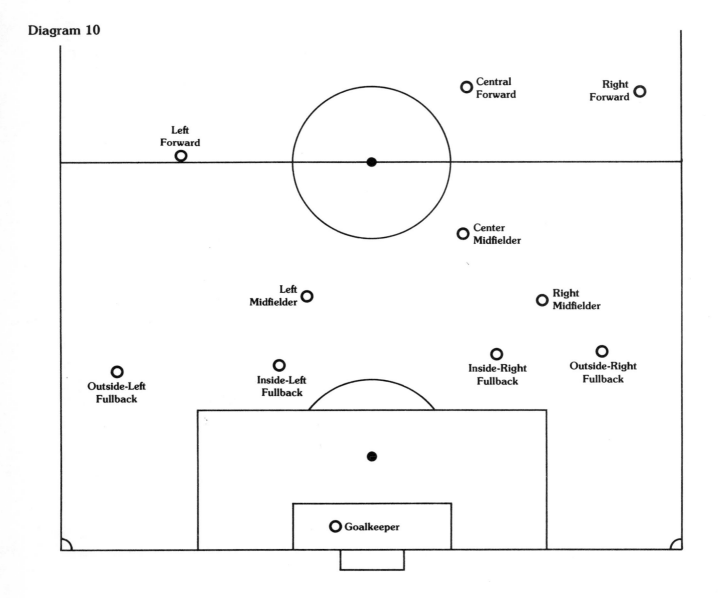

Diagram 11

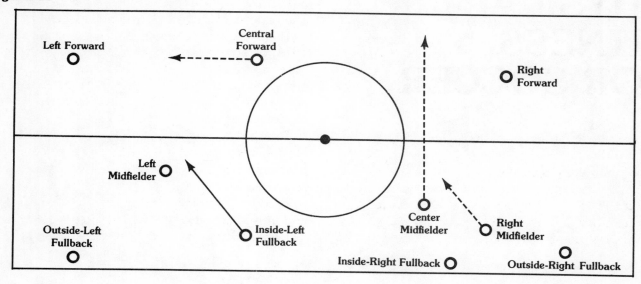

Left Forward

Central Forward

Right Forward

Left Midfielder

Center Midfielder

Right Midfielder

Outside-Left Fullback

Inside-Left Fullback

Inside-Right Fullback

Outside-Right Fullback

run ----->   path of ball ------>   Attack

Diagram 12

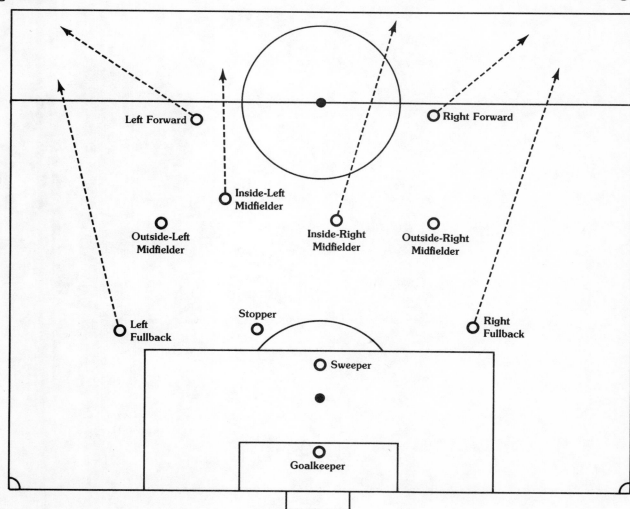

Left Forward

Right Forward

Inside-Left Midfielder

Outside-Left Midfielder

Inside-Right Midfielder

Outside-Right Midfielder

Left Fullback

Stopper

Right Fullback

Sweeper

Goalkeeper

PART IV
PHYSICAL
FITNESS
FOR SOCCER

CHAPTER 12
TRAINING
FOR ENDURANCE
AND STRENGTH

A soccer player covers between 5,500 and 6,000 yards during each game. About half of this distance is covered by sprinting and jogging. So obviously, he must be in excellent physical condition to complete a game. The better his condition and the greater his stamina, the more able he will be to execute the soccer skills and play to his full potential. Although conditioning is essential in all sports, no game requires more physical endurance than soccer.

Fitness training for soccer may be done with or without the ball. The rule of thumb is that the higher a player's technique level, the less need there is for fitness training with the ball. If his technique level is low, a ball should be provided. In the early stages of a player's development the coach should conduct 80 percent of fitness training with the ball.

To prepare soccer players for the rigors of the game, fitness training should be designed to develop the following: general endurance, local muscle endurance, muscle strength, and flexibility. A mode of training that develops fitness and technique at the same time is known as *circuit training*. This unique and rewarding method is discussed and illustrated at the end of this chapter.

GENERAL ENDURANCE TRAINING

A wide range of general endurance exercises and workouts is available to the coach. These may be taken from programs used in other sports as well as from general routines practiced in gyms and health clubs. Coaches working with players under the age of 16 should be more concerned with improving technique than with fitness training. But coaches dealing with older players who already have acquired a fair amount of soccer skill should place heavy emphasis on fitness training.

Basically, exercises that involve short sprints and medium-distance runs are ideal for soccer players. Remember, higher-level players average 90 to 100 sprints during only one-half of a game. It is absolutely essential that each player be trained to the point where he is able to perform for 90 minutes under game conditions.

Warm-up

A warm-up may be any exercise or set of exercises preceding participation in a more strenuous physical program. Although one of the major reasons for a warm-up is the psychological preparation for exertion, a number of important and beneficial physiological adjustments occur in the body that enhance its consequent physical performance. Some of these major adjustments are increase in body temperature, dilation of blood vessels supplying muscles being used, increased flow of blood to these muscles and resulting increase in muscle temperature, increase in heart rate and blood pressure, increase in the pulmonary blood flow, deeper and faster respiration, and conversion of stored glycogen into glucose that passes into the general circulation.

A warm-up should consist of stretching exercises for flexibility as well as exercises involving specific skills or tactical movements of the game. The more related the warm-up exercises are to the activity following them, the better the players' performance in that activity will be. The duration of a warm-up can vary from 5 to 20 minutes or more, depending on the individual, the intensity of the exercises, and external conditions such as temperature. One reason frequently given for warming up is to diminish the chance of injury during training or play; however, a good warm-up will not eliminate the chance of injury.

Warm-down

A warm-down is an exercise that gradually diminishes the player's physical activity after a period of intense exertion. Any exercise or activity of a severe, prolonged nature should always be followed by a warm-down. Its purpose is to help the body's circulatory system return to the pre-exercise state and to decrease the total amount of time it will take the body to recover. A warm-down allows the bloodstream to eliminate lactic acid and other waste products that have accumulated in the muscle tissue during exercise and to decrease the oxygen debt created when the muscles were not supplied with as much oxygen as they required. A good warm-down exercise is slow jogging for a period of 5 to 15 minutes.

Interval Training

General endurance training for soccer players can be accomplished most efficiently and economically through interval training. During this type of training athletes generally remain in an aerobic state, which means that they are working with an adequate supply of oxygen to their muscles.

Aerobic interval training involves exercises that have a particularly beneficial effect on the condition of the heart, lungs, and blood vessels. A program that has been researched extensively includes vigorous running, swimming, or cycling for a work period of 3 to 5 minutes with a heart response—for those under 20 years of age—of 160 to 180 beats per minute. A period of relative rest involving slow walking or jogging until the heart rate recovers to 120 beats per minute should follow each work period. The work and recovery intervals are repeated for 30 to 60 minutes, and the program is scheduled for every other day. For a player aged 20 to 30, the beginning work heart rate would be somewhere between 140 and 160 beats per minute. The recovery heart rate would be between 100 and 120 beats per minute initially and thereafter stabilized at 120 beats per minute.

At the beginning of an interval training session, an all-out sprint over a short distance or a fast run over a longer distance will bring the heartbeat up to the target work rate. As the player's fitness improves, it will take longer for his heart rate to increase to the specified number of beats per minute, and the work intervals should be increased in distance and/or time. Initially, the work-to-rest ratio is 1:3, but gradually it is increased to 1:2 or even 1:1. With the added work load, the heart rate could reach 180 beats per minute, which should be allowed to return to 120 beats per minute during the rest period, before the next work period is begun.

Generally, the interval training program is designed around the concept of sets. A set is a group of work and recovery intervals, with each work period followed by a rest period. There are a certain number of repetitions in each set, and each repetition is performed over a certain training distance and within a specific amount of time.

A more game-related interval training exercise would require players to change the direction of their runs on a soccer field. For example, at a given starting signal, players who are lined up along the goal line can sprint to the other end of the goal area and return to the goal line; then without stopping they can turn and sprint to an imaginary line drawn through the penalty spot and return to the goal line. Again without

Sprinting Exercise

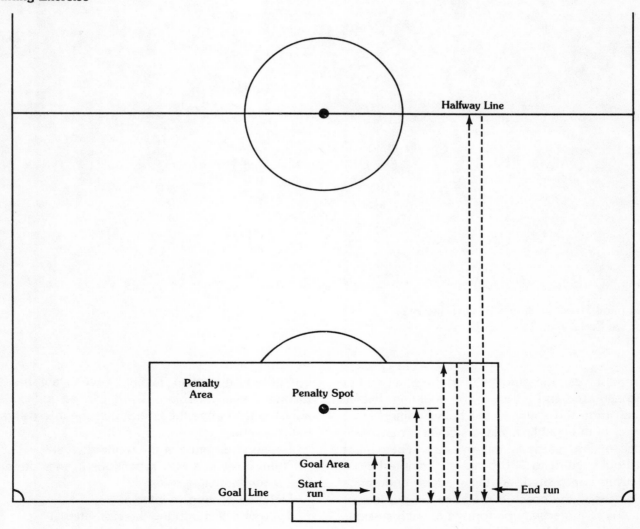

**Jogging and Heading Between Work Intervals
During an Endurance Training Session**

stopping they can turn and sprint to the other end of the penalty area and return to the goal line. Finally they can turn and sprint to the halfway line before returning to the goal line. Players cover a maximum distance of 336 yards in this exercise. Their heart rates should return to 120 beats per minute before the activity is repeated. As the players' endurance level increases, the coach can add to the number of repetitions of the activity performed at each session.

Edward Fox and Donald Mathews, both respected authorities on interval training, have established the following five variables, which can be individually adjusted to change the intensity of the interval training program:

Rate and distance of the work interval

Number of sets and repetitions in sets during each training session

Duration of the rest interval

Type of activity during the rest interval

Frequency of training per week

Interval training can also be performed with the ball. In this case the main object is not to cover a certain distance but to do a certain amount of work with the ball. The work—juggling, dribbling, heading—must be performed at a pace that will cause the heart rate to go up to between 160 and 180 beats per minute. Then the rest period should allow it to return to 120 beats per minute. At the beginning, a 1:3 work-to-rest ratio is recommended. For instance, players dribble a ball very rapidly in a restricted space for 20 seconds, then rest for 1 minute. During the rest period they may stretch, pass the ball back and forth, or jog slowly in place.

Fartlek

Another form of endurance training is *Fartlek*, which literally means "fast play" in Swedish. It consists of distance-running at various paces over different levels and types of terrain. For example, the athlete might sprint across a meadow, jog up a hill, and then coast down the other side.

Continuous Training

As the name implies, this type of training involves continuous activity without rest intervals. The intensity of the pace is just below competition level and is usually maintained over distances farther than those an athlete would cover during actual competition. Continuous training is very demanding and can be used to prepare players for the soccer season.

Slow Long-Distance Training

Here the athlete performs at a relatively slow run and the heart rate seldom goes above 160 beats per minute. The object of slow long-distance training is to cover distance—between 15 and 30 miles per day—and not to be concerned about speed. This program is only applicable to soccer during the post-season phase of endurance maintenance.

LOCAL-MUSCLE-ENDURANCE TRAINING

Muscle endurance, as the term implies, is the ability of a muscle or group of muscles to sustain an effort for a prolonged period of time. Training for muscle endurance is completely different from training for muscle strength, and generally, one will not accomplish a development of muscle endurance while training for muscle strength, and vice versa. In working with weights, for example, endurance can be improved by performing a high number of repetitions at very low resistance, but in strength training a low number of repetitions and high resistance are required.

An effective program for the development of local muscle endurance would consist of 3 to 6 sets of a weight-training exercise (see the following pages for specific weight-training exercises) and between 15 and 25 repetitions per set. Once 25 repetitions can be performed, the resistance should be increased and the number of repetitions again reduced to 15. A rest period should always follow a work interval to allow the heart rate to return to normal. Local muscle endurance can also be developed by having 2 players repeatedly press their body weights together.

When balls are used instead of weights to improve local muscle endurance, 2 or 3 players can serve in rapid succession to 1 receiver. The receiver must send the balls back to the servers, using only one foot and one technique, for example, the outside-of-the-foot pass. When the exercise is performed over a period of 30 seconds, the player who is receiving and returning the balls reaches a condition of muscle overloading that leads to the development of local muscle endurance. It must be pointed out that this type of pressure-training is anaerobic, which means that the player's oxygen intake is lower than the amount of oxygen required for the activity. Skill learning is not the object of this exercise, which should be performed only after the player has mastered the specific technique being used.

MUSCLE-STRENGTH TRAINING

In order to stimulate the development of muscle strength, the muscle group involved must be "overloaded," that is, it must be required to work against resistance greater than that to which it is accustomed. Most of the research on the subject indicates that the use of high resistance combined with a low number of repetitions will achieve maximal muscle-strength development. As muscles become stronger, and thus larger in functional size, the resistance used must become progressively heavier. For example, a player should begin a weight-lifting program by using a weight that he can lift no more than 6 times during 1 exercise. Three sets of this exercise should be performed during a workout, which should take place every other day. A player should increase the resistance, that is, choose a heavier weight, when he finds that he can lift the starting weight 8 times in a row; again, he should choose a weight that he can lift only 6 times. The greatest increase in strength will occur during the first month of training. After that, strength will continue to improve but at a much slower rate.

Basic Weight-Training Program to Develop Muscle Strength

A basic program with weights should take 6 weeks. Individuals work out on alternate days, and each work day is followed by a rest day, which may be used for skill and tactics training with the ball. Three sets of exercises are performed during a workout,

THE MUSCLES A SOCCER PLAYER MUST DEVELOP

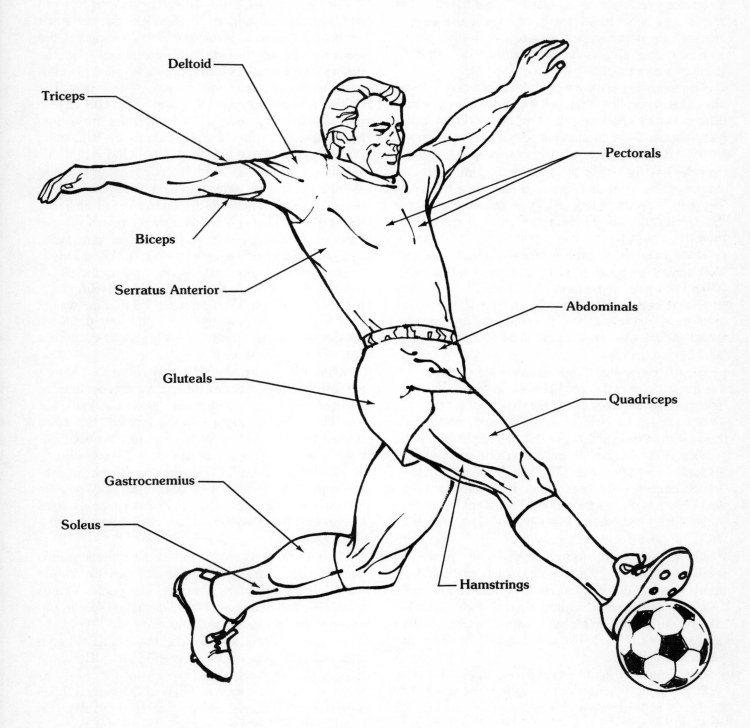

Deltoid

Triceps

Pectorals

Biceps

Serratus Anterior

Abdominals

Gluteals

Quadriceps

Gastrocnemius

Soleus

Hamstrings

with a set usually consisting of 6 to 8 repetitions of each exercise. Stations (similar to those described at the end of this chapter) are set up for the performance of a particular exercise to develop a specific muscle group, and usually a maximum of 8 stations complete a circuit.

The following are the exercises recommended and the muscle groups that will be affected by each. Equipment needed includes barbells and dumbbells plus standard weight-lifting accessories.

Military press (deltoids, triceps, serratus anterior muscles)—The player is in a standing position and bends at the waist and knees to pick up a barbell at his feet. With his palms facing down as he grips the bar, he lifts the weight first to his chest, then over his head.

Knee flexion (hamstring group)—Holding a barbell behind his head or in front of him at about mid-thigh level, the player flexes his knees.

Curl (biceps)—With his palms facing up as he grips a barbell at waist level, the player lifts the weight to his chest and then lowers it, keeping his forearms straight and flexing his elbows.

Bent-knee sit-ups (abdominals)—The player lies on his back, moving his heels close to his buttocks and putting the soles of his feet flat on the floor. His hands should be held behind his head, and his elbows should be pointing out. Sit-ups require a curling motion, with the backbone curled out and the chin tucked close to the chest. The player sits up and then lowers himself to the floor. When he reaches a certain level of strength, he should hold a weight behind his head while performing the exercise. The feet must NOT be held down by a partner.

Knee extension (quadriceps)—The player is seated, with a weight attached to each ankle. He extends one leg, then the other, straight ahead of him.

Heel raise (gastrocnemius, soleus, abdominals)—The player is lying on his back, with a weight attached to each foot. He slowly raises one foot, then the other, off the floor.

Hip extension (gluteal group)—Lying on his side, with a weight attached to his top leg, the player lifts his leg as high as he can. He repeats the exercise with the other leg.

Bench press (pectorals)—Lying on his back, the player lifts a barbell off a rack above him. Keeping his palms facing forward, he lowers the weight to his chest and then raises it an arm's length above him.

For goalkeepers, the *wrist roll* or *reverse forearm curl* should be added to develop the extensor (straightening) and flexor (bending) muscles of the forearms. To do the wrist roll, the player grips the barbell with his palms facing down; keeping his arms taut, he moves the weight by flexing his wrists. The reverse forearm curl involves gripping the barbell with the palms facing down. The player lifts the weight from the waist to the chest and then lowers it, keeping the forearms straight and flexing the elbows.

Warm-up exercises must precede the workout and should consist of static stretching of the muscle groups to be used. (See the discussion of flexibility training on a following page for definitions of the two types of stretching.) Running in place, jumping jacks, and other total body exercises may also be included.

On the first day of basic weight training the player is tested to determine the maximum load with which he can accomplish 5 repetitions of each of the weight exercises. The fifth repetition should be very difficult for him to execute, and the sixth should be almost impossible.

When the player returns to weight training after a day off, he should complete at least 6 repetitions at each of the stations, using the maximum load that was lifted during testing. Once a circuit has been started, the player is not allowed to rest between stations. He should take 2-minute rests between sets 1 and 2 and sets 2 and 3. The goal for the player is to accomplish 8 repetitions at each station. When he achieves this, he is tested again to determine the load he can lift 6 times at each station. The duration of the workout should not exceed 1 hour.

Players soon will realize that some muscle groups gain strength more quickly than others. This should not affect the program, however. The goal is always to achieve 8 repetitions at the determined weight before proceeding to a heavier weight.

In doing bent-knee sit-ups, the player's target should be to perform 60 repetitions in a 2-minute period. During the early workouts, he should do as many sit-ups as he can in 3 sets of 30-second intervals, with a rest period following each one to allow his heart rate to return to normal. When the target is reached, the player should add a 5-pound weight to be held behind his head; again, he should aim for the 2-minute target of 60 repetitions.

Isometrics

Muscle strength development can also be accomplished through an isometric training program. In this type of training, muscles attempt to shorten as they encounter a stationary force such as a wall or a pole, but because the resistance is so great, no movement or change in muscle length can occur. Isometric exercises develop a muscle's strength at specific points and angles only. They do not increase the muscle's total strength and capability of movement. Furthermore, in doing isometric exercises an individual is only capable of exerting himself at about 85 percent of capacity.

An isometric training program would consist of a number of 6-second contractions, followed by 2-second rests. For example, when performing an isometric exercise to strengthen the legs, the player remains in a standing position and places the inside part of one foot against an immovable object. He then pushes his leg toward that object. The push must be as hard as possible and must be held for 6 seconds. The player rests for 2 seconds, then places the outside of the same foot against the object and again pushes hard, holding for 6 seconds and resting for 2 seconds. He repeats this activity 6 times and then does the same thing with his other leg. The inside-of-the-foot exercise is used to develop the adductor muscles of the leg (those muscles that pull toward the median of the body); the outside-of-the-foot exercise develops the leg's abductor muscles (muscles that pull away from the median of the body). Isometrics have recently been found to be dangerous for individuals with a history of circulatory

and respiratory problems and therefore should not be practiced by such persons.

FLEXIBILITY TRAINING

Flexibility—which refers to the range of motion possible at a joint—is a very important component of physical fitness since it is necessary for the performance of basic motor as well as highly specialized skill movements. Flexibility exercises should be a part of any conditioning program and can consist of either static or ballistic stretching.

Static stretching involves locking the joints, stretching muscles and tendons to the greatest extent possible, and holding for 20 to 30 seconds. *Ballistic stretching* makes use of bobbing and bouncing movements to stretch muscles by momentum at the end of the range of motion. Static stretching is a more advantageous flexibility exercise because it involves less danger of muscle soreness or tissue tear and a more extensive stretch can be achieved.

Players should be advised to begin with a series of static stretching exercises and then move on to the ballistic type. Here are a few guidelines to keep in mind concerning flexibility training:

It is not important how flexible a player is. What is important is that he can stretch his muscles properly.

An individual should not compare himself with others. Each player is different. Stretching is not a contest to see who can reach out the farthest, but rather an individual *exercise.*

A player should become aware of the difference between the feeling of stretch and that of pain. When stretching, he should do so to the point where he feels an easy stretch. He should hold this position and relax into it. As he relaxes, he should reach out a little farther until he feels the stretch more strongly. If he reaches out too far, however, the stretch will hurt, and he will not be able to relax. Remember that straining is not stretching.

CIRCUIT TRAINING

The circuit-training method to improve strength and power is a unique way for the coach to achieve a number of objectives at the same time, and it also gives him a chance to enliven the practice routine. A soccer circuit consists of a number of stations at which different exercises are to be performed. It can be set up on a playing field or in a gymnasium (with improvised goals), using a variety of equipment—cones, flag posts, benches, for example. An imaginative coach will be able to design a circuit on which fitness and technique training can be combined. The number of stations in a circuit is determined on the basis of the players' previous training and ability levels. Between stations, players should rest long enough to regain their breath, and a thorough warm-up should always precede the exercises. Advise your players, in advance, of the sequence of the exercises, the length of time allowed for each, and the number of repetitions required.

Experienced soccer coaches recommend that pairs of players start at different stations and proceed in a clockwise or counterclockwise fashion around the circuit until every exercise has been performed. A squad of 20 players would require a circuit of 10 stations. Each pair of players should be given 4 minutes at a station and 1 minute to change stations. The 4 minutes may consist of 1 minute of work and 1 minute of rest, alternated. For example, player A should work for 1 minute and then rest for 1 minute. While A rests, player B, who may have been watching, assisting, or resting, becomes active. Then again their roles are reversed. Working and resting intervals can vary from 30 or 45 seconds to 1 minute, depending on how physically fit the players are. A well-organized circuit of 10 stations should consume about 1 hour of practice time.

The circuit system is intended for use over a period of 4 weeks, with gradual increases in the number of repetitions and the length of time spent at each station. However, the coach may also wish to use the circuit for a change of pace during the season or when weather conditions impede other activities. During the off-season, circuit exercises may be performed daily, especially when the team is unable to practice together or to begin training at the same time. The circuit allows players who arrive late to begin working out without requiring the immediate attention of the coach.

Each of the following exercises can be set up at any station within the circuit. The coach may make changes in the circuit exercises and adapt the equip-

10-STATION TRAINING CIRCUIT

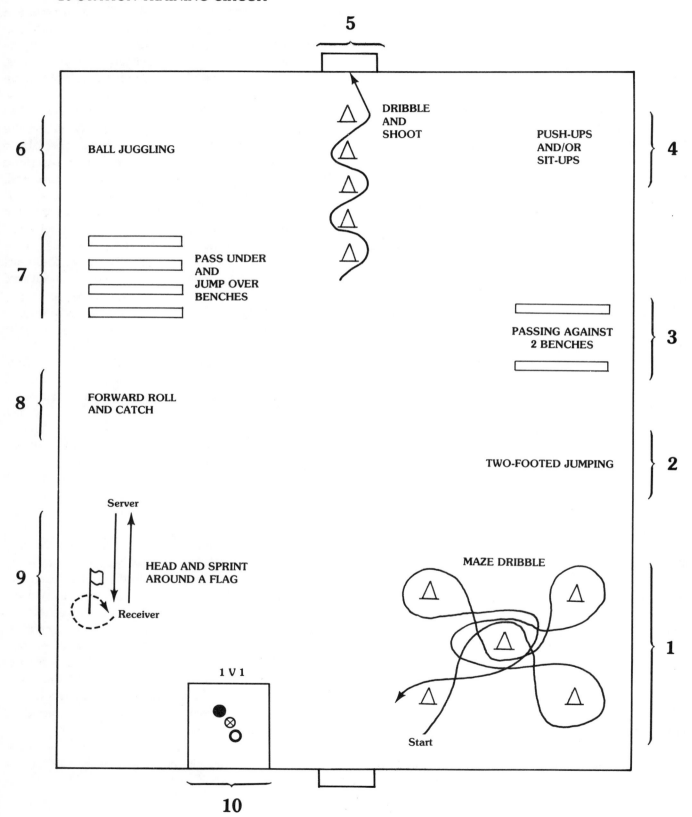

5

6 BALL JUGGLING

DRIBBLE AND SHOOT

PUSH-UPS AND/OR SIT-UPS **4**

7 PASS UNDER AND JUMP OVER BENCHES

PASSING AGAINST 2 BENCHES **3**

8 FORWARD ROLL AND CATCH

TWO-FOOTED JUMPING **2**

9 Server

HEAD AND SPRINT AROUND A FLAG

Receiver

MAZE DRIBBLE

1

1 V 1

Start

10

ment to meet his team's needs. Stations should be set up so that difficult and less difficult exercises are alternated. A typical 10-station training circuit includes:

1. *Maze Dribble.* Place 4 cones to form a 10-yard square and a fifth cone in the middle. The player dribbles counterclockwise, starting around a corner cone, then around the center cone, around the next corner cone, back around the center cone, around the next corner cone, etc., until the time is up.

2. *Two-Footed Jumping.* The player jumps sideways or forward and backward over a ball.

3. *Passing Against 2 Benches.* Place 2 benches opposite each other, approximately 20 to 30 yards apart, on their sides. The player passes the ball on the ground to 1 bench, intercepts the rebound, turns and passes to the opposite bench, and again intercepts the rebound. The activity is repeated.

4. *Push-ups and/or Sit-ups.* The player does as many push-ups as he can, followed by sit-ups in rapid succession.

5. *Dribble and Shoot.* Place 5 cones or flag posts 5 yards apart in a line just outside the penalty area and at a right angle to the goal (or their equivalents if a gymnasium is being used). Have 10 balls ready near the cone that is closest to the center circle. The player starts with the first ball, dribbles around the cones, shoots on goal, and sprints back to another ball. He then repeats the activity.

6. *Ball Juggling.* The player juggles the ball 3 times, then kicks it high and wide and sprints to collect it. He repeats the exercise.

7. *Pass Under and Jump Over Benches.* Place 4 to 6 benches 10 to 15 yards apart. The player passes the ball under the first bench, jumps over the bench, and collects the ball on the other side. He repeats the activity, passing under and jumping over the other benches.

8. *Forward Roll and Catch.* The player throws the ball high, does a forward roll, and catches the ball before it hits the ground. He repeats the exercise.

9. *Head and Sprint Around a Flag Post.* Place the post 10 to 15 yards in front of a server and about 5 yards to the left of a receiver. The server sends a ball in the air to the receiver, who must leap and head it back to him. The receiver must then sprint around the flag. The exercise is repeated.

10. *1 V 1.* Two players play 1 V 1 in a 10- to 15-yard square. Since both players are working at the same time, both will rest at the same time.

CHAPTER 13
FITNESS
EXERCISES
AND GAMES

FITNESS EXERCISES

The following exercises are easy and fun to do, yet they will help to prepare players for competition. They are designed to exercise the muscles used in soccer and to increase the overall agility, flexibility, and endurance of players. Most of the exercises are done with a ball.

Jump with both feet from side to side over the ball. Repeat for a given time.

Jump with both feet from front to back over the ball. Repeat for a given time.

Pinch the ball between your ankles, lift it to your hands by jumping, and then bend to place it on the ground. Repeat.

Pinch the ball between your ankles, jump, arch your back, and loft the ball over your head. Catch it on the rebound and repeat. (Can be done by passing to a partner.)

While holding the ball in your hands, jump with both feet, arch your back, and push the ball up into the air from your chest. Jump again, catch the ball, and push it up again before touching the ground. (Can be done while passing to a partner.)

While holding the ball in your hands, jump with both feet, pike at the waist, and throw the ball up with an underhand motion. Jump again, catch the ball, and throw it up again before you touch the ground. (Can be done while passing to a partner.)

Bounce the ball 3 times, jump, and bounce it backward between spread legs. Turn around and catch the ball. Then repeat the activity in the opposite direction.

While holding the ball in your hands, jump with both feet, arch your back, put the ball behind your neck, and slam it to the ground in front of you. Jump again to catch it over your head. (Can be done while passing to a partner.)

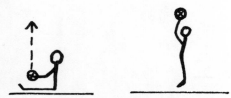

While sitting straight-legged, throw the ball up underhand. Get up, jump, and catch it over your head. Sit again and repeat.

While sitting with your legs stretched out in front of you, kick the ball up. Get up, jump, and catch it over your head. Sit again and repeat.

Bounce the ball 3 times with your right hand. Jump in a vertical scissors position and bounce it under both legs to your left hand. Bounce the ball 3 times with your left hand and repeat the scissors jump, bringing the ball back to your right hand.

While standing, throw the ball up, do a squat thrust or push-up, return to a standing position, and catch the ball. Repeat. (The same exercise may be done using a backward roll, forward roll, or sit-down-and-get-up.)

Throw the ball up, jump, and collect it with your head. Let it drop to your feet and then dribble it for 10 yards. Repeat. (This exercise may also be done with the chest instead of the head.)

Throw the ball up, jump off your left foot, scissor your thighs, and collect the ball on your right thigh. Let it drop to your feet and then dribble it for 10 yards. Repeat. (This exercise may also be done with the instep.)

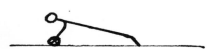

Place both hands on the ball in a push-up starting position. Touch your chest to the ball and push back up to the starting position. Repeat.

Assume a push-up starting position with the ball resting under your waist or hips. Do a push-up, but move your hips to the outside of the ball by putting pressure on your right arm. Do the same to the left.

Sitting with the ball pinched between your ankles, lift it from the ground, keeping your legs straight. Then bring your knees to your chest and extend your legs again. Repeat. (Can be done without the ball.)

Lying flat on your back with the ball pinched between your ankles and your arms stretched behind your head, raise your legs, arms, and back to a "V" position and lower them again. Repeat. (Can be done without the ball.)

Sitting straight-legged and with your arms stretched out behind you, pinch the ball between your ankles and raise your heels 6 inches off the ground. Move your legs to the right and your arms to the left. Repeat in the opposite direction, arms to the right, legs to the left. (Can be done without the ball.)

Sit straight-legged and pinch the ball between your ankles. Lie back with your arms stretched behind your head, and bring legs and ball over your head to your hands. Place the ball in your hands, sit up, and return it to your ankles.

Sit straight-legged with the ball at your feet. Using your hands, roll it around behind your back and down to your feet again. Repeat.

Stand with your legs straight and the ball at your feet. With your hands roll it around your feet. Repeat.

Stand with your legs spread and slightly bent. Hold the ball in both hands, with the right hand in front of the left. Flip the ball up slightly and switch the position of your hands. Repeat.

Stand erect, throw the ball up, squat as it comes down, and catch it with your hands below and between your knees. Repeat.

Stand erect with the ball in your hands and legs spread. Bend over, put the ball between your legs, and throw it backward and upward over your head. Catch it in the erect starting position. (Can be done by passing to a partner.)

Place the ball on the ground and roll it backward between your legs. Run to catch up and roll it backward between your legs in the opposite direction. Repeat. (Can be done by passing to a partner.)

In a push-up starting position, head the ball forward along the ground. On your hands and feet, crawl to catch up with it. Repeat.

In a supine position, use your hands to pass the ball under your back and over your stomach while arching and straightening your back. Repeat.

In a push-up starting position, place the ball behind your neck and do push-ups while keeping the ball balanced there.

While lying on your stomach, arch up with the ball in your hands, keeping your knees, legs, and elbows off the ground. Bounce the ball with both hands while remaining arched. (Can be done with a partner: after 3 bounces, pass to partner 10 yards away.)

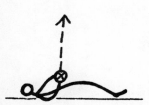

While lying on your back, arch up on your heels and shoulders. Throw the ball up with both hands, and catch it at your chest. Repeat.

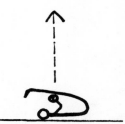

While lying on your back, bring your legs over your head and hold this position. Throw the ball up with both hands, and catch it at your chest. Repeat.

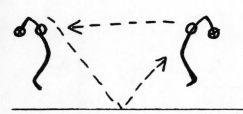

Two players, each with a ball, jump and hang in the air at the same time. One slams the ball to the ground, passing to the other. The other passes by throwing directly to his partner. Repeat, switching roles. (Can be done standing.)

Two players start with balls held on their left-hand sides. Both throw at the same time to the other's right side. Each returns the ball to his left-hand side to throw again.

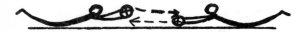

Two players face each other in prone positions, with their backs arched and their knees and elbows off the ground. They pass balls back and forth, one throwing in the air, the other rolling the ball along the ground. Repeat, switching roles.

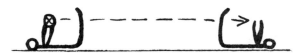

Two players lie on their backs with their legs spread and raised straight up. They pass the ball back and forth to each other.

Two balls are placed side by side and touching on the ground, with each player assuming a push-up starting position on his own ball. The players push and pull their balls, trying to knock each other off-balance.

Two players stand facing away from each other, 10 yards apart. Each holds a ball. One player throws his ball through his legs; the other throws his ball over his head. Each turns to catch the pass. Repeat, switching roles.

Two players face each other and roll balls in front of them, each trying to knock the other's ball away while keeping one hand on his own ball.

One player gets down on his hands and knees to form a wicket. The other player rolls a ball under him and jumps over him to retrieve it. Repeat, switching roles.

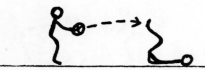

One player tosses the ball to a supine partner, who plays it back with the soles of his feet by bringing his knees to his chest and then thrusting his legs toward the thrower. Repeat, switching roles.

One player holds another in a "wheelbarrow" position. The held player heads the ball while walking on his hands. Repeat, switching roles. (Can be done without heading the ball.)

Two players lie flat on their backs with their heads toward each other. One player places the ball between his ankles and throws it, using his feet and legs, to the hands of his partner, who returns the ball in the same manner.

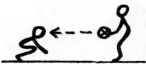

Two players, one standing and one squatting, face each other. The standing player throws the ball to his partner, who dives as he heads the ball back to the thrower. Repeat, switching roles.

One player, lying on his back with legs raised, holds the ball between his ankles. He throws the ball, then does a forward roll. The second player runs to retrieve the ball. Repeat, switching roles.

One player stands over the ball with his legs spread. The other player dives between his legs and heads the ball forward. He then gets up, chases it, and stands over it with spread legs so the first player can dive and head the ball between his legs.

Two kneeling players face each other and, with their arms wrapped around the ball, wrestle for possession.

One player lies flat on his back while the other throws the ball toward him from a standing position. The first player sits up and heads it back to the thrower. Repeat, switching roles.

One player throws the ball up while the other does a backward roll, jumps up, and heads the ball back to the thrower. Repeat, switching roles.

One player holds the ball between his knees and jumps around on both feet. The other player, while holding his left ankle with his left hand, crawls after him, trying to knock the ball loose with his other hand. Repeat, switching roles.

Two players sit facing one another, each gripping the ball with both hands. Each player leans back and stands up. Repeat.

Two players sit facing each other, holding hands while pinching the ball between their foreheads. They both stand up, keeping it between their foreheads, and then sit back down. Repeat.

One player moves the ball around on the ground with his hands, attempting to maintain possession, while a second player tries to steal it away. When he does, the roles are reversed.

The first player tosses the ball toward the second player, who heads it back. The first player rolls the ball through the spread legs of the second player, then crawls through after it and retrieves it. Repeat, switching roles.

With a partner on his back, a player passes the ball forward 10 to 15 yards, sprints after it, and stops it with his feet. Repeat, switching roles.

Two players stand 10 yards apart. One player slings the ball with a straight arm to the chest of the second player, who returns it in like manner. Repeat.

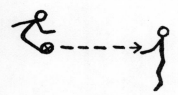

One player pinches the ball between his feet, jumps, pikes at the waist, and passes the ball to the chest of his partner, who returns it in like manner. Repeat.

One player lies on his back with his knees raised. The second player sits on the knees and does sit-ups. Repeat, switching roles.

One player straddles the hips of a standing player, who holds him up. The supported player does sit-ups. Repeat, switching roles.

The first player lies flat on his back and holds the ankles of a second player, who is standing behind him. The supine player extends his legs toward his partner, who pushes them down. The first player stops the momentum 6 inches from the ground by tensing his stomach muscles. Repeat, switching roles.

The first player is on his hands and knees. The second player lies on his back and, with knees bent and ankles and calves on the back of the kneeling first player, does sit-ups. Repeat, switching roles.

The first player holds on to the hips of the second player and pulls back on him as he springs forward. The first player is allowed to run for 20 yards, but only with a continuous struggle. Repeat, switching roles.

The first player faces the second player and pushes against the man's shoulders with his hands. The second player runs forward under pressure as the first player holds him back. Switch roles after 20 yards.

Two players interlock their arms and lean against each other. Both push hard against each other and then sprint forward in the interlocked position.

Two players stand back-to-back with arms interlocked and push against each other, each trying to move the other backward.

Two players stand facing each other, then jump up and bump their chests together. Repeat.

One player stands behind another, with his hands on his partner's shoulders. He jumps and for 1 second holds himself stiff-armed on the shoulders of the other player. Repeat, switching roles.

The first player jumps over the back of the second player in leapfrog manner, then crawls back through his partner's legs. Repeat, switching roles.

Two players "box" by touching each other on the chest.

Two players stand facing each other. Each player tries to get behind the other to slap him on the buttocks.

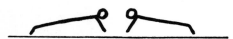

Two players in push-up starting positions try to slap each other's hands. Each keeps his hands moving, trying to get into position to counterattack.

The first player gets on the back of the second player and works his way around the man's body. Repeat, switching roles.

The first player does a handstand with his legs resting on the shoulders of the second player. The first player does push-ups. Repeat, switching roles.

The first player leans back against the second player, who puts his arms under him, lifts him, and spins him from right to left, then from left to right. Repeat, switching roles.

Two players stand back-to-back and interlock their arms. The first player lifts the second player onto his back in a piked position and then lets him down. They continue, reversing roles. (The player being lifted may go completely over the head of his partner and land on his feet.)

The first player stands and moves about. The second player, on all fours, chases him, trying to touch his feet. Repeat, switching roles.

Practicing the Wall Pass, or Give-and-Go, Combines Exercises in Physical Fitness, Basic Skills, and Tactics Training

CONDITIONING GAMES

The following games have the double advantage of promoting physical fitness and providing competitive fun. They are soccer oriented and allow players to use and practice soccer skills. Games such as these will keep players interested and alert while improving their endurance and overall body fitness.

Hand Soccer

Set up a half field with 2 goals and divide the players into 2 teams. Players must roll the ball on the ground using only their hands. Striking on goal and combination play should be encouraged in the game, but

throwing the ball through the air and kicking the ball are not permitted.

Dozen Balls

Divide the players into 2 groups of 8 without goalkeepers. The entire soccer field with 2 goals should be used, but the goals should remain unguarded. Place 12 soccer balls in the center circle. When a starting signal is given, each team tries to shoot as many balls as possible into the opponent's goal. If a ball goes out-of-bounds, it is put back into play by a throw-in. When all the balls have been shot into the goals, the game is over. Count the number of balls in each goal to determine which of the teams has won,

Week One of Pre-Season Training Program

	MONDAY Heavy Activity	TUESDAY Very Heavy Activity	WEDNESDAY Maximum Activity
Morning: 7:30–8:30	Static stretching exercises Ball gymnastics Goalkeeper training	Static stretching exercises Ball gymnastics Goalkeeper training	Static stretching exercises Ball gymnastics Goalkeeper training
Morning: 10:00–11:30	Inside-foot passing; collecting; rolling balls in motion	Outside-foot passing; collecting; rolling balls	Dribbling and tackling 1 V 1
Afternoon: 3:00–4:00	1 V 1, restricted: 1 goal, 2 goals, with goalkeepers	1 V 1 review 2 V 1, restricted: 1 goal, 2 goals, with goalkeepers	2 V 1 review 2 V 2, restricted: 1 goal, 2 goals, with goalkeepers
Evening: 7:00–8:30	11 V 11 on a full field with no restrictions	6 V 4 on half the field; functional tactical patterns	4 V 4 V 4, restricted: 2-touch; all players must touch the ball in the midfield
Evening: 8:30–8:45		Sprinting exercise, 3 sets pure-speed training	2 sets of interval training on half the field

then place the balls back in the center circle and repeat the game.

Moving Goals

Use the entire soccer field and divide the players into 2 teams with 6, 7, or 8 on each side. Pick 1 player from each team to serve as "goalposts." The "goalposts" carry a 16-foot rope or crossbar over their heads and should move around the field, in any direction, attempting to stay away from the ball and the action. The 2 teams play regular soccer, and the object is to score through a moving goal. Shots may be taken from in front of or from behind the goal. All players take turns serving as goalposts.

Handball

Divide the players into 2 equal teams with goalkeepers. Players are permitted to throw or punch the ball to each other, but they may only take three steps with the ball in their hands. Kicking is not allowed. Goals may be scored by heading only.

THREE-WEEK TRAINING PROGRAM

Physical fitness exercises, practice in basic skills, and tactics training all have the same ultimate objective: the creation of a winning soccer team. They should be integrated into a single soccer training program, based on the players' fitness and ability levels.

THURSDAY Light Activity	FRIDAY Heavy Activity	SATURDAY Maximum Activity	SUNDAY Light Activity
Static stretching exercises Ball gymnastics Goalkeeper training	Static stretching exercises Ball gymnastics Goalkeeper training	Static stretching exercises Ball gymnastics Goalkeeper training	Off
Dribbling and collecting airborne balls	Heading	Shooting	Off
3 V 1 (with ball possession), 4 V 2 (ball possession, penetration of the defense), both restricted: 1 and 2 goals	4 V 2 with 2 goals 5 V 5 with 4 goals	3 V 2, restricted: 1 goal, 2 goals, with goalkeepers	Off (Optional skill work on the field)
8 V 8, restricted: 2-touch, low passes only; functional tactical patterns	8 V 8, restricted: give-and-go 2 V 1, restricted: give-and-go	11 V 11 with local opponent if possible	Skill contests for prizes
	2 sets of interval training on half the field		

Week One of Three-Week Program

The first week's schedule of the US National Youth Team's pre-season three-week training program is given here as an example of an integrated approach to soccer training. This schedule may be used by coaches as a guideline for their own teams during the pre-season.

It is important to keep in mind that skill-training sessions should be scheduled in the mornings, when players are well rested and better able to perform the muscular movements that the mastery of soccer skills demands. In the afternoons they should perform tactical exercises such as 1 V 1, both with and without restrictions. The night before the training proper begins the players should participate in stretching, jogging, and ball gymnastics, followed by a film.

Weeks Two and Three

In the second and third weeks of the program, mornings are devoted to functional training for goalkeepers, fullbacks, midfielders, and forwards. The afternoon sessions consist of tactical training in groups and of training in the various restart situations, such as the throw-in, the corner kick, and the direct free kick.

Games, such as soccer-tennis and soccer-baseball, should be included in the afternoon sessions and may also be played during the evenings. As the three-week program draws to a close, the emphasis should be on functional training and team tactics. Scrimmages against local opponents are strongly recommended over intra-squad scrimmages because they heighten the element of competition.

CHAPTER 14
NUTRITION
FOR
SOCCER PLAYERS

Athletes make special demands on their bodies and must be physically prepared to meet these demands. Yet even dedicated athletes often ruin their chances to excel with inefficient and sometimes harmful diets. With some basic knowledge of food and how it supplies the body's needs, an athlete may greatly enhance his abilities.

In physiological terms, food satisfies three fundamental needs: the need for energy, the need to build new tissue and to repair old tissue, and the need to regulate metabolic functions (the chemical processes taking place in the body). These needs are filled by specific chemical components of food called nutrients. There are six classes of nutrients, each having precise chemical characteristics to meet specific body needs. The six classes of nutrients are *water, minerals, vitamins, proteins, carbohydrates,* and *fats*. A diet that supplies adequate amounts of these nutrients is essential for health and physical fitness.

Water. The only "food" that contains no calories, water is essential for energy production, temperature control, and cell metabolism. The average adult requires 2½ quarts of water every day, and active athletes need more.

Minerals. These are divided into two groups: those needed by the body in relatively large amounts—macromineral elements—and those needed in very small amounts—micromineral, or trace, elements. Calcium and phosphorus make up three-fourths of the body's mineral content. Minerals play an important role in the body's regulatory activities.

Vitamins. These chemical regulators are necessary for growth and the maintenance of life. A well-balanced diet contains all of the vitamins needed by the body. Some are needed in such small quantities that even poor diets provide sufficient amounts.

Vitamins govern the hundreds of biochemical reactions involved in organ function, growth, and energy metabolism. The need for vitamins is usually not greater in an athlete than in a sedentary person.

Proteins. The fuels for the human body come from three sources: proteins, carbohydrates, and fats. Protein is a major structural component of all body tissue and is needed for growth and repair. Carbohydrates and fats are useless without it, and lack of protein causes listlessness and fatigue. It is also a component of enzymes, hormones, antibodies, and blood plasma. The digestion of protein requires water, and when large amounts of protein have been consumed, dehydration sets in faster. Young athletes need more protein than older ones, but it is not true that participating in active sports increases a person's need for protein. Excessive amounts, especially of animal protein, should be avoided.

Carbohydrates. Most carbohydrates are formed by the union of simple sugars, such as glucose and fructose. During digestion and metabolism, carbohydrates are eventually broken down and converted to glucose. Much of this glucose is then transported by the blood to different parts of the body. A relatively small amount is converted to glycogen, or animal starch, which is stored in the muscles and the liver until the blood sugar level drops, when it is broken down to glucose again and returned to the bloodstream. An inadequate supply of carbohydrates causes weakness, hunger, nausea, and dizziness.

Carbohydrates cannot be stored in significant amounts by the body; only about a half-day's supply of glucose can be stored. The active person must take in a regular supply of carbohydrates throughout the day. It has been found that during the strenuous exertion of a soccer game the muscles are not supplied with large amounts of oxygen. About 20 percent of the muscle work that takes place during a game is done with oxygen present (aerobically), and about 80 percent is done without oxygen (anaerobically). This means that the soccer player's body must rely on carbohydrates as its main energy source, since they can be utilized anaerobically. Thus it is extremely important that players increase their glycogen stores to the highest possible level before a game. This can be done through a carbohydrate-buildup program commonly known as *carbohydrate loading*.

Fats. Like carbohydrates, fats are a significant energy source for working muscles. They are, in fact, the most concentrated source of energy, containing more than twice as many calories per unit of weight as either carbohydrates or proteins. Fats are also well suited for storage. But since their utilization as an energy source requires the presence of sufficient oxygen in the muscle tissue, the soccer player cannot rely on them as his main energy source.

A BALANCED DIET

A balanced daily diet consists of servings from each of the four basic food groups:

The milk group, containing protein, calcium, and riboflavin (B2)

The meat group, which includes eggs and nuts as well as fish and meat, all with a high protein content

The vegetable-fruit group, containing minerals, vitamins, and cellulose to promote bowel movements

The bread-cereals group, containing protein, minerals, and vitamins; this is the most economical source of energy

In addition, it is essential that an athlete develop the habit of drinking water. Soft drinks and even milk are inadequate substitutes.

If weight reduction is desired, the athlete should be guided by a realistic time schedule. The recommended weight loss per week is two pounds and should not exceed four pounds. The athlete should limit his caloric intake but consume enough food to provide him with sufficient energy for his activities. To keep the body functioning properly, a person weighing 175 pounds needs 1,800 calories per day.

HIGH-PERFORMANCE DIET— CARBOHYDRATE LOADING

In recent years it has been discovered that glycogen storage can be greatly increased when a high-carbohydrate diet is followed during the week preceding competition. The initial research in this field was done by Swedish physiologists who found that on a normal diet the average concentration of glycogen in the muscle tissue is approximately 1.75 grams per 100 grams of muscle. They discovered, however, that if a diet is restricted to fat and protein for three days, the glycogen level drops to 0.6 gram of glycogen per 100 grams of muscle, thus resulting in glycogen depletion. When the diet is changed to one with a large carbohydrate intake over three days, the glycogen level increases to 3.5 grams—twice as much as on a normal diet.

The researchers found further that if the process of glycogen depletion during the first phase of the diet is accompanied by strenuous exercise, the glycogen level rises even higher during the second phase of carbohydrate loading. In fact, it rises as high as 4.7 grams per 100 grams of muscle.

It is recommended that athletes start a program of carbohydrate buildup approximately five days prior to the day of a game. The program requires heavy workouts and a diet high in fats and proteins for the first two days. Training activities should be reduced to normal on the third and fourth days while the diet is changed to one with very high carbohydrate content so that the body may replenish and build up its glycogen stores.

On the day before the game the workout should be light to avoid depletion of the glycogen stores. Food intake should be balanced and contain protein, fats, and carbohydrates. The intake of liquids should be increased since water is necessary for storing carbohydrates.

ONE-WEEK MEAL PROGRAM PRIOR TO A GAME

Day	Training	Diet
Monday	Heavy	High Fat and Protein (Plan 1)
Tuesday	Heavy	High Fat and Protein (Plan 1)
Wednesday	Normal	High Carbohydrate (Plan 2)
Thursday	Normal	High Carbohydrate (Plan 2)
Friday	Light	Balanced
Saturday	Game	Balanced Plus Pre-Game Meal

Recommended Diets During Pre-Game Week

PLAN 1
High in fats and proteins,
low in carbohydrates

Breakfast
Eggs (fried or scrambled)
Bacon, ham, or sausage
Toast (buttered)
Milk, coffee, or tea
Fruit juice

Lunch
Cold cuts, cheese
Lettuce salad (with dressing)
Jello
Milk, other beverages

Dinner
Meat, fish, or poultry
Rice
Lettuce salad (with dressing)
Broccoli, asparagus, etc.
Fruit cake, fruit pie, etc.
Beverages

PLAN 2
High in carbohydrates,
low in fats and proteins

Breakfast
Cereals with milk and sugar
Pancakes or waffles with syrup
Fruit
Fruit juice

Lunch
Soup—bean, chicken, split-pea, vegetable, etc.
Tuna casserole
French fries, potato chips, etc.
Cookies, pudding
Fruit
Beverages

Dinner
Spaghetti, lasagna, or other pasta with meat sauce
Rice, potatoes
Salad
Corn, peas, etc.
Dessert—fudge, cake, fruit pies, etc.
Beverages

PRE-GAME MEAL
High in carbohydrates and liquids,
low in fats and proteins

Cereal with milk, sugar, and fruit
Pancakes or waffles with syrup (optional)
Toast with jelly
Fruit, particularly bananas or peaches
Fruit juices
Other beverages

Daily Balanced Diet

FOOD GROUP	FOOD	NUMBER OF SERVINGS
Milk	Milk, cheese, ice cream, and other milk-based foods	4 or more glasses or equivalent
Meat	Meats, fish, poultry, eggs, dry beans, peas, nuts	3 or more servings
Vegetables and Fruits	Dark-green, light-green, and yellow vegetables; potatoes; tomatoes	4 or more servings
	Citrus fruits, apples, bananas, peaches, plums, etc.; juices	3 or more servings
Breads and Cereals	Whole grain, enriched	4 or more servings

This diet should provide adequate amounts of all nutrients. Servings of
all foods except fruits may be increased to add more calories.

On game day the pre-game meal should be consumed a minimum of three hours, preferably four to five hours, before the game. This will allow adequate time for the food to be absorbed into the body. Bland foods and fluids that contain above-normal amounts of carbohydrates should be consumed. Large amounts of fats and proteins should be avoided because they are too difficult to digest and very little of their available energy will be utilized. Foods that irritate the stomach lining, such as cabbage, cucumbers, nuts, salads, oils, spices, and rough or seedy vegetables, should also be avoided.

Nutritionists sometimes recommend a completely liquid pre-game meal because it will pass through the stomach more quickly. The liquid meal should have a high carbohydrate content and be consumed no later than two hours before the game. During a prolonged competition, such as a soccer game, simple sugar solutions, dextrose tablets, and sugar-based candy bars are quick-acting energy suppliers that are easily digested and absorbed.

With the exception of the special carbohydrate-loading diet, an athlete should consume a balanced diet of approximately 10 to 20 percent protein, 30 to 35 percent fat, and 50 to 55 percent carbohydrates. During the season, the soccer player should keep his daily caloric intake at a minimum of 4,000 and a maximum of 6,000 calories.

CHAPTER 15
SOCCER INJURIES
AND
THEIR CARE

Since soccer is a contact sport and, at times, a collision sport played at high speed, all players face the possibility of various types of injuries. These may involve muscles, bones, ligaments, the skin, or any other part of the body. They may range in severity from simple scrapes and bruises to torn ligaments or tendons.

Anatomy and physiology are part of the USSF National Coaching School curriculum, and coaches attending the school are examined in these two areas. Every coach should know how to recognize and deal with injuries once they have occurred, including those that his athletes may attempt to disguise in order to play.

The coach also has the responsibility for making a field decision concerning an injured player's status. Based on the seriousness of the injury, he must decide whether or not to allow further competition. If there is any chance of aggravating a potentially dangerous situation, the coach, of course, should withdraw the player from the game even if he is still playing well. Again, if the injury is not serious but limits full participation, the coach probably should sideline the player. Only when an injury is neither potentially dangerous nor limiting of full participation should a player be allowed to continue.

In the event of an injury, the coach should take the following four steps:

Remove the player from the field
Examine the injury
Administer immediate care
Initiate emergency procedures if necessary

Following are descriptions of the most common soccer injuries and ailments, along with recommended first-aid measures and treatment procedures. At the end of the chapter is a list of medical supplies that should be on hand at all times.

STITCH

A stitch is a short-lasting but sharp pain in the side of the abdomen that occasionally occurs during heavy exertion. It generally is considered to be a cramp in a portion of a muscle in the abdominal region, probably the diaphragm muscle. To alleviate this condition, the athlete should breathe as deeply as possible through both nose and mouth and perhaps slow down his exercise rate for a while. A stitch might also be relieved by having the athlete "grunt" while he is exercising or playing.

MUSCLE CRAMP

Muscle cramps are strong, involuntary contractions of a muscle or a group of muscles. They can be caused by a number of factors, including a sharp blow to a muscle, such as a kick in the calf; excessive fatigue caused by over-exercising; an inadequate or improper diet; or the misuse of a muscle or a muscle group. Cramps can also occur in cold weather or when a player has not warmed up properly. In hot weather they may be caused by dehydration and salt loss. The most common areas for cramps are the calf and the hamstring muscles.

A player who suffers a cramp should stop playing or exercising immediately. He should stretch the muscle slowly to relax the spasm. He should not massage a cramp until its cause has been determined. If the cause was a blow to the muscle, ice should be applied to the area and the player should continue to stretch. If the cramp was not caused by a blow, the muscle should be massaged and heat should be applied after the muscle is stretched and relaxed.

SPRAIN

The sprain is the most frequent injury suffered in soccer, with the knee and ankle most often involved. A sprain is a stretching or tearing of a ligament beyond its normal limits. A ligament is the band of tough tissue that connects the bones and holds the joints together. There are varying degrees of sprains, depending on the amount of ligament fiber torn and the resulting degree of instability. The immediate care procedure for any sprain is "RICE": *Rest, Ice, Compression, Elevation.* Each of these four procedures must be followed because their physiological side *effects* help to localize the injury and promote healing.

Rest. Take the player out of the game or practice session without permitting him to put his full weight on the injured leg. Never tell him to walk or run a sprain off. No sprain will improve with immediate activity. The player should sit down.

Ice. The application of ice or a cold pack is the most important of the four treatment steps. By applying ice to the injury, you accomplish several things. You help the player feel relief immediately, and you assist in speeding his recovery and eventual return to play. The ice causes the blood vessels in the damaged area to constrict, or become narrower, thereby limiting the amount of blood flowing to the area. This helps to decrease the swelling. The ice also serves to reduce the painful spasm that usually accompanies a sprain and anesthetizes the area by making it numb.

The ice should be applied directly to the injured and surrounding areas for 30 minutes at a time, at least 4 times a day for the first 48 hours following the sprain or until all swelling has stopped.

Compression. Whenever a sprain occurs, blood vessels and other tissues are damaged and fluid is released into the surrounding area. This causes a disruption of the fluid pressure in that region, which in turn causes more swelling. One of the primary aims of applying a compression bandage is to try to restore the fluid pressure balance and limit the amount of swelling. Compression is applied most easily with an elastic bandage (Ace or Tensor). Make sure to apply the compression in such a way that the wrapping is tighter at the bottom and looser higher up. This forces the swelling into the muscles above the sprain so that the unaffected muscles can help "pump out" excess fluid from the injured area.

Elevation. The purpose of this step is to limit the amount of swelling and promote drainage of existing swelling. Elevation simply means raising the sprained joint so that it is higher than the injured player's heart. With an ankle or knee sprain, for example, elevation would call for the athlete to sit or lie on the ground with something propped under his calf to keep the injured part higher than his heart.

To review these four steps, consider a hypothetical case during a game. A player appears to have sprained his ankle and is lying on the field in pain. After the game is stopped, check to see if the ankle is grossly deformed. If it is, the athlete should be carried from the field. Once he is on the sideline, carefully and gently remove his shoe and sock and apply a wet Ace bandage if possible. If this is not possible, apply an ice bag directly to the skin. After applying the ice and securing it to the ankle, have the athlete elevate his foot, either on the bench or some other object, so that it rests higher than his heart.

After the game, take the athlete to a doctor for X rays, any necessary medical treatment, and, ultimately, a rehabilitation program for the ankle. Remember, a complete recovery of the injured joint can be attained through an exercise program prescribed by a qualified person.

STRAIN

The second most common injury in contact sports is a strain of a muscle or tendon (see Tendon Injuries). This injury—caused by a violent contraction, excessive forcible stretch, or poor coordination of assisting muscle groups—usually is referred to as a "pull" when it occurs in a muscle. The most frequent strain in soccer is the groin pull. Strains present a difficult problem and must be treated immediately. Delayed or improper treatment will increase the amount of inelastic scar tissue the body deposits in the muscle. The more scar tissue the athlete has, the greater his chances of straining the muscle or tendon again.

The immediate treatment of a strain, as with a sprain, is "RICE." A physician should be consulted to determine whether there is damage to the bones or to any of the other body structures. Ice should be applied 4 times a day for 48 hours; if the muscle is not severely damaged, the ice may then be replaced with moist heat and light exercise may be resumed. This exercise must include flexibility or stretching movements for the injured muscle. Static stretching will drastically reduce the chance of reinjury.

Since the strain represents a complex medical problem, everything must be done to prevent such an injury. A complete static stretching routine for all the muscles of the trunk and the lower extremities should be part of every warm-up and warm-down as well as of halftime exercises.

TENDON INJURIES

The strong, nonelastic fibrous cord or band that connects the muscles to the bones or other body structures is called a tendon. Tendon injuries are not as common in soccer as they are in some other sports, but they do occur, and they are serious. Some of the long tendons are enclosed in sheaths of connective tissue. When these tendons are overstrained, inflammation or infection in the sheaths may result—one of the reasons a physician should always be consulted if a player suffers a strain (see Strain).

Damage to the Achilles tendon occurs in a "tripping from behind" situation, in which a player attempting to tackle from behind misses the ball and strikes his opponent above the heel instead. There is pain in that area, and the injured man, unable to flex his ankle, can hardly walk. Ice should be applied, the foot elevated, and a doctor called immediately. If the tendon is ruptured, the calf muscles are drawn up tensely toward the bend of the knee. Surgery is necessary, to sew the ends of the torn tendon together, followed by immobilization in a cast.

CARTILAGE INJURIES

The tough, gristly connective tissue that covers the bone ends in the joints is known as cartilage. Within certain joints there are also thin disks of cartilage that function to reduce friction between the joint surfaces and to act as shock absorbers between two bones. The crescent-shaped cartilages in the knee are those most often injured. Treatment depends on the severity of the injury. The first step is again "RICE."

A physician should be consulted for cartilage injuries. If a piece of cartilage has broken off and moves within the knee, it may cause the knee joint to lock, click, buckle, or give way. In this case, surgery is usually the only effective treatment. Some cartilage injuries can be treated by applying a cast to immobilize the area and allow the cartilage to heal. Other injuries respond to a well-designed knee-exercise program.

Following the treatment of any injury to the knee, the involved leg must be rehabilitated. The rehabilitation program should provide for the redevelopment of strength, power, endurance, and flexibility in the affected muscles of the joint.

CONTUSION

When a player is kicked in the leg, especially the thigh, the skin and all tissues under it are bruised, an injury called a contusion. If the force of the blow is strong, a considerable amount of internal bleeding will occur in the muscle. The collection of blood and other fluids in the muscle is known as a hematoma.

The immediate care of a contusion should consist of slow stretching of the affected muscle to the point of pain and ice application with the muscle in a stretched position. An elastic bandage should be applied over the ice, and the area should be kept elevated. The ice applications and stretching should continue until the hematoma, visible as a lump, has completely disappeared. Gentle exercises should follow. Generally, it takes about 10 days for a contusion to heal, depending on its severity.

WOUNDS

A wound is any break in the continuity of body tissues. There are four types of open wounds commonly encountered in soccer: abrasions, lacerations, incisions, and punctures. If any of these wounds appear to be serious, provide first aid and secure immediate medical attention.

An *abrasion* occurs when the skin scrapes against a

hard surface and only its outer layers are damaged. A *laceration* is an irregular or jagged break or tear in the skin, usually caused by great force being exerted against it. There may be immediate and profuse bleeding. An *incision* is a cut caused by glass, rough edges of metal, or other sharp objects. Again, heavy bleeding may occur at once. If the cut is deep, there may be damage to muscles, tendons, or nerves. A *puncture wound* results from an object piercing the skin layers and causing a small, but sometimes deep hole in the tissues. There is usually little external bleeding, and the hazard of infection is therefore increased. First aid for all of these types of wounds consists of the following measures:

Stop the bleeding. This can be accomplished by direct pressure, using a pressure bandage, or by applying pressure to the artery supplying the injured area. The injured part also should be elevated.

Protect the wound from contamination and infection. When bleeding is not severe, first cleanse the wound, using soap and water, and make sure to cleanse the surrounding area as well. Then rinse the wound thoroughly by flushing it with clean water, preferably running tap water. Blot the wound dry with a sterile gauze pad or clean cloth. Next apply a dry sterile bandage or clean dressing and secure it firmly.

Remind the player to watch the area closely and to see a doctor promptly if an infection occurs. Some symptoms of infection are:

Swelling of the affected part
Redness of the affected part
A sensation of heat in the affected area
Throbbing pain in the affected area
Tenderness to the touch

If any of these symptoms are overlooked and the wound is allowed to go unattended, the following may occur: fever; formation of pus, either collected beneath the skin or draining from the wound; swollen lymph glands, especially in the armpit, groin, or neck; and red streaks leading from the wound. These are indications that the infection is spreading and may lead to blood poisoning, a serious condition.

FRACTURES

A fracture is defined as a break in the continuity of a bone. It can be the result of a direct blow, such as a kick from another player. Falls or twisting the body may also cause fractures. In addition, a forceful muscle contraction will sometimes cause a tendon to pull a piece of bone free, resulting in what is called an avulsion fracture.

Fractures are broadly classified into two types: open or closed. An open fracture is one producing an open wound as a result of a bone piercing through the skin—also called a compound fracture. If the skin is not broken, the fracture is closed.

Signs and Symptoms

It is important to note that there are several signs and symptoms which when present should lead one to suspect a fracture, although not all signs and symptoms need be present to justify the diagnosis of a fracture. Remember, a fractured bone might not prevent the player from moving the injured part. Therefore, do not ask the player to move to determine whether a fracture has occurred. It is important to be aware of all possible injuries before making a decision about what to do with the player, and whenever you are in doubt about whether he has a fracture, you should assume that he does.

A break in a bone should be suspected and the part treated accordingly if one or more of the following signs are present:

Deformity. The arm or leg is in an unnatural position or angulated where there is no joint.

Tenderness. Usually sharply localized at the site of the break, this is known as "point tenderness." It can be checked by gently pressing along the bone with the tip of a finger.

Grating. This is a sensation that can be felt internally where the broken ends of the bone rub together. *Do not seek this sign manually!*

Swelling and discoloration. Swelling to some degree will be present in all fractures. The discoloration usually will not occur for several hours. At first, the area is bluish-black, later fading to greenish-yellow because of chemical changes in the blood.

Loss of use. A person who has sustained a fracture usually guards the injured part and will not attempt to use it. There may be partial or complete loss of motion in the adjacent joints.

One of the most important determining factors in diagnosing a fracture is the *history of the injury.* Have the player describe what happened, and be alert to factors that frequently cause fractures. Let the injured party provide the information. Do not ask leading questions such as "Did you hear it crack?" or, "Did you feel it snap?" These types of questions might put false ideas in the mind of a player in pain or under emotional stress.

Many factors can be determined only by X-ray examination. Therefore, it is important to refer *all* suspicious cases to the attention of a doctor.

First Aid

Immobilize the injured part before moving or transporting a player with a suspected fracture. Follow the old axiom: "Splint it where it lies." Immobilization reduces pain, helps prevent or control shock, and prevents additional damage to nerves, blood vessels, and soft tissue.

If the fracture is open, the first priority is to control bleeding from the wound. Be careful not to contaminate the wound further. Use a sterile dressing and apply the bandage before moving the player or immobilizing the part of the body with the fracture.

Immobilization is accomplished by applying splints and bandages—and using a sling if the arm area is involved—to keep the body part from moving. Follow these general guidelines for first aid procedures:

Immobilize the joints above and below the fracture site

Make sure bandages or splints do not interfere with normal circulation

Pad the splints where they come in contact with the body to prevent undue pressure and injury

Transport the player on a stretcher

Treat him for shock

Transport the player to medical attention

DISLOCATION

When a bone is displaced from the opposing connective surfaces that constitute a joint, the condition is called a dislocation. The injury occurs most often in the shoulder and finger joints. A hard blow or a fall is the usual cause, but it may also result from violent muscular effort. The joint has a markedly deformed appearance, and there is intense pain at the site. If the bone is pulled out of place only slightly, the injury is known as an incomplete dislocation, but in either case the joint should not be touched.

The dislocated part should be immobilized and the player removed on a stretcher unless he can walk. Prompt medical attention should be secured.

UNCONSCIOUSNESS

If a player is completely unaware of what is going on around him and unable to make any meaningful or purposeful movements, he is in a state of unconsciousness. The cause might be either injury or illness. The primary concern in dealing with an unconscious player is to keep his windpipe open and unobstructed. If the athlete is not breathing at all, he should be given artificial respiration.

The unconscious player, if allowed to lie on his back unassisted, is in danger of asphyxiation and death. His tongue will drop backward, forming an obstruction to his windpipe. This can often be detected by noisy, "snoring" breathing. To place a pillow or support under the player's head will only aggravate the condition.

As a first step, lift and hold the unconscious player's lower jaw forward; place him on his side or with his face down. Cleanse the mouth and throat with suction. Remember that the player may have a neck injury, so the neck must be protected. It should not be extended, flexed, or twisted. The player should not be given any liquids. If there is bleeding or leaking of fluids from the mouth or ears, turn the player's head to the side to aid the flow. When dealing with an unconscious player, the coach must:

Watch the player's breathing carefully, using artificial respiration when necessary

Keep the patient lying down even when he regains consciousness

Put nothing in the patient's mouth

Not move the head if a neck injury is suspected

Call for emergency medical assistance to transport the player

Call on medical assistance to treat the patient for shock

Keep track of the duration of unconsciousness, if possible, and report it to the physician

Not attempt to move the player himself

THE GAME WILL WAIT!

CONVULSIONS

Convulsions are violent, jerky, purposeless movements caused by the sudden stimulation of a large number of brain cells. These movements may occur in only one arm or leg, one-half of the body, or the entire body. Most persons are unconscious during convulsions and may remain unconscious for 5 to 10 minutes after the seizure has stopped.

Take all available precautions to prevent the patient from hurting himself. He might seem to have a windpipe obstruction and might even become slightly bluish in the face. This is usually not a serious problem. He will start to breathe normally after the attack has passed and as soon as the relaxation period has begun.

Occasionally, a person having convulsions may clamp his teeth and bite his tongue. A bite-stick, or padded wooden tongue depressor, or suitable substitute should be placed between his teeth. However, if help can be administered only by force, it is better not to attempt it. On the other hand, if the player has swallowed his tongue—a life-threatening situation—the mouth may be opened by using an "oral screw." Once the mouth is opened and secured, place a pair of tongue forceps into the side of the mouth and grasp the tongue with the forceps. *Never put your hand in the player's mouth!*

The patient's body and especially his head should be protected at all times during convulsions. Remove any objects that he might strike, and do not try to restrain him. Once the player has regained consciousness, do not move him. Secure emergency transport to a hospital.

HEAT EXHAUSTION

Heat exhaustion is the most common of the heat-related injuries. This condition may occur during situations of heavy muscular work in hot temperatures. It may be caused by dehydration or salt depletion or by both conditions.

Signs and Symptoms

Although the player usually will remain conscious, it is not uncommon for fainting to occur in a case of heat exhaustion. The following symptoms should be looked for:

The player becomes weak and is unable to exercise or play

Skin will be moist and clammy

Pupils might be dilated

Skin will be pale or ashen gray

Body temperature will usually be normal or subnormal

Pulse might be slightly more rapid than normal and weak

Player might suffer from heat cramps

First Aid

Heat exhaustion is an emergency situation, but usually it is not life-threatening.

Have the player lie down and rest in the coolest available place

Give the player *cold* drinks and encourage him to drink as much as possible

The player should be taken to a hospital in case there are other complications

HEAT STROKE

Heat stroke is caused by a high body temperature and by salt depletion and dehydration. The body's mechanisms for dissipating heat have ceased functioning, and therefore a tremendous increase in body temperature will occur very quickly.

Heat stroke is a life-threatening situation and should be treated as an emergency. Secure medical help immediately!

Signs and Symptoms

The signs of heat stroke are different from those of heat exhaustion, and the coach should make a special effort to memorize the differences.

Body temperature will be extremely high, ranging between 105°F and 109°F

Skin will feel hot to the touch

Skin will be extremely dry

Skin will appear flushed and red

Pulse rate will be strong and rapid

Player is dizzy and weak

Player is mentally confused, euphoric, or overcome with a sense of impending doom before
becoming unconscious

Player might become unconscious with little
warning

First Aid

Make immediate arrangements for transporting the
player to a hospital or clinic. Until the victim arrives at
the medical facility, the coach should do the following
to preserve life:

Remove all of the player's clothing

Move the player to the coldest available place

Cool the player's body by any means possible,
but preferably in an ice bath (If no ice bath is
available, improvise to help lower body
temperature—use cold water or chemical
cold packs; rub ice vigorously over body; etc.)

If the patient is conscious and can cooperate,
give him cold drinks to aid in heat loss

PREVENTING HEAT INJURIES

Sports activities involve a high risk of heat injuries.
The three major types of heat injuries are heat
cramps, heat exhaustion, and heat stroke. Athletes
are especially prone to these problems because their
physical activity is strenuous and they often exercise
in hot or humid environments. Since most sports activities are planned, however, it is possible for the
coach to greatly reduce the risk of serious heat injuries by taking proper precautions. Temperature and
humidity are the critical factors. The relative humidity
can be measured with a sling psychrometer. Heat
stroke and exhaustion can occur in the shade!

Athletes should go through a pre-season conditioning program for many reasons, not the least of
which is that a well-conditioned athlete is better able
to cope with heat stress. Practice should take place
under conditions similar to those that will be present
during actual games. It is also important to provide for
gradual acclimatization of players to hot-weather activity. A quick explanation to them before practice
about the dangers of heat is a good idea.

The following are suggestions to help coaches prevent heat injuries during hot weather:

Have each player get a checkup before beginning practice, and require from each a medical history

Schedule workouts during cooler hours, that is,
mornings and evenings in hot weather

Acclimate players to hot weather activity by
graduated practices

Provide 15- to 30-minute rest periods out of the
sun during workouts in hot weather

Supply or suggest clothing that is white, loose
enough to permit heat escape, and perme-
able to moisture to allow heat loss by evaporation of perspiration

Supply adequate liquids for drinking during all
workouts

Do not allow the use of rubberized sweatsuits or
other such apparel in hot weather

Watch players for signs of trouble, particularly
those who tend not to report discomfort

NOSEBLEEDS

Most episodes of nasal bleeding can be controlled by
pinching the lower half of the nose between the
thumb and index finger for 10 minutes. The player
should be kept in a sitting position whenever possible.
If the bleeding does not stop, ice packs should be
applied to the nasal and facial area. In addition, a
gauze pad can be moistened with water and gently
inserted into the bleeding nostril. The nose is then
pinched, using the thumb and index finger, for 10
minutes. If this does not control the bleeding, medical
attention should be obtained.

GENERAL CARE OF THE FEET

In soccer any foot problem is bound to diminish a
player's performance in games and limit his ability to
practice. Foot problems also cause an athlete to alter
his normal walking and running patterns and to place
undue pressure on other areas of the foot; this pressure can lead to ankle strains and/or sprains. To help
the players avoid problems before they occur, here
are some recommendations for proper foot care:

Wash the feet thoroughly with soap and water
after each practice and dry them well before
putting on socks and shoes

Use clean socks every day

For burning sensations, "hot spots," etc., use a combination of pre-tape spray and talcum powder

Cut toe nails straight across (Do not taper them) and keep them long enough to prevent the edges from penetrating side tissues yet short enough to prevent irritation from socks and shoes

Wear proper fitting shoes

Even when all of these precautions are followed, foot problems may still develop, since the soccer player by necessity subjects his feet to considerable wear and tear. Immediate attention will usually minimize his discomfort.

Athlete's Foot

Athlete's foot is a fungus disease that can lead to a bacterial infection. The recommended care is to keep the feet clean and dry; to wear clean socks; and to apply fungicidal powder, ointment, cream, or liquid between and around the toes. In an especially persistent case, the athlete should be referred to a physician. To prevent the disease from spreading, players should wear slippers or clogs in the locker and shower rooms and refrain from using each other's towels, socks, shoes, and sneakers. The locker room and shower floors should be disinfected daily. Athlete's foot is very contagious.

Blisters

A blister is a separation of the layers of the skin with fluid accumulation between the layers. A combination of pre-tape spray and talcum powder applied daily is effective in the prevention of blisters. There are closed and open blisters. When caring for a closed blister, clean the area thoroughly with soap and water. Use a sterilized needle or scalpel to puncture the first layer of skin. Drain the fluid by pressing down with a sterile gauze pad. Apply an antiseptic ointment and cover the area with a sterile gauze pad taped in place.

With open blisters, the skin is torn and the fluid has usually already drained. Cut the loose skin away and round off any rough edges that could cause further irritation. Clean the entire area with soap and water. Apply antiseptic ointment and a gauze pad.

Calluses

A callus is an accumulation of dead tissue. Blood blisters may appear under calluses to add to the discomfort. To care for calluses, first carefully shave off the dead skin with a callus knife, emery paper, sandpaper, or scalpel. If the area is tender, put a donut pad around the callus and secure it with tape. If a blood blister has formed under the callus, send the player to a physician. The use of an emery board or a pumice stone after showering will help to keep calluses from forming.

Corns

A corn is caused either by the pressure of improperly fitted shoes or by faulty posture. Corns, which usually form on the tops of the toes, are a thickening of the soft tissue, which is inflammatory and painful. A corn should be removed only by a professional podiatrist, although the use of a donut pad may cause one to slowly disappear.

Ingrown Toe Nails

It must be remembered that nails do not grow in; they are forced into the surrounding skin by pressure. An ingrown nail can be cared for by soaking the toe in warm water for 20 minutes, 3 times a day. A piece of gauze or cotton should be placed under the edge of the nail to lift it away from the skin. If there is an infection and it does not subside, a physician should be consulted.

Toe Injuries

Toe injuries are very common in soccer. They may be caused by running or kicking on uneven surfaces, by striking the ball improperly, or by striking the ground before the ball. The toe will be tender and painful; it may swell or look deformed. Treatment consists of applying ice and immobilizing the injured member by taping it to an adjacent toe. X rays are recommended, so the patient should see a physician.

MEDICAL SUPPLIES AND EQUIPMENT

The following is a list of the basic supplies a coach should have in his medical kit at all games and practice sessions. He should also carry a first-aid manual.

Ace or Tensor Bandages	
3 in.:	2
4 in.:	2
6 in.:	2
Adhesive Tape	
½ in.:	2 rolls
1 in.:	2 rolls
1½ in.:	4 rolls
Alcohol:	1 bottle
Ammonia Caps (Ampules):	1 doz.
Analgesic Balm:	1 lb.
Antacid Tablets:	12
Antiglare Black:	1 tube
Aspirin Tablets:	1 bottle (100)
Band-Aids	
1 by 3 in.:	2 doz.
extra large:	1 doz.
Bite-Stick (Padded Tongue Depressor):	1
Cold Packs, Instant:	3
Cotton Balls:	25
Cotton Tip Applicators (Q-tips):	1 box
"Elastikon" Tape	
3 in.:	2 rolls
Germicide Solution:	1 bottle
Medicated Ointment:	1 tube

Moleskin Adhesive Felt	
6-in.-sq. sheet:	1
Oral Screw:	1
Oral Thermometer:	1
Pre-Tape (Benzoin) Spray:	1 can
Safety Pins:	Assorted sizes
Salt Tablets:	1 bottle (100)
Skin Lube (Vaseline):	1 lb.
Splints	
air:	1 set
wood:	Assorted sizes
cardboard:	Assorted sizes
Sponge Rubber	
¼ in.:	1 6-in.-sq. sheet
½ in.:	1 6-in.-sq. sheet
Sterile Bandages	
1 in.:	4 rolls
2 in.:	4 rolls
Sterile Gauze Pads	
2 in. sq.:	10
3 in. sq.:	10
4 in. sq.:	10
Tape Scissors:	1
Tongue Depressors, Wooden:	50
Triangular Bandage:	2

PART V
COACHING
IS MORE
THAN
ATHLETICS

CHAPTER 16
COACHING
YOUTH

A youth coach is anyone coaching boys or girls between the ages of 6 and 18. He has a double responsibility inasmuch as he not only teaches the game but also has to take into consideration the mental and physical development of his charges. The 6-to-14-year age range is an ideal time for learning soccer skills. During those years, youngsters are highly competitive and possess a tremendous amount of energy and enthusiasm. The coach, therefore, should channel these characteristics into positive development. But remember, in dealing with youth players the coach must always base his plans on the maturity, strength, fitness, and attention spans of his players.

It is always better to coach by example rather than by command. This is especially true when working with youngsters. If a coach pays attention to his appearance, maintains good communication with his players, and teaches skills by demonstrating them, he will probably have a team that is happy to return to the practice field. Here are some general guidelines, designed to assist those who coach youth:

Coach yourself before you coach others. Practice your skills so that you can give competent demonstrations. This is the most convincing method of teaching skills.

Do your homework. Analyze previous games. Prepare your practice schedules beforehand. Keep your team organized, both on and off the field.

Have players practice their weaknesses. First have them practice the basic skill or skills in which they are

deficient. Gradually increase the level of difficulty of the practice sessions and, finally, put the players to the test by having them play a game.

Watch the training load. Too much and too little are equally bad. A balanced training program takes into account the players' needs for improvement, their ages, and their physical and mental abilities.

Be alert to individual needs and be flexible. Don't impose the same exercises and practice times on all players; allow each to concentrate on individual weaknesses. This requires one-to-one coaching wherever possible.

Simplify. Complexity is confusing. Use simple and specific explanations rather than soccer terminology on an advanced level.

Make practice fun. Use a variety of exercises and drills and break them up by introducing games.

Do not over-coach. Avoid talking too much or "preaching" to the players while they are seated. Most of the coaching should be done while they are practicing, and they learn faster by performing.

Remain aware of the stage of physical and mental development of each player. They may all be the same calendar age, but that does not mean they are the same biological age. Some youngsters mature sooner than others.

COACHING PROGRAMS

Generally, the following programs are recommended for coaching youth groups of varying ages and levels of development:

Ages 6 to 8

Stage of development. Players in this group are very self-conscious, have a very limited attention span, and need constant movement.

Teaching program. Encourage movement through soccer-related children's games such as playing tag with a soccer ball. Also use small grids for games involving 5 V 5, 7 V 7, etc. The emphasis should be on having fun. There should be no competitive pressure.

Training program. Two 40-minute practice sessions per week. One game per week, with 7 to a side on a small field (70 by 50 yards; goals 5 yards high and 2 yards wide) and 15-minute halves.

Ages 8 to 10

Stage of development. Players in this group have better-developed circulatory and muscular systems. They also have a longer concentration span and great eagerness for learning.

Teaching program. Introduce the basic techniques and use small grids for games involving 2 V 2, 3 V 3, etc. The emphasis should now be on increasing enjoyment through improving play.

Training program. Two 50-minute practice sessions per week. One game per week, with 7 to a side on a small field (70 by 50 yards; goals 5 yards high by 2 yards wide) and 20-minute halves.

Ages 10 to 12

Stage of development. These players are perhaps better balanced physically and mentally than any other age group. They have a great sense of team loyalty, are quite competitive, and learn skills eagerly.

Teaching program. Introduce all techniques— dribbling, juggling, collecting, passing, shooting, heading, and tackling—and team play, with more intensive exercises (3 V 3, 4 V 2, 5 V 5).

Training program. Two 60-minute practice sessions per week. One game per week, with 8 to a side on a small field (70 by 50 yards; goals 5 yards high by 2 yards wide) and 25-minute halves.

Ages 12 to 14

Stage of development. Players in this group are just entering the first, or physical, phase of puberty. This is a period of physical change, usually accompanied by mental unrest, which may be a disadvantage as players try to learn the basic techniques. There is a tendency at this stage for players to form social groups.

Teaching program. Work more intensively on the techniques introduced at the 10-to-12-year level. Channel the players' inclinations to form groups into the creation of tactical units for team play.

Training program. Two 70-minute practice sessions per week. One game per week, with 11 to a side on a regular-size soccer field and 30-minute halves.

Ages 14 to 16

Stage of development. These players are still essentially in the physical phase of puberty but are in the process of entering the psychic phase, in which they discover their own personalities, personal preferences, and styles.

Teaching program. At this point, the players' ability to perform the basic skills must be perfected. They must be able to apply all of the skills under pressure from an opponent and with restrictions of time and space. A thorough knowledge of the principles of play and of team tactics is now demanded. It is also time to introduce a heavier physical-fitness training schedule to improve endurance and strength.

Training program. Two 80-minute practice sessions per week. One game per week, with 11 to a side on a regulation field and 35-minute halves.

Ages 16 to 18

Stage of development. Players in this group are in the second (psychic) phase of puberty. They now become more set in their ways, and this can be seen partly in the way they express themselves and perform on the field. They are becoming young adults and must be treated accordingly.

Teaching program. Players should perform at close to their maximum potential. Their techniques must be polished under game conditions, and their tactical training should be completed. Some players of this age group should be ready for professional-level play if they have received proper coaching throughout their earlier development.

Training program. Two or three 90-minute prac-

tice sessions per week. One game per week, with 11 to a side on a regulation field and 40-minute halves.

"ECONOMICAL" TRAINING METHODS

Soccer is a very demanding sport. It requires a player to play 90 minutes or more, to execute the basic skills under the most severe pressure, and to concentrate in order to play a tactically sound game. Thus, the efficient use of training time is essential to the proper development of youth players. The coach must always seek the most "economical" training methods, that is, those that involve more than one of the four components of soccer: fitness, skill, tactics, and mental alertness. When two or three of these components are incorporated in a single workout, the coach is using his and his players' time to best advantage, and he is speeding up the development process.

Fitness training, for instance, can be included in technique training. If heading is being practiced, the coach can require heading with vertical jumping within a time frame, say, 20 jumps within one minute. In the same manner, it is economical to combine tactics and fitness training. During a tactical workout employing an 8 V 8 alignment on a full field, a player can be required to sprint in the direction of his choice—but one that is tactically constructive—after he gives up the ball or passes to a teammate. This immediately adds greater mobility to the 8 V 8 exercise, while it helps to improve each player's fitness and speed.

Because of the short soccer season and the limited preparation time in many states, economical training

is of crucial importance. It not only allows the coach to accomplish more in a shorter period of time but also helps him avoid preparing players for specialized positions. His object should be to develop total players, not positional players. Today, each member of a soccer team must be capable of playing both defensively and offensively in all parts of the field.

Much can be accomplished in a one-hour practice session if time is used intelligently and full participation is demanded of all players. The following one-hour program includes warm-up, skill training, and tactics exercises. Players should be kept moving and the various training phases completed within the stated times.

Typical One-Hour Youth Practice Session

5 minutes	Static Stretching
10 minutes	Individual Technique
	ball lifting—standing; in motion
	instep juggling—standing; in motion
	thigh juggling—standing; in motion
	head juggling—standing; in motion
10 minutes	Technical Training
	passing with the inside of the foot while standing
	passing while in motion
	diagonal passing with partners
5 minutes	Individual Tactics
	1 V 1
	—5 minutes rest; water break—
10 minutes	Group Tactics
	3 V 3 with 2 small goals on 20-square-yard grid
15 minutes	Team Tactics
	8 V 8 on a full field with goalkeepers
	8 V 8 adding restrictions
	8 V 8 varying positional organization

Follow the same general pattern during each practice session. However, from week to week add new fitness exercises, such as ball gymnastics, and introduce different skills and other group and team tactics exercises. Devise similar time tables during the course of the season to cover all phases of training. And remember to allow the players to have as much fun as possible, particularly when they are playing games in small grids.

CHAPTER 17
THE COACH-PLAYER RELATIONSHIP

WHAT IS YOUR COACHING STYLE?

In recent years many researchers have tried to define the ideal coach. They have compared the personalities of coaches and have identified different styles and methods of coaching. Dr. Thomas Tutko and Dr. Jack W. Richards, both noted sports psychologists, have defined five types of coaches and have pointed out the advantages and disadvantages inherent in the personalities of each. Without classifying yourself, see if you can find any of your own traits in the following descriptions of coaching styles.

The "hard-nosed," or authoritarian, coach believes strongly in discipline, is rigid about schedules and plans, and is very well organized. He often uses punitive measures to enforce rules, resorts to threats to motivate players, and does not get too close, personally, to his athletes. The "hard-nosed" coach usually has a disciplined, well-organized, aggressive, and physically rough team, with good team spirit when things are going well. However, dissension and unnecessary tension are likely to occur through the coach's inability to handle sensitive players.

The "nice guy" coach uses positive means to motivate his athletes and is often experimental, sometimes allowing flexibility to turn into chaos. Usually, the "nice guy" coach has a relaxed and cohesive team. He is often characterized as weak because he is unable to handle those players who try to take advantage of him.

The "intense," or driven, coach is frequently worried and constantly pushes himself. He spends hours on preparations. He often considers setbacks as personal affronts. His demands might be unrealistic, and his team might burn itself out before the end of the season or before crucial games. His intense involvement often leads to emotional displays, which tend to embarrass his players, school, club, or organization.

The "easygoing" coach does not take things too seriously, but he gives the impression that everything is under control. He puts little pressure on his team, and there is little complaining about the work required. In this relaxed atmosphere players feel free to question, for instance, the usefulness of a training phase, and they often profit from the uninhibited discussion that follows. On the other hand, the "easygoing" coach is sometimes too casual about training. He may, for example, produce a team that is not in top physical condition, and such a team will often panic when under pressure.

The "businesslike" coach approaches his sport in a calculating manner, using a sharp intellect and logic to solve problems and outguess opponents. This coach, however, lacks compassion. He is unable to motivate his team emotionally and has little rapport with those athletes who need his personal support and attention.

All of the preceding traits can be found in different combinations and to different degrees among a great many coaches. And, indeed, there is no single coaching style that can be held up as a perfect example. Rather, each of the styles has its place in handling particular situations or athletes.

If a coach pays attention to details, is specific and

realistic in setting long- and short-term goals, is knowledgeable about soccer and applied psychology, is sensitive to the needs of his players, can be strict when necessary, has charisma and the talent for leadership, has self-confidence, and, above all, can teach and motivate his players, then he might become that fortunate person: the successful coach.

ATHLETES ARE MORE THAN BODIES

Competition can be viewed as the struggle between individuals, groups of individuals, or teams to achieve some common goal. Success in competition often is viewed as winning, but it can also be evaluated in terms of the enjoyment, self-improvement, satisfaction, or self-confidence that players derive from the experience. Thus, while winning certainly is more exhilarating than losing, the players (as well as the coach) may find other rewards in competition. The coach should help each athlete to understand this and should be aware of the many personal needs that are being met through the medium of the game.

Players need recognition as they proceed to develop their own physical stamina, skills, and tactical ability as members of a team. To provide them with meaningful recognition, the coach must have insight into their personalities, and this requires observation of their behavior over a period of time. As players learn, overcome weaknesses, and attain higher performance levels, the coach should communicate his awareness of their achievements. It is important too to gear recognition to the individual's personal potential and rate of development rather than to an absolute standard of performance that might be beyond the reach of many players, if, indeed, it is attainable by any one of them.

The coach not only teaches, evaluates, and physically prepares his athletes, but he also must be able to motivate them to fulfill their potential. He wants his players to participate in practice sessions with enthusiasm, to achieve the goals they set for themselves (often with his guidance), and to be in a positive state of mind before a game. Coaches may best motivate athletes by appealing to their self-respect and common sense rather than to old-fashioned concepts such as loyalty to a group. He must arouse the individual's desire to act, achieve, and persist in the face of adversity.

Sports psychologist Brian J. Cratty identifies the variables that motivate athletes as the following:
Seeking and overcoming stress
Achieving excellence
Seeking status
The need to belong
Because of the varying experiences and emotional characteristics of players their reasons for joining a team differ greatly. A coach who always seeks to motivate his players as a group is doomed to failure. Players are individuals first and must be motivated individually. Subsequently, small group motivation and, finally, full team motivation may be employed.

A coach must also understand—especially when dealing with youth and high-school players—that many people choose to play on the team either for social reasons or to stay in shape. A player who participates for social reasons often needs love and the feeling of belonging. Just making the team might provide him with a great deal of satisfaction. By recognizing this, the coach might be able to motivate him even further to strive to excel.

TRAITS OF SUCCESSFUL ATHLETES

Certain personality traits seem to prevail among better players. These traits are listed here for the guidance of coaches in choosing athletes as well as in training them. The wise coach will try to enhance his players' winning characteristics.

Desire Factors. These factors relate to a player's expectations from athletics and his willingness to work hard toward fulfilling them.

Drive. The player has a great desire to win or to be successful. He will work hard in practice. He is very competitive.

Determination. The player will not give up easily. He will work very hard to improve his performance.

Aggression. The player knows that in order to win he must play hard. He is physical; he enjoys physical contact. He often becomes angry. He hates to be beaten.

Emotional Factors. These factors relate to the player's attitudes and feelings about himself, his coach, and how he is coached.

Coachability. The player respects his coach and willingly accepts his advice and instructions. He is a good team player.

Emotionality. The player can control himself. He is not upset by bad breaks and bad calls or by his teammates' mistakes.

Self-Confidence. The player feels sure of his ability and knowledge. He is not upset by unexpected situations or pressure. He accepts criticism, yet will speak up if he thinks he is right.

Mental Toughness. The player usually is insensitive to the feelings and problems of others. He accepts strong criticism, booing, losing, and even playing badly. He does not need much encouragement and usually is quite consistent.

Conscientiousness. The player always attempts to do things correctly. He does not have to be supervised constantly. He is a team player.

Responsibility. The player does what he says he will do and accepts responsibility for what he does. He will work to improve his weaknesses. He is a team player.

The coach should take the necessary time to evaluate his players in terms of these personality traits. He might wish to rate each player in each of the above areas and ask them to rate themselves as well. The coach might even devise a standard test that can be used to discover the extent to which his players (or potential players) possess the characteristics of successful athletes.

In the pre-season it is wise to have each player fill out a form, including information about his family, his hobbies, reasons for wanting to join the team, and vocational and academic interests. The form might also ask him to list the players and teams he most admires and to state his personal goals for the season as well as for the next few years. The purpose for collecting such information is to make the coach more aware of his players' backgrounds and aspirations so that he will be in a better position to help them help themselves. If the coach needs assistance in preparing such a questionnaire or in interpreting and applying the information the players provide, it is often possible, especially in a school setting, to obtain help from a person skilled in conducting polls.

CHAPTER 18
PRE-GAME
TO POST-GAME
RESPONSIBILITIES

A coach cannot expect to motivate his team in an atmosphere of chaos. It is as important to handle all practical arrangements efficiently and smoothly as it is to prepare the players physically and mentally for the game. Only if external factors are under control, will the game itself be a true measurement of the team's ability.

Tiring bus trips, noisy hotels or motels, uncomfortable beds, and unprepared-for changes in climate often have caused the defeat of an otherwise able team. The coach must try to anticipate adverse conditions and be ready with alternative plans in case they arise.

He should prepare thoroughly for out-of-town games, taking into account the equipment changes or repairs that might be necessary. Uniforms should be chosen according to the climate and the time of day or night the game is to be played. The inventory of equipment should include 1 ball for every 2 players, plus an air pump and pin to regulate air pressure. It is strongly recommended that in the pre-game practice the team use the same balls that will be used in competition. Remember: last-minute changes for games on the road are difficult to make, so plan ahead.

One hour before a game the coach should assemble the team in the locker room. Before the meeting he should have acquainted himself with the field and weather conditions so that he can announce any necessary changes in strategy or in the boots and uniforms to be worn. The coach must also be ready for all questions or problems that players might bring up in the pre-game session.

The chief purposes of this meeting are to discuss the game plan, to make sure all members of the squad are familiar with key plays, and to diagram and illustrate new plays or those needing reemphasis. (It is certainly an asset if the coach is a creative speaker who can use his voice effectively and underline his points with expressive gestures.)

During a game, coaches often become spectators or, even worse, cheerleaders or referee-baiters. Needless to say, such emotional involvement is destructive and should be avoided. The coach needs all the concentration he can muster to analyze the game in detail. In this, he should seek the cooperation of the reserve players. The coach's concentration will be further enhanced if the players' bench is placed at a safe distance from the field, away from distracting interferences from spectators or officials.

APPOINTMENT OF A TEAM CAPTAIN

In soccer, coaching from the sidelines is not allowed. This makes it imperative that a competent team captain be appointed to serve as "second coach" both on and off the field. The captain must be thoroughly prepared to make decisions on the field that are compatible with the coach's own thinking. Off the field, one of the captain's duties is to make sure there is open communication between the players and the team's management. The captain should be included in all discussions concerning such matters as planning and organization.

The team captain should be selected on the basis of his qualifications as a player and the contributions he can make to effective team management. Since he must be respected by the other players, and serve as an example to them, the captain should be a superior performer, capable of playing the full 90 minutes. He also must have insights into coaching and an understanding of the personalities, strengths, and weaknesses of his teammates. Under no circumstances should the captain be picked on the basis of tradition, favoritism, seniority, or popularity with the other players or with the fans.

SUBSTITUTES

Substitutions during a match must always be made with a definite objective or tactic in mind. But the coach must be realistic in his expectations when he sends a player into the game. No single player can change a game situation unless he is given an idea of how to proceed and is allowed the time necessary to execute his mission.

A substitute can be sent in because of his experience or because of another player's injury. Younger or less experienced players should be used when they cannot endanger the outcome of a game, in order to further their development and permit them to acquire seasoning under game conditions. All players should be made to understand the importance of substitutes to the team as a whole so that unnecessary rivalries and bitterness between players and other misunderstandings can be prevented.

POST-GAME PSYCHOLOGY

It is considered poor timing to go over the specifics of a game immediately after it has been played, especially if the coach has reason to criticize the players. Instead, he should present a short résumé of the game, without criticism, and should make sure in-

juries are identified and treated. The coach should also announce or post the practice schedule for the following week.

It is very important psychologically to avoid any player-coach confrontations in the presence of the entire team. Such confrontations can be damaging to the team's morale and can undermine mutual respect between players and coach. A player's confidence depends upon encouragement, and all criticism should be constructive rather than abusive.

The day following a game should be one of rest and regeneration. Some stretching exercises, games such as soccer-volleyball or soccer-tennis, and relaxation in a sauna or steam bath will help the players unwind and recover from bruises to body and spirit. During this day of rest, the coach may hold individual talks to go over a player's performance or prepare him for the criticism he might encounter at the next team meeting.

As soon as a game is over, the coach must begin thinking about the next contest. The match will have indicated the necessary changes to be made, and he must decide how much additional practice is needed to overcome any tactical weaknesses he spotted during the game. As a general rule, the interval principle should be applied for the week's training schedule, with two peaks of intensive physical work and two valleys of less demanding work and with emphasis on the team's shortcomings.

PUBLIC RELATIONS

Part of the coach's duties, whether he likes it or not, is to educate the public about soccer. The more that spectators understand and appreciate the finer points of the game, the firmer will be their support of the team.

Lectures and clinics will help to get the message across that soccer is a thrilling sport to watch and a body- and character-building sport in which to participate. If the coach makes himself available to the people in his community and actively tries to promote soccer, he will be able to count on better rapport with the crowd during games as well as sustained ticket sales, which, after all, are necessary for the support of the team.

APPENDIX A
THE LAWS OF SOCCER SUMMARIZED AND WITH COMMENTARY

There are 17 laws, or rules, of soccer as laid down by FIFA. These provide guidelines for playing the game. The laws are simple, flexible, yet specific. It is the responsibility of the coach to know and understand these laws thoroughly and to pass this knowledge on to the players. In addition to maintaining the spirit of the laws, the coach must be concerned with their tactical application. He can use them to his team's advantage, while staying within their limits. The brief commentary that follows the summary of each law suggests ways in which to do this.

LAW I. THE FIELD OF PLAY

The soccer field is rectangular, its length not more than 130 yards nor less than 100 yards and its width not more than 100 yards nor less than 50 yards. At each end are a goal, a goal area, and a penalty area with a penalty spot. In addition, the field is marked with a center circle, center spot, penalty arcs, corner areas, and a halfway line. Flags are placed at each corner of the field and, optionally, just outside each touchline, or sideline, opposite the halfway line.

Commentary: Depending on the broad characteristics of a team, the size of the field can be an asset or a liability. A very fit, fast team with mediocre technique will be more effective on a large field. On the other hand, a slower, less fit team with excellent technical skills will perform better on a small field.

LAW II. THE BALL

The ball is made of leather or other approved material. Its circumference is between 27 and 28 inches and the weight, at the start of the game, between 14 and 16 ounces. The ball cannot be changed during a game without the referee's permission.

Commentary: The size, weight, air pressure, and material of the ball should be determined by the skill levels of the players. Players with poor skills will find it easier to control a big, heavy ball inflated to minimum pressure. Youth players should use smaller balls. The balls used in practice should be the same as those used in games.

LAW III. NUMBER OF PLAYERS

Teams have 11 players, one of whom is the goalkeeper. Any of the field players may change places with the goalkeeper, provided the referee is informed of the switch and the change is made during a stoppage of play. In international competition no more than 2 substitutes are allowed, but in other matches up to 5 substitutes may be allowed as long as the 2 teams agree on the number beforehand and inform the referee prior to the match. The referee must be informed of all substitutions, and once replaced, a player may not return to the game. A match is not considered valid if there are fewer than 7 players on either team.

Commentary: The selection and role of substitutes is an important consideration for the coach. The game situation itself will indicate when substitution is required, and the coach should be ready to make the decision. In youth games the number of allowed substitutions is higher than the number permitted by the international body, in order to give more players time to participate. The coach should be ready with at least 1 substitute for each of the following positions: goalkeeper, forward, fullback, attacking midfielder, and defensive midfielder.

LAW IV. PLAYERS' EQUIPMENT

A player shall not wear anything that is dangerous to another player. Bars of leather or rubber may be worn

across the soles of the shoes as long as they are at least ½ inch wide. Studs are permitted on the soles of the shoes, but they must be rounded, at least ½ inch in diameter, and not more than ¾ inch long. Studs molded as part of the sole must be of soft material and, if there are at least 10 on a sole, have a minimum diameter of ⅜ inch. The goalkeeper must wear colors that distinguish him from the other players and the referee.

Commentary: Shoes should be selected according to the surface of the field and its condition. On soft fields long studs are preferred; in fact, the softer the field, the longer the studs should be. Shoes with studs molded into the soles are preferred for harder fields. For artificial surfaces, sneakers should be considered. Shin guards should be worn by all players. Shirt material depends on climatic conditions; in hot, humid weather short-sleeved perforated shirts are recommended.

LAW V. REFEREES

The referee is in complete charge of the game. He is the timekeeper and keeps a record of the contest. The referee is empowered to stop play for injury or other reasons and to restart it when ready. He also may end the game due to inclement weather, spectator interference, etc. The referee administers penalties and cautions or expels players for misconduct. His decisions are final.

Commentary: Courteous behavior toward the referee brings better results than confrontation. Antagonism breeds antagonism, and an amiable manner is usually returned. Furthermore, a player who disputes the referee's decision incurs a penalty.

LAW VI. LINESMEN

There are 2 linesmen. Their chief duty is to indicate when the ball is out of play and which side is entitled to the corner kick, goal kick, or throw-in. The linesmen are equipped with flags, which they use to signal to the referee. By signaling, they assist him in controlling the game. See Chapter 4 for illustrations of both the referee's and the linesmen's signals.

Commentary: The linesmen are an extension of the referee and should be treated as such. The coach can use them to communicate with the referee when, for instance, he wishes to make a substitution.

LAW VII. DURATION OF THE GAME

Soccer is played in 2 periods of 45 minutes each. Time lost due to injury or other causes is added on to the playing times at the discretion of the referee. Time is extended at the end of a period, if necessary, to allow for a penalty kick. The halftime interval shall not exceed 5 minutes, except by consent of the referee. For durations of youth matches, see Chapter 4.

Commentary: The coach must prepare the team to perform at top efficiency during the entire game. The psychological, physical, and tactical intensity during the last minute of play should be equal to that of the first minute of play. However, the team should be coached to adjust its tactics as time is running out. For example, if it is winning and there are only 10 minutes left in the game, maintaining possession of the ball should be the team's objective; if it is losing, more fullbacks should be sent into the attack.

LAW VIII. THE START OF PLAY

A kickoff is used to start play at the beginning of the game, after a goal has been scored, and after halftime. The ball is placed on the center spot, and the kicker must send it into the opponent's half of the field. All other players must remain in their half of the field, and no opposing player may be within the center circle (that is, within 10 yards of the ball). The ball is in play after it has traveled the distance of its own circumference. The kicker may not play the ball again until it has been touched by another player.

The toss of a coin determines which team gets to decide whether to kick off first or to have its choice of ends at the beginning of the game. After a team scores a goal, the other team kicks off. Following halftime, ends are changed and the kickoff is made by the team that did not kick off to start the game.

When restarting play from causes other than those just mentioned or those mentioned elsewhere in the laws, and providing the ball has not passed over the touchline or goal line, the referee drops the ball at the place where it was when play was suspended, and it is in play when it touches the ground.

Commentary: The coach must determine whether it is to his team's advantage to gain the choice of ends or possession of the ball at the start of play. The condition of the field, the direction and intensity of the wind, and the position of the sun are some of the factors that should influence the choice of ends. Usually, the advantageous end is chosen at the start of a game in hopes that the team will be able to take an early lead. Besides, conditions may change in the second half of the game. The team should have set plays for kickoffs, drop balls, and other restart situations.

LAW IX. BALL IN AND OUT OF PLAY

The ball is out of play when it has wholly crossed the goal line or touchline, whether on the ground or in the air, and when the game has been stopped by the referee. The ball is in play at all other times, including when it rebounds from the goalposts and off officials who are on the field of play.

Commentary: Too often players stop when only a part of the ball has crossed a boundary line. Remember: the entire ball must cross the line before play is halted.

LAW X. METHOD OF SCORING

A goal is scored when the whole of the ball has passed over the goal line, between the goalposts and under the crossbar, providing it has not been thrown, carried, or propelled by hand or arm by a player of the attacking side. The team scoring most goals wins. If no goals are scored or if an equal number of goals are scored by each team, the game is declared a draw.

Commentary: Scoring goals is the essence of soccer. Any method can be used to shoot provided it is not specifically prohibited by the laws.

LAW XI. OFFSIDE

A player is offside if he is nearer his opponent's goal line than the ball at the moment the ball is played unless: he is in his own half of the field; at least 2 opponents (including the goalkeeper) are nearer their own goal line than he is; or he received the ball directly from a goal kick, corner kick, throw-in, or drop-ball situation. The penalty for being offside is an indirect free kick by a player of the opposing team from the place where the infringement occurred. Even though a player may be technically in an offside position, the penalty is not called unless, in the opinion of the referee, he is interfering with play or with an opponent or is seeking to gain an advantage by being offside. See Chapter 4 for diagrams that illustrate several of the basic offside positions.

Commentary: On attack, players should always be aware of their position as it relates to the offside rule. Defensively, the offside trap—luring an attacker into an offside position—can be used to tremendous advantage. If the attacker is declared offside, the defensive team will not only gain possession of the ball but will also disrupt the rhythm of their opponents. The defensive team should be ready with backup plays in the event that the referee does not call the offside.

LAW XII. FOULS AND MISCONDUCT

A player who intentionally commits any of the following offenses shall be penalized by awarding a direct free kick to the opposing side from the place where the offense oc-

curred: kicking or attempting to kick an opponent; tripping an opponent; jumping at an opponent; charging an opponent in a violent or dangerous manner; or charging from behind unless the opponent is obstructing; striking or attempting to strike an opponent; holding or pushing an opponent; and carrying, striking, or propelling the ball with the hands or arms (except for the goalkeeper within his own penalty area).

Should a defending player intentionally commit one of these offenses within the penalty area, a penalty kick is awarded the opposing team.

A player committing any of the following offenses shall be penalized by awarding an indirect free kick to the opposing side from the place where the offense occurred: playing in a dangerous manner; charging fairly when the ball is not within playing distance of the players concerned and they are not trying to play it; when not playing the ball, intentionally obstructing an opponent; charging the goalkeeper except when he is holding the ball, obstructing an opponent, or has moved outside his goal area; and when playing as goalkeeper, indulging in tactics designed to delay the game to his team's advantage.

A player is cautioned if he enters, reenters, or leaves the field without the referee's permission; persistently infringes the laws; shows by word or action dissent from a decision made by the referee; or is guilty of ungentlemanly conduct. An indirect free kick results from the last three cautions and, at the referee's discretion, may result from the first.

A player is sent off the field if he is guilty of violent conduct or serious foul play; uses foul or abusive language; or persists in misconduct after receiving a caution. If play is stopped when a player is ordered off the field, the game is resumed by an indirect free kick awarded to the opposing side from the place where the infringement occurred.

Commentary: Every player should know the offenses that result in direct and indirect free kicks. This awareness can be instilled in 1 V 1 training.

LAW XIII. FREE KICK

There are two types of free kicks: *direct* (from which a goal can be scored) and *indirect* (from which a goal cannot be scored unless the ball has been played or touched by a player other than the kicker before it passes through the goal). When a player is taking a free kick inside his own penalty area, all opposing players must remain outside the area and at least 10 yards from the ball. When he is taking a free kick outside his own penalty area, all opposing players must be at least 10 yards from the ball unless they are standing on their own goal line between the goalposts. On free kicks the ball is in play once it has traveled the distance of its own circumference, and the ball cannot be played again by the kicker until it has been touched by another player.

Commentary: As with other still-ball situations, the attacking team has a better chance of scoring on a free kick if they have set plays, or predetermined moves, to follow up the kick. Set plays require correct timing, proper execution, and deception. On direct free kicks, players with the ability to bend, or curve, balls around an opposing wall of defenders are especially useful. On defense, the organization of the wall should take place quickly and without the assistance of the goalkeeper.

LAW XIV. PENALTY KICK

If a defending player is within his own team's penalty area when he intentionally commits any one of the nine offenses that result in the awarding of a direct free kick (see Law XII), the opposing team is granted a penalty kick. The penalty kick is taken from the penalty spot, and all players (except the defending goalkeeper) must stay outside of the penalty area and at least 10 yards away from the ball. The defending goalkeeper must remain stationary on his goal line between the goalposts until the kick is taken. The person making the kick must propel the ball forward and cannot play the ball a second time until it has been touched by another player.

Commentary: Players on the attacking team should position themselves around the penalty area in anticipation of the ball rebounding off the goalkeeper, the goalposts, or the crossbar. Players should be given experience in making penalty kicks, and the shooter must be prepared for the psychological pressure that accompanies this situation.

LAW XV. THROW-IN

To restart play after the whole of the ball has passed over a touchline, the ball is thrown in from the point where it crossed the line by a player of the team opposing that of the person who last touched the ball. The thrower must use both hands and deliver the ball from over his head, while keeping part of each foot either on or outside the touchline. He cannot again play the ball until it has been touched by another player. A goal may not be scored directly from a throw-in. Opposing players are not allowed to dance about or try to impede the thrower.

Commentary: Because the offside law is not in effect during throw-ins, they can be an effective attacking

weapon. Individuals capable of making long throws are especially valuable on a team. Set plays should be designed according to the location of the throw-ins and the abilities of the players.

LAW XVI. GOAL KICK

When the whole of the ball passes over the goal line (excluding that portion of the line between the goalposts) and it was last played by a member of the attacking team, it is kicked into play by a member of the defending team from a point within that half of the goal area nearest to where it crossed the goal line. The ball must be kicked beyond the penalty area, and players of the opposing team must remain outside that area while the kick is being taken. The kicker cannot play the ball a second time until it has been touched by another player, and a goal may not be scored directly from a goal kick.

Commentary: Although any member of the defending team may take the goal kick, the goalkeeper usually performs this duty in order to maintain the numerical balance of players downfield. The main objective of the person making the goal kick is to enable his team to retain possession of the ball. Thus long, high kicks downfield are not in order. It is safer for the kicker to play the ball short, allowing time for his team to build up the attack.

LAW XVII. CORNER KICK

When the whole of the ball passes over the goal line (excluding that portion of the line between the goalposts) and it was last played by a member of the defending team, the attacking team is allowed a corner kick. The ball is kicked from the quarter circle (corner area) at the nearest corner flag post, which must not be moved. A goal may be scored directly from a corner kick. Opposing players must remain at least 10 yards from the ball until it is in play, or has traveled the distance of its own circumference. The kicker may not play the ball a second time until it has been touched by another player.

Commentary: Set plays should be developed to capitalize on corner-kick situations. The ball can be kicked to a teammate or propelled directly into the goal area. Players should practice bending, or curving, the ball around the defenders and kicking at varying speeds and heights. Since the offside law is not in effect during corner kicks, the players' runs are not restricted.

APPENDIX B
ADMINISTRATION
AND ORGANIZATION
OF SOCCER

Soccer is governed by a strict organizational structure on the international and national levels. The Fédération Internationale de Football Association (FIFA), or the International Federation of Association Football, is the governing body of soccer. All national federations are eligible for membership in FIFA, and at the present time there are more than 140 members. The world headquarters of FIFA is in Zurich, Switzerland.

The member countries of FIFA are subdivided into six continental confederations: Africa, Asia, CONCACAF, Europe, Oceania, and South America. The United States is part of CONCACAF—the Confederation of North and Central American and Caribbean Association Football. All national and international competitions are played under the rules and laws established by FIFA, and any changes in rules must be approved by the organization.

THE WORLD CHAMPIONSHIP

All national federations in good standing are eligible for participation in the World Championship, or World Cup, which is conducted every four years under the auspices of FIFA. Preliminary qualification competitions begin in the continental confederations two years prior to the finals. Which country will serve as the site of the finals is determined eight years in advance, and this is changed for each championship. Sixteen teams qualify for the final games. The host country and the reigning champion are automatic qualifiers. The other 14 teams must win preliminary competitions in order to qualify.

UNITED STATES SOCCER FEDERATION

The United States Soccer Federation (USSF) is the internationally recognized national federation of soccer in the United States and is an official member of FIFA. Founded in 1913, the USSF is composed of all state associations in existence today. The USSF is responsible for regulating American soccer on the youth, amateur, semiprofessional, and professional levels. It must sanction all international competitions that involve a team from the United States or a foreign team playing in the United States. The USSF conducts the following national competitions: the National Junior Challenge Cup, National Amateur Cup, and National Open Challenge Cup.

The USSF serves as a source of information about soccer. It publishes *Soccer Monthly*, which deals with all aspects of the game on the national and international levels. This magazine is available by subscription from the USSF headquarters, located at 350 Fifth Avenue, Suite 4010, New York, NY 10001. Telephone: (212) 736-0915. Books and pamphlets on soccer are also available, and films can be either purchased or rented. These materials are intended for use by players, coaches, and administrators. Further information can be obtained from the USSF.

Affiliations

All state associations in good standing are affiliated with the USSF with equal rights and responsibilities. The following institutions are also affiliated with the USSF:

North American Soccer League
American Soccer League
Intercollegiate Soccer Association of America
National Soccer Coaches Association
USSF Coaches Association

State associations are responsible for the administration of the game within their borders. In some cases, generally due to the physical size of the state, two state associations exist within a state. Examples include the California Soccer

Association, North, and the California Soccer Association, South; the Eastern Pennsylvania and the Western Pennsylvania soccer associations; the Southern New York State Soccer Association and the Northwestern New York State Soccer Football Association.

The National Coach

The final preparation and coaching of all teams representing the United States in international competitions is the responsibility of the National Coach, who is ultimately responsible to the president of the USSF. The teams in this category include under-19-year-olds, or Youth; Olympic; Pan-American; and World Cup teams, as well as teams competing in invitational and developmental games.

In his role as Director of Coaching, the National Coach is responsible for the organization and conduct of the USSF National Coaching School System. As part of this system, the Director of Coaching, in consultation with the state associations, appoints state and regional coaching staffs to conduct state licensing courses.

The USSF National Coaching School System

One of the important aims of the USSF is to standardize and improve the quality of coaching in the United States, which entails keeping up-to-date on coaching expertise as it is developing around the world. With this consideration in mind, the USSF established the USSF National Coaching School in 1969.

The school operates throughout the year at various regional sites. Its organization and conduct are the responsibility of the Director of Coaching and the National Coaching Staff. The purpose of the school is to train both state and national coaches. There are three levels of preparation and licensing for both groups: "C," "B," and "A" for national coaches and "F," "E," and "D" for state coaches. The theoretical and physical requirements for licensing increase in complexity from level to level, progressing from fundamental to advanced and incorporating new developments in the game. The courses designed for the parent-coach and the beginner-coach on the state level are the least demanding. Postgraduate credit is available to candidates. Refresher courses are required of all coaches every five years in order to maintain license certification.

The United States Youth Soccer Association

In July, 1974, at the Annual Convention of the USSF, the constitution of the new United States Youth Soccer Association (USYSA) was approved. The purpose of the USYSA, as stated in its constitution, is "to develop, pro-

mote, and administer the game of soccer among players under 19 years of age." The association holds its own Annual General Meeting, attended by representatives of all affiliated state youth associations in much the same way as the senior state associations hold their Annual Convention. These representatives constitute the National Youth Council.

The age-group classifications in youth soccer are: Under 19, Under 16, Under 14, Under 12, Under 10, and Under 8. These are based on skill level, not age.

World Youth Tournament for the Coca-Cola Cup

FIFA recently established an international competition for Under-19 teams that is comparable in structure to the World Cup—the World Youth Tournament for the

Coca-Cola Cup, which was held for the first time in 1977. Sponsored by the Coca-Cola Company, this tournament will be held biennially. The 16 national teams that have survived the preliminary elimination rounds compete for a silver trophy, the Coca-Cola Cup. Players must be USSF-affiliated to qualify for the American team.

USSF Development Camps for Youth

The USSF Development Camps for Youth are conducted by the National Coach and the National Coaching Staff for outstanding players from all regions of the country, usually

ORGANIZATIONAL
CHART OF SOCCER

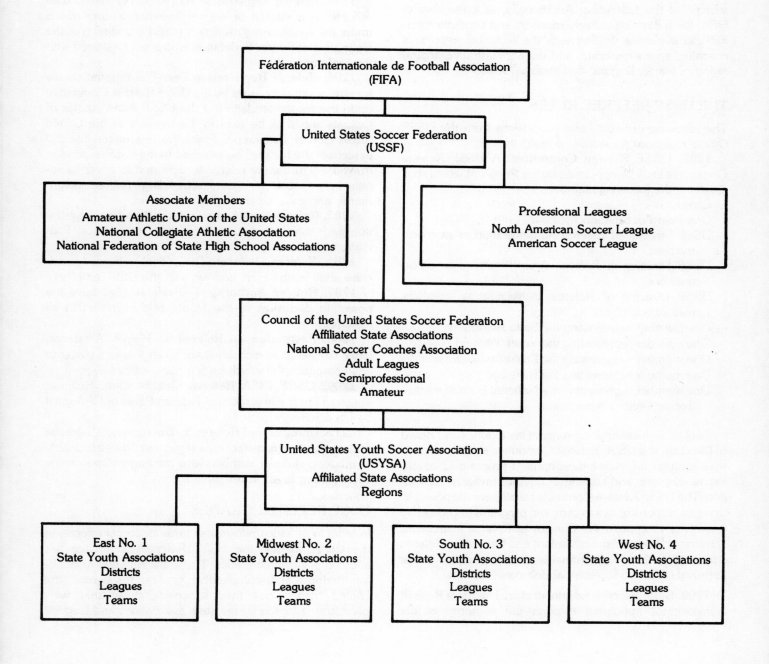

in conjunction with the USSF Coaching School. The camps have been developed for the purpose of identifying and evaluating a pool of promising and talented players for international competition. The selection of players is based on the recommendations of the state associations, the state coaching staffs, and the National Coaching Staff.

Clinics and Workshops

The National Coach and his staff are available for clinics and workshops for players, teachers, coaches, and administrators to familiarize them with the developmental scheme of the federation. Additionally, as a member of FIFA, the federation actively sponsors and conducts international symposia dealing with the technical aspects of coaching, sports medicine, and the administrative organization of teams, leagues, and state associations.

THE USSF REFEREE RULES

The following excerpts have been taken from the *USSF Official Rulebook for Administration*.

1201. USSF Referee Committee. A USSF Referee Committee shall be appointed by the President which shall consist of the following members:

Chairman
One Board of Directors member
USSF Director of Referee Administration as *ex-officio* member
USSF Director of Referee Assessments as *ex-officio* member
USSF Director of Referee Instruction as *ex-officio* member
One member representing the State Association
One member representing the Youth Division
One member representing the Professional Division
One member representing the Referees
One member representing the National Intercollegiate Soccer Officials Association

Subject to the overall authority of the Council and Board of Directors, the USSF Referee Committee shall be responsible through its referee development program to coach, examine, grade, and administer referees under its jurisdiction. The USSF Referee Committee shall have the power to delegate responsibilities to carry out programs approved by it, such as to appoint the Director of Referee Instruction, Director of Referee Administration, and Director of Referee Assessment; these appointments shall be subject to the approval of the USSF National Board of Directors.

1202. State Referee Administrator. The State Referee Administrator appointed through the authority of the USSF Referee Committee with the consent of and upon consultation and cooperation with the local state association (or other responsible organization if there is no state association) shall be the delegate of the USSF Referee Committee to the state association, shall administer the USSF referees within the state association, shall work in cooperation with the state association, shall serve as liaison between the state association and the USSF referees registered in its territory, and may be a member of the executive committee or equivalent board of directors of the state association.

1203. Referee Registration Required. No person shall officiate as a referee or neutral linesman in any match under the sanction or jurisdiction (direct or indirect) of the United States Soccer Federation who is not registered with this Federation.

1204. Referee Registration Fee. The registration fee for referees shall be as set by the USSF Referee Committee upon the recommendation of the USSF Administrator of Officials and shall be paid to the treasury of the United States Soccer Federation. From the registration fee, 50 percent of the fee shall be returned to the state association in whose territory the referee is registered to cover its administrative costs for game scheduling, referee assignments, and other referee-related expenses.

1205. Referee Registration Cards. All referee registration cards shall be issued by the United States Soccer Federation.

1206. Referee Uniform. The official uniform for referees shall be the FIFA uniform with the USSF emblem.

1207. Referee Authority. The referee shall have the power to decide as to the fitness of the ground in all matches.

1208. Restriction on Referee as Player. A referee, when registered as such, shall not be eligible as a player in any competition in which he is a game official.

1209. USSF FIFA Referee Qualification. Referees appointed to the International Referee Panel of FIFA must be US citizens.

1210. Unregistered Referee in Emergency. If, because of unforeseen circumstances, a registered referee is unable to officiate, clubs or combinations may agree upon some other person to act in the emergency.

USSF REFEREE GRADES

In order to provide uniform standards for soccer referees in the United States, the USSF Referee Committee has adopted five referee grades. These are intended to establish uniform and comparative grading throughout the United States, and they supersede those that were previously adopted by the state associations and leagues.

OFFICIAL USSF REFEREE UNIFORM

(FIFA Uniform with USSF Referee Badge)

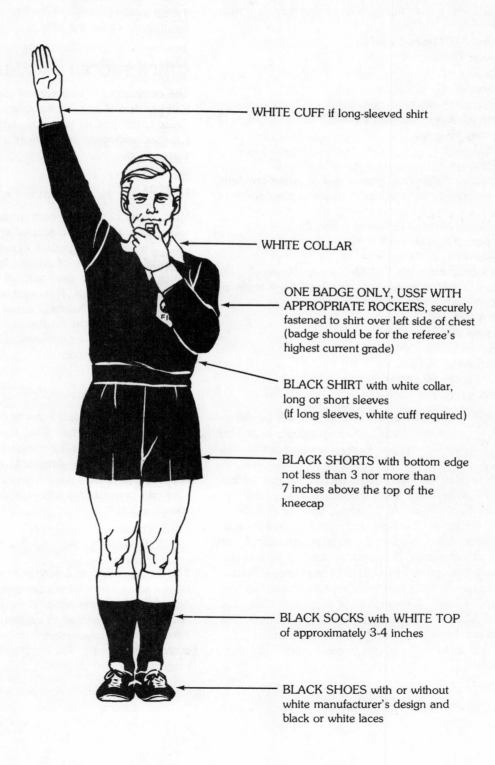

WHITE CUFF if long-sleeved shirt

WHITE COLLAR

ONE BADGE ONLY, USSF WITH
APPROPRIATE ROCKERS, securely
fastened to shirt over left side of chest
(badge should be for the referee's
highest current grade)

BLACK SHIRT with white collar,
long or short sleeves
(if long sleeves, white cuff required)

BLACK SHORTS with bottom edge
not less than 3 nor more than
7 inches above the top of the
kneecap

BLACK SOCKS with WHITE TOP
of approximately 3-4 inches

BLACK SHOES with or without
white manufacturer's design and
black or white laces

The five grades are:

USSF Referee Trainee
Minimum age: None
Badge: USSF
Competence level: Beginning referee for novice youth games

USSF Referee (Classes 1 and 2)
Minimum age: None
Badge: USSF
Rocker: Referee
Competence level: All youth games

USSF State Referee (Classes 1 and 2)
Minimum age: 19 years
Badge: USSF
Rocker: State
Competence level: All youth games and all senior amateur games except interstate games in senior national competitions

USSF National Referee (Classes 1 and 2)
Minimum age: 19 years
Badge: USSF
Rocker: National; brass pin "USSF National Referee"
Competence level: All games except formal FIFA international matches

USSF FIFA Referee
Minimum age: 25 years
Badge: FIFA or USSF
Rocker: National; FIFA pin
Competence level: All games
US citizenship required

The USSF grade and class of an official will be determined solely by the standards and examinations issued by the USSF Referee Committee. Annual reexaminations will be required.

The USSF Referee Committee recognizes that within each USSF grade there will be some referees who are more skilled than others. Accordingly, the USSF Referee Committee recognizes the right of the professional leagues and state associations to select the most skilled officials for their most critical games. In particular, each state association will have the option (through its state referee administrator) to designate each Youth Referee and State Referee as Class 1 or Class 2 for assignment purposes. Class 1 is higher than Class 2. Any class designation for Youth and State Referees, however, must be determined only by the standards and assessment criteria issued by the USSF Referee Committee.

If there is a shortage of officials at a particular competence level, officials at the next highest level may be used, except in national and professional competitions. Beginning referees are permitted as USSF Referee Trainees in novice youth games if there are not enough USSF Youth Referees to cover the games.

OTHER SOCCER ORGANIZATIONS

The organizational structure of soccer in the United States is unlike that of any other country in the world. In addition to the USSF and its state associations, high schools, junior colleges, colleges, and universities also sponsor soccer competitions.

High Schools and Junior Colleges

Most states have their own athletic association, which is responsible for the conduct of sports on the high school level. The central organization on the national level is the National Federation of State High School Associations, which publishes its own annual rulebook on soccer for member associations. The organization's headquarters is in Elgin, Illinois. The National Junior College Athletic Association controls soccer on the junior college level. The association sponsors a post-season tournament to determine the national champion.

Colleges and Universities

The National Collegiate Athletic Association (NCAA), with headquarters in Kansas City, Kansas, governs soccer on the collegiate level. It is organized into University and College divisions. A post-season tournament determines the national champion for each division. The National Association of Intercollegiate Athletics also governs soccer on the collegiate level.

National Soccer Coaches Association

The National Soccer Coaches Association is the oldest and largest association for soccer coaches. Although its membership consists mainly of college coaches, coaches from all levels are admitted. The association holds an annual convention in conjunction with the largest soccer coaching clinic in the country. The organization publishes a quarterly magazine, *Soccer Journal*.

GLOSSARY

Advantage Rule: Applied by the referee when in his judgment penalizing an infraction would give an advantage to the offending team. He signals that play is to continue, and no penalty is called.

Backs: See Fullbacks.

Ballistic Stretching: A flexibility exercise using bobbing and bouncing movements to stretch the muscles.

Ball-Side: Pertaining to that side of the field where the ball is.

Banana Pass: See Curving Pass.

Beat: To avoid a tackle by feinting, or faking out an opponent.

Bending the Ball: The technique of kicking the ball so that it curves in one direction or the other. Also called "curving the ball."

Bending Pass: See Curving Pass.

Bending Run: Running in a curving pattern, usually to arrive at a specific point just as the ball does.

Blind-Side Run: A run made away from the opponent's field of vision.

Block Tackle: Attempting to dispossess an attacker of the ball by blocking it with the inside of the foot at the same time he attempts to kick it in the opposite direction.

Boots: Traditional name for soccer shoes.

Carbohydrate Loading: A high-energy diet, rich in carbohydrates, recommended by nutritionists for players during the week before a game.

Catenaccio: A defensively oriented system of play incorporating tight, man-to-man marking of opponents and providing for a free man called a sweeper, or libero, who stands behind the last line of defense and covers every teammate in the defensive third of the field.

Caution: A disciplinary action taken by the referee—signaled with a yellow card and officially recorded—against a player guilty of misconduct; a second offense warrants ejection from the game (red card).

Center Circle: The circle at the center of the field, drawn with a radius of 10 yards from the center spot.

Center Fullback: See Stopper.

Centering: Passing the ball into the goal from a wing area of the field. Also called "crossing."

Center Pass: See Cross Pass.

Center Spot: The point in the center circle (the midpoint of the halfway line) from which kickoffs are taken.

Central Forward: See Central Striker.

Central Striker: The central forward, the player who usually leads the attack and scores most of the goals.

Charging: Use of the shoulder to charge the shoulder of an attacking player in order to dispossess him of the ball—the only time deliberate body contact is allowed in soccer.

Checking Run: A feinting technique that involves taking a few quick steps in one direction before turning and sprinting in another.

Chip Pass: A pass in which the ball is kicked steeply over the head of an opponent or over the heads of a group of opponents to a teammate. Also called the "lob pass."

Circuit Training: A system for combining fitness and technique training employing a number of stations on a field at which a series of different exercises is performed.

Clearing: Throwing (by the goalkeeper only), kicking, or heading the ball high and wide to move it out of the goal area or the penalty area.

Collecting: The technique of first receiving a ground or airborne ball, then bringing it under control before putting it into play.

Combination Passes: A series of short, low passes used by 2 or more players to maintain possession of the ball while they move toward the opponent's goal. Also called "combination play."

Combination Play: Passing between players at short distances, followed by abruptly sending the ball long in another direction.

Corner Area: An arc, or quarter circle, with a radius of 1 yard, drawn at each corner of the field, from which corner kicks are taken.

Corner Flags: The flags located at each corner of the field to mark its boundaries. They are not to be removed for corner kicks.

Corner Kick: A direct free kick taken from a corner area by a member of the attacking team if the ball goes out-of-bounds across the goal line and was last touched by a member of the defending team.

Cover: A defensive concept that involves taking a goal-side position to support, or back up, a teammate who is challenging an opponent for the ball.

Cross Pass: A pass from one side of the field to the other or toward the center, usually taken to set up a teammate for a shot on goal.

Curving the Ball: See Bending the Ball.

Curving Pass: Kicking the ball to the right or left of center to send it in the opposite direction. Also called the "bending pass" and the "banana pass."

Cutting Down the Angle to the Goal: A tactic used by a goalkeeper when confronted by a single attacker on a breakaway. The goalkeeper comes out of the goal and toward the shooter, thus obstructing more of the goal from the shooter; in other words, he confines the shooter's visual target to the smallest possible part of the goal.

Dead Ball: A ball lying still on the field, but playable; a ball out-of-bounds; a ball on the field when the referee stops play.

Dead Space: For the attacking team, areas of the field occupied by players of the opposing team.

Direct Free Kick: A free kick that may score a goal directly; that is, without the ball first being touched by another player. Also a specific penalty called for fouls and misconduct. See Corner Kick; Free Kick; Penalty Kick.

Diving: A method used by the goalkeeper to stop or deflect low and medium-high balls aimed at the goal.

Diving Pit: A surface of foam rubber or sawdust used to absorb impact when a goalkeeper or other player practices diving saves, diving headers, or scissors kicks.

Double Marking: A defensive strategy using 2 players to guard 1 attacker.

Double Pass: A continuation of the "give-and-go" (see Wall Pass) in which the player who sprints through to receive the pass returns it to the passer, who, in turn, dashes ahead to receive it again.

Dribbling: Using soft touches of the feet to control and propel the ball on the ground without the aid of teammates. Also called "improvisation."

Drop Ball: A ball dropped by the referee between 2 players, 1 from each team, to restart the game after he has purposely stopped play for a no-penalty situation. The ball is dropped at the spot where it was last in play unless this happens to be in the penalty area, in which case it is dropped at the nearest point outside the penalty area. A goal may be scored directly from a drop-ball kick.

Dropkick: See Half-Volley.

"Economical" Training: Training sessions that combine at least two of the four basic components of soccer—fitness training, technique training, tactics training, and the psychological dimensions of the game.

Ejection: Sending a player off the field. A disciplinary action taken by the referee—signaled with a red card and officially recorded—against a player guilty of a personal foul or handballing. Usually results in expulsion from at least one future game.

Fair Charge: See Charging.

Far Post: The goalpost farthest from the ball.

Fartlek ("fast play" in Swedish): A form of endurance training consisting of distance-running at various speeds over different levels and types of terrain.

Feinting: The use of deceptive moves to put an opponent off guard.

First-Time Passing: Passing the ball, either by kicking or heading, without stopping it first.

Forwards: Players who function primarily in the attacking third of the field and whose main responsibility is to score goals. Also called "strikers."

Free Kick: A placekick awarded to a team when a player of the opposing team is penalized. A free kick is either a direct kick, called for a serious offense, or an indirect kick, called for a minor infraction. Players on the offending team must remain 10 yards away from the ball until it is put into play, unless they are on their own goal line between the goalposts. See Direct Free Kick; Indirect Free Kick.

Fullbacks: Players forming the last line of defense, immediately in front of the goalkeeper. Their main job is to repel attacks on goal. Also called "backs."

Functional Training: (1) Specialized training in the particular skills necessary for playing a specific position; (2) training, under game conditions, that stresses a player's technical or tactical weakness.

Ghost Drill: Practicing soccer skills with no opposition other than the goalkeeper.

Give-and-Go: See Double Pass; Wall Pass.

Goal: The 8-yard-wide by 8-foot-high area into which field

players must send the ball in order to score. Two goal-posts, a crossbar, and netting form the goal, which is positioned midway along each goal line and extends beyond the official playing field.

Goal Area: The 6-by-20-yard area directly in front of each goal, from which goal kicks are taken.

Goalkeeper: His team's last line of defense, whose primary responsibility is to prevent the opponent's ball from entering the goal for a score. He is the only player allowed to use his hands, provided he is within the penalty area.

Goal Kick: A placekick taken from the goal area by a member of the defending team when the ball goes out-of-bounds across the goal line and was last touched by a member of the attacking team or when it goes straight into the defenders' goal after a kickoff. All opposing players must stay outside the penalty area until the ball is in play. A goal cannot be scored directly from a goal kick.

Goal Line: The boundary line at each end of the field. When the ball completely crosses the goal line between the goalposts and under the crossbar, a goal is scored. When the ball completely crosses the goal line elsewhere, play is stopped and restarted either by a corner kick or a goal kick.

Goal-Side: A position between the ball and the defending team's goal (the attacking team's target).

Grid: A marked-off area, smaller than the entire soccer field, used to teach techniques and tactics in a confined space.

Halfbacks: See Midfielders.

Half-Volley Kick: A kick taken just as the ball bounces up from the ground. Usually the instep or the inside of the foot is used. Also called a "dropkick."

Halfway Line: The line drawn across the center of the field, parallel with the goal line, and separating the attacking and defending zones. Also called the "center line."

Handballing: A major violation, the intentional use of the hands other than by a goalkeeper. The penalty is a direct free kick.

Heading: Using the forehead, between the eyebrows and the hairline, to propel and direct the ball.

Heel Pass: A kick made with the heel to send the ball backward.

High Overhead Volley: A volley kick that sends the ball over the head of the kicker. The ball is struck when it is about waist level, and the leg is kicked high to help curve the ball backward.

Holding: Using the hands or arms to impede an opponent's movements. A personal foul, and the penalty is a direct free kick.

Improvisation: See Dribbling.

Indirect Free Kick: A free kick that cannot score a goal without the ball first being touched by a player other than the kicker. Also a specific penalty called for minor infractions. See Free Kick.

Inside Forwards: The forwards chiefly responsible for scoring goals, they play inside of the wingers, or outside forwards, and on either side of the central striker.

Isometrics: Physical exercises done by exerting stationary force against an immovable object. Less effective than regular exercises.

Jockeying: A maneuver in which a tight-marking defender gives ground, leading the player in possession of the ball into a less dangerous area of the field. Also called "shepherding."

Juggling: Keeping the ball in the air continuously by using various parts of the body except the hands. Juggling is a training technique used to teach ball control.

Kickabout: An informal, or pickup, game of soccer for fun and exercise.

Kickoff: A placekick taken from the center spot to start the game and the second half or restart play after a goal has been scored. Opposing players must remain outside of the center circle until the ball is in play. A goal may not be scored directly from a kickoff.

Killer Pass: See Through Pass.

Lateral Pass: See Square Pass.

Libero: See Sweeper.

Linesmen: The 2 officials who assist the referee. The linesmen patrol the touchlines and carry flags to signal the referee when a ball has gone out-of-bounds, there is an offside, or a foul has been committed that the referee might not have seen.

Linkmen: See Midfielders.

Live Space: Open, or free, space created for a teammate by enticing an opponent away from an area.

Lob Pass: See Chip Pass.

Low Overhead Volley: A volley kick that sends the ball over the head of the kicker. It is executed with both legs in the air and the body in an almost horizontal position. Also called the "scissors kick."

Man-to-Man Defense: A defensive strategy requiring each defender to assume responsibility for marking, or guarding, a specific attacker.

Marking: Guarding an opponent. Marking may be tight (close) or loose. See Double Marking; Man-to-Man Defense; Zone Defense.

Midfielders: Players who function primarily in the central part of the field and whose main responsibility is to link the defense and the attack. There are three types of midfielders: defending, playmaking, and attacking. Also called "halfbacks" and "linkmen."

Near Post: The goalpost closest to the ball.

Obstruction: Deliberately impeding the progress of an opponent instead of playing the ball. The penalty is an indirect free kick.

Off the Ball: Offensive or defensive players who are not in the vicinity of the ball.

Offside: A player is offside if he is between his opponent's goal line and the ball at the moment the ball is played unless: he is in his own half of the field; at least 2 opponents (including the goalkeeper) are nearer their own goal line than he is; he received the ball directly from a corner kick, goal kick, throw-in, or drop-ball situation. The penalty is an indirect free kick.

Offside Position: A situation in which a player is technically offside but because he is not interfering with the play or an opponent and is not gaining an advantage, the referee will not call a penalty.

Offside Trap: A defensive maneuver designed to lure an attacker into an offside position in order to gain ball possession with the penalty call. See Offside.

One-Touch: Passing or shooting on goal without stopping the ball first; that is, on the first touch.

On-Side Run: Running to avoid being caught in the opponents' offside trap.

Out of Play: The ball is out of play when it has wholly crossed the goal line or a touchline and when the game has been stopped by a referee.

Outside Forwards: The forwards usually positioned near the touchlines, whose responsibility is to work the ball into scoring range for the inside forwards or the central striker. Also called "wingers."

Outside Fullbacks: The fullbacks usually positioned near the touchlines, who with the sweeper, stopper, and goalkeeper form the last line of defense. Also called "wingbacks."

Overhead Kick: See High Overhead Volley; Low Overhead Volley.

Overlapping Run: When on attack a player runs from behind the teammate in possession to receive a pass from him. Also called an "overlap play."

Own Goal: A goal scored for the opponents by a defending player sending the ball into his own goal.

Passing: Propelling the ball to a teammate by heading it or kicking it. See Centering; Cross Pass; Double Pass; Possession Pass; Square Pass; Through Pass; Wall Pass.

Penalty Arc: An arc drawn outside the penalty area at a radius of 10 yards from the penalty spot. No players are allowed within this arc when a penalty kick is being taken.

Penalty Area: An 18-by-44-yard area located directly in front of each goal. The goalkeeper may handle the ball in this area, and penalty kicks are taken from here.

Penalty Kick: A direct free kick taken from the penalty spot. It is awarded to the attacking team if a defender commits a major offense within his own penalty area. A goal can be scored directly from a penalty kick. Except for the goalkeeper, who must remain stationary between the goalposts on his own goal line while the kick is being taken, all players must be outside of the penalty area and at least 10 yards from the penalty spot until the ball is in play.

Penalty Spot: The place 12 yards in front of the center of the goal line from which penalty kicks are taken. Also called the "penalty kick mark."

Pendulum: A highly effective device used by coaches for technique training.

Penetrating Pass: See Through Pass.

Penetrating Run: An offensive player's run through the line of defensive players.

Pitch: The traditional name for the soccer field.

Placekick: A kick taken when the ball has been placed in a stationary position for starting the game and for restart situations.

Poke Tackle: Use of the toe to poke the ball away from the person in possession. The poke tackle can be executed from the side or the rear of the opponent.

Positionless Soccer: See Total Soccer.

Possession Pass: Usually a square (lateral) or backward pass that has little chance of being intercepted.

Punching: A means of saving a goal or deflecting a ball by hitting it with the fists. Can only be used by the goalkeeper, but he must be in the penalty area.

Punt: A kicking technique used by goalkeepers. The goalkeeper drops the ball and kicks it before it touches the ground.

Push Pass: A short pass executed with the inside of the foot.

Quarter Circle: See Corner Area.

Referee: The official in complete charge of a soccer game. He is assisted by 2 linesmen.

Restart: A term that includes all methods of recommencing play after it has been stopped. These are the drop ball, the placekick, and the throw-in.

"RICE": Rest, Ice, Compression, Elevation—the four basic first-aid procedures the coach must follow when a player suffers the most common soccer injuries. (NOTE: Soccer injuries, and first-aid treatment, are described in Chapter 15.)

Save: A successful effort by the goalkeeper to prevent a possible score by stopping or deflecting a ball aimed at the goal.

Scissors Kick: See Low Overhead Volley.

Screening: See Shielding.

Set Play: A predetermined maneuver, usually employed

in restart situations such as throw-ins and free kicks.

Shadow Dribbling: A training exercise that involves a trailing player, without the ball, imitating the moves of the dribbler.

Shadow Drill: Practicing soccer skills with opponents providing passive resistance (not attempting to gain possession of the ball).

Shepherding: See Jockeying.

Shielding: When dribbling, staying between the ball and an opponent to prevent him from claiming the ball. Also called "screening."

Shooting: Heading or kicking the ball on goal with the intent of scoring.

Shoulder Charge: See Charging.

Sidelines: See Touchlines.

Slalom Dribbling: A training exercise requiring players to dribble around or between cones or flag posts.

Slide Tackle: Dispossessing an attacker of the ball by sliding into the ball and kicking it away. The slide tackle can be executed from the front, rear, or side of an opponent.

Space: See Dead Space; Live Space.

Square Pass: A pass made laterally to a waiting or moving teammate across the field.

Static Stretching: A flexibility exercise that involves locking the joints and stretching the muscles and tendons to the greatest extent possible, then holding for a short time.

Still Ball: A ball in position for a placekick that starts and restarts the game.

Stopper: One of the central defenders. His main responsibility is to mark the central striker of the opposing team. Also called the "center fullback."

Strikers: See Forwards.

Sweeper: Often the last player, except for the goalkeeper, on defense. His main responsibility is to prevent attacks on goal. Also called a "libero."

Tackling: Trying to dispossess an opponent of the ball by using the feet or a shoulder charge. See Block Tackle; Charging; Poke Tackle; Slide Tackle.

Target Player: Usually the central striker, who is tall and especially skilled in receiving air balls.

Through Pass: Moving the ball between or over the defending players to a teammate who is in a good position to shoot on goal. Also called the "penetrating pass" and the "killer pass."

Throw-In: The method of putting the ball back into play after it has gone out-of-bounds over the touchline. A member of the team opposing the team that last touched the ball must throw it onto the field from over his head, using both hands and keeping a part of each foot on the ground either behind or on the touchline. The ball is thrown in from the point where it went out-of-bounds. A goal cannot be scored directly from a throw-in.

Total Soccer: A system of play involving constant changes of players' positions as the teams gain and lose possession of the ball. Also called "positionless soccer."

Touchlines: The boundary lines at each side of the field. If a ball goes completely over the touchline, play is stopped and restarted by a throw-in from the place where it went out-of-bounds. Also called "sidelines."

Trapping: A term incorrectly used to mean stopping the ball and controlling it after gaining possession. Trapping involves pressing the ball to the ground, a method of controlling it that is not to be encouraged.

Two-Touch: Passing or shooting on goal on the second contact with the ball; that is, on the second touch.

Volley Kick: A kick taken before the ball touches the ground. Usually the instep or the inside of the foot is used. See High Overhead Volley; Low Overhead Volley.

Wall: A human barrier of at least 3 players, used to aid the goalkeeper in defending against free kicks—when they are specifically so awarded. Players may line up 10 or more yards from the ball to form a barrier between the kicker and the goal.

Wall Pass: A pass in which a receiver is used as a "wall" to redirect the path of the ball. The first player makes a short pass to a teammate, then sprints into open space to receive a return pass. Also called the "give-and-go." See Double Pass.

Warm-Down: An exercise that gradually diminishes the player's physical activity to help the body recover after a game or other periods of intense exertion.

Warm-Up: An exercise or a set of exercises devised to enhance the player's physical performance in the game or a strenuous training session that follows.

Weak-Side: Pertaining to the side of the field away from the ball.

Wingbacks: See Outside Fullbacks.

Wingers: See Outside Forwards.

Wings: The parts of the field near the touchlines.

Zone Defense: A defensive strategy requiring each defender to assume responsibility for guarding opponents in a particular area of the field.

BOOKS FOR FURTHER STUDY

Anderson, Bob. *Stretching*. Box 1002, Englewood, Colorado, 1975.

Banks, Gordon. *Gordon Banks' Soccer Book*. London: Pelham Books, 1973.

Bauer, Gerhardt. *Der Fussball*. Munich: Blu Verlagsgesellschaft, 1974.

Colson, John H., and Armour, William J. *Sports Injuries and Their Treatment*. London: Stanley Paul, 1975.

Cottrell, John A. *A Century of Great Soccer Drama*. London: Hart-Davis, 1970.

Csanádi, Arpad. *Soccer*. Budapest: Corvina Press, 1975.

FIFA. *Laws of the Game and Universal Guide for Referees*. Zurich: International Federation of Association Football, 1976.

Hughes, Charles. *Tactics and Teamwork*. London: E. P. Group, 1973.

Jago, Gordon. *Football Coaching*. London: Stanley Paul, 1974.

Lodziak, Conrad. *Understanding Soccer Tactics*. London: Faber and Faber, 1966.

Miller, Al, and Wingert, Norm. *Winning Soccer*. Chicago: Henry Regnery, 1975.

Morgan, R. E., and Adamson, G. T. *Circuit Training*. London: G. Bell and Sons, 1961.

Muse, Bill, and White, Dan. *We Can Teach You to Play Soccer*. New York: Hawthorn Books, 1976.

Shilton, Peter. *Shilton in Goal*. London: Stanley Paul, 1974.

Tutko, Thomas, and Richards, Jack. *Psychology of Coaching*. Boston: Allyn and Bacon, 1971.

USSF. *Handbook for Youth Soccer*. New York: United States Soccer Federation, 1976.

Wade, Allen. *Football Association Guide to Training and Coaching*. London: Heinemann, 1967.

Watson, Bill. *Football Fitness*. London: Stanley Paul, 1973.